THE LONG GOODBYE
Khe Sanh Revisited
©2016 Michael Archer

Published by Hellgate Press
(An imprint of L&R Publishing, LLC)

Hellgate Press
PO Box 3531
Ashland, OR 97520
email: sales@hellgatepress.com

Editor: Harley B. Patrick
Interior and cover design: Michael Campbell
Cover photo by Bob Cook

ISBN: 978-1-55571-794-0

Library of Congress Cataloging-in-Publication Data available on request

Printed in the United States of America
First edition 10 9 8 7 6 5 4 3 2 1

OTHER BOOKS BY MICHAEL ARCHER

A Patch of Ground: Khe Sanh Remembered

"The best first-hand account of the battle of Khe Sanh."
— *VIETNAM MAGAZINE*

"A must read for anyone interested in knowing what it was really like at Khe Sanh."
— *RAY SMITH, Major General, USMC (Ret.) and company commander at Khe Sanh*

"An intelligent, courageous, sensitive book about an historic battle in a controversial war."
— *KENNETH J. CAMPBELL, Professor of Political Science and International Relations, University of Delaware*

A Man of His Word: The Life & Times of Nevada's Senator William J. Raggio

"Mr. Archer has rendered the people of Nevada a fascinating history lesson."
— *HARRY REID, U.S. Senate Minority Leader*

"Archer's thorough research reveals his intellectual honesty and literary balance."
— *JUDGE DAVID HARDY, Second Judicial District-Nevada*

WHAT OTHERS SAY ABOUT THE LONG GOODBYE

"Michael Archer established himself as a worthy spokesman for Vietnam War veterans in 2004 with publication of his poignant combat memoir, *A Patch of Ground: Khe Sanh Remembered*. Now, Archer has delivered a powerful sequel in *The Long Goodbye*, a brutally honest and impassioned work of nonfiction that takes us even deeper inside America's faltering war in Vietnam in early 1968. The focal point of *The Long Goodbye* is Archer's best friend from high school, Lance Corporal Thomas Patrick Mahoney III, who survives his combat debut at Hue City, only to disappear under mysterious circumstances at Khe Sanh. *The Long Goodbye* builds to a climax in contemporary Vietnam, with Archer playing the role of relentless cold-case detective, driven by loyalty and devotion to unravel the mystery of Tommy Mahoney's disappearance, and to bring home his beloved friend. Many Americans would rather not remember the anguish of our lost crusade in Vietnam. In *The Long Goodbye*, Michael Archer reminds us why we should never forget."

> — *GREGG JONES has been a foreign correspondent, investigative journalist and Pulitzer Prize finalist author. His critically acclaimed works of nonfiction include* Last Stand at Khe Sanh *and* Honor in the Dust.

"Marines don't leave their dead behind, goes the adage, and in *The Long Goodbye* Mike Archer demonstrates the truth of that statement and the double-edges of its meaning. The dead stay with us. They demand to be recovered and remembered and for us to find meaning in their sacrifice. This is the task that Archer, himself a veteran of the bloody siege of Khe Sanh, took upon himself and in this tale of his search for a lost comrade and his journey into the Vietnam of the past and the present, he gifts us with the vivid, utterly compelling story of his stubborn devotion to a friend and of the grim reality of war and its long echoes into the lives of veterans. This is a book that will leave its grip on your heart. It deserves to stand with the classics not only of the Vietnam War but of all wars."

— WAYNE KARLIN *is an award-winning author and editor. His numerous works of fiction and nonfiction include* Wandering Souls: Journeys With the Dead and the Living in Viet Nam. *A Marine veteran of combat in Vietnam, Wayne teaches languages and literature at the College of Southern Maryland.*

"A wonderfully written account by a Marine veteran of the siege of Khe Sanh, who refused to let the memory of a buddy be forgotten. Mike's gripping description of the decade long search for his friend's remains speaks volumes about the motto of the Corps, *Semper Fidelis*--Always Faithful. His description of the realities of service in Vietnam and its effects on those who served there are spot on. He writes plainly of his own fight to slay the dragon of post-traumatic stress and his discovery that human dignity and loyalty is a common thread among those who experience the horror of war."

— DICK CAMP *is a retired Marine Corps colonel, former company commander at Khe Sanh, and formerly Deputy Director of the Marine Corps' History Division. He has authored numerous books, both fiction and non-fiction, including* Boots on the Ground *and* Battleship Arizona's Marines at War.

"Skillfully blending history and biography, Michael Archer tells a compelling story of the Vietnam conflict and its aftermath. His timely revisiting of the epic battle of Khe Sanh reminds us that for those who experience combat a war may never end."

— GEORGE HERRING, *Alumni Professor of History Emeritus at the University of Kentucky, is a leading authority on U.S. foreign relations. His books include* America's Longest War *and* From Colony to Superpower.

"Michael Archer writes the simply gripping and astounding story of the death of his childhood friend and fellow Marine in *The Long Goodbye*, one that goes to great lengths to place that terrible event into its proper personal, historical, and geopolitical context. Everyone who dies in the service of their country deserves a friend like Archer who can write their story so powerfully and so beautifully."

— *CALEB CAGE is a West Point graduate, decorated for his leadership and courage in combat during Operation Iraqi Freedom II and coauthor of the book* The Gods of Diyala. *He is director of Nevada's Office of Homeland Security and an advisor to Governor Brian Sandoval.*

THE LONG GOODBYE

Khe Sanh Revisited

🙰 🙰

MICHAEL ARCHER

In memory of Robert J. "Doc" Topmiller:
healer, teacher, friend

CONTENTS

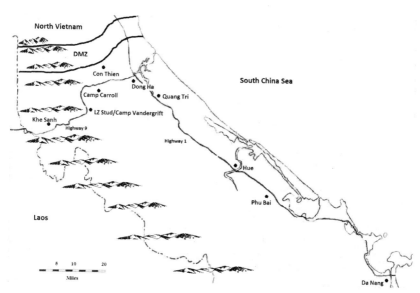

Map of northern I Corps, South Vietnam, 1968.

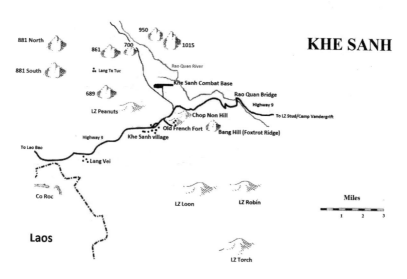

Map of Khe Sanh area, 1968.

PROLOGUE

On the stifling, summer afternoon of July 6, 1968, twenty-three-year-old warrant officer Nguyen Van Luong squirmed uncomfortably within the tight confines of a camouflaged foxhole he'd dug the night before. His scout team from the 246th Independent Regiment of the People's Army of Vietnam had been ordered to move as close as they could to the U.S. Marines on Hill 881 South without being detected. Luong complied, as he always did, expertly and silently leading his men through a hundred yards of land mines, tanglefoot barbed wire traps and trip flares, now so close he could hear conversations coming from the American bunkers and smell their cigarette smoke.

The previous March, when Luong led his platoon from North Vietnam into the vicious fighting around the remote American combat base at Khe Sanh, he commanded over forty soldiers. Death, wounds, disease and desertion had now reduced that number to just five. The "glorious liberation" of Khe Sanh, he mused, had taken longer, and cost more, than their political cadres had assured them it would; but now, four months after arriving, the mission was nearly completed. Five miles to the east, the large American base and airfield had been abandoned just fourteen hours earlier, and only three undermanned hill outposts now remained. It was the job of Luong's team that day to block Marines on this hill from going to the aid of others, less than two miles away, who were now battling his regiment's main force.

As he raised up out of his hole and peered through the tall, pale-green grass toward the bunkers, Luong was astonished to see a lone, unarmed American standing just forty feet away. He would later report him to be "a young, male Caucasian, tall and with a large build," who may have been in some emotional distress because "his face was red and his eyes were blue like a mean animal."

1

The American, Lance Corporal Tom Mahoney, did not appear to be looking for anything in particular when his gaze suddenly fixed upon an odd flickering in the grass. It was Luong blinking perspiration from his eye as he now took aim at him along the barrel of a Kalashnikov. Tom's fellow Marines heard his stunned cry—"Oh my God, help me!"—an instant before Luong squeezed the trigger, hitting him twice in the heart.

Tom Mahoney was unquestionably the most popular member of his platoon, known for his quick smile, courage and composure under fire, and a perpetual concern for the safety of his fellow Marines, often fretfully counting heads after a combat engagement until all were accounted for. So it was with anxious fury that his buddies fought the remainder of the day to recover his body from under the effective gunfire of Luong's well-hidden team; even resisting orders from senior Marine officers to discontinue the rescue effort and immediately carry out the scheduled abandonment of the hill. As darkness began to fall, making it impossible to continue the fight, they reluctantly left their friend behind—never forgotten and always wondering what had led to his mysterious walk into oblivion.

PART I

They were willing to guard something more precious than my life. They would have carried my reputation, the memory of me.

~ MICHAEL NORMAN, *These Good Men* ~

1
TOM MAHONEY

TOM MAHONEY AND I met about the time of his fifteenth birthday in early October 1962 while attending Saint Mary's College High School in Berkeley, California. Later that month, two events would be burned into our memories forever. The first occurred in the bottom of the ninth inning during Game Seven of the World Series across the bay at Candlestick Park when, down by a run with two out and runners at second and third, Willie McCovey scorched a line drive into the glove of shortstop Bobby Richardson ending our dreams of a local championship by the San Francisco Giants over the haughty and much-despised New York Yankees.

The second would affect our lives much more profoundly. With national midterm elections looming, and to preempt accusations by Republicans that he was soft on the threat of Soviet missiles in Cuba capable of reaching U.S. soil, President John F. Kennedy ordered a naval blockade of the island to prevent further such armaments from arriving. Kennedy and Soviet Premier Nikita Khrushchev soon exchanged dire public warnings of imminent nuclear war.

A pall descended over the nation as Americans became fixated on televised news footage of Russian cargo ships, escorted by war vessels, steaming resolutely toward the American blockade. Each passing hour without a resolution reinforced our belief that we were about to be incinerated in an atomic holocaust from which there was no escape. Secret negotiations eventually ended the crisis, and evidence declassified years later indicated the actual situation may not have been that grim; but the trauma of those frightening days left me, Tom and much of our generation convinced that the communist world was a real and very immediate threat to ourselves and our families.

Throughout his childhood Tom had been naturally adept at sports, particularly basketball and baseball, and possessed an adventurous spirit that often distressed playmates. One recalled that on several occasions as a third grader Tom explored the city's sewers alone, because others refused to join him, gaining access through a loose storm drain grate near his grade school and later telling unsettling stories of eerie noises and rats scurrying about in the dank, shadowy tunnels.[1]

By fifth grade, the girls in his class at Saint Leo's parochial school in Oakland developed a collective crush on the handsome and confident boy, altering the pronunciation of his last name to "My honey" when they talked about him among themselves. One classmate, Kathleen (McCorry) Lopes, later my high school sweetheart, recalled that her close friendship with Tom in grade school was not solely due to his charm, but because each were being raised by single mothers who shared the prevailing social stigma of that time, particularly among Catholics, that came with being divorced. They also shared a first kiss at age seven, which Kathleen never forgot. "Tommy would stop by each morning," she said, "and we would walk together to school, truly a gentleman, even as a boy."[2]

Tom's mother, Patricia, instilled such chivalrous behavior early on. Another Saint Leo's classmate, Bill Corporandy, recalled a shopping trip with him and his mother in downtown Oakland, and how she insisted they walk closest to the curb "when with a lady" and never forget to open doors. "I remember feeling inadequate," Bill said, "not like Tom, who seemed so suave and self-assured."[3] But life had not always been easy for Tom or his mother.

A native of Oakland, Patricia (Waterman) Mahoney was raised by her mother, Ruby, who had come from Montana alone about the time of the First World War. Little was ever said about Patricia's father. By the late 1930s, Ruby owned a small corset shop on Grand Avenue in Oakland and had purchased an imposing Queen Anne style home at 677 Fairmount Avenue, with a dark, redwood shingle exterior, latticed windows and an elegant front staircase with a leaded-glass entry door. The home was located in a fashionable area of the city, near the small upscale community of Piedmont, and Ruby saw to it that Patricia was provided all the benefits of upper middle-class society.

Tom's paternal great-grandfather, Patrick Mahoney, emigrated from Ireland to Ohio in 1851 and his son, Thomas Patrick Mahoney, moved to Oakland around the turn of the century. His wife Gertrude would bear eight children. Thomas Jr., the youngest and only boy, was born in October 1918. He showed an early aptitude for mechanical design and, after graduation from high school, the handsome and gregarious Thomas Mahoney Jr. attended San Francisco Junior College where he was soon smitten by classmate Patricia Waterman, a lithesome, blue-eyed, blonde. The two were married in September 1942, with a reception for over two hundred guests at Ruby's home.

Thomas enlisted as a private in the U.S. Army Air Corps the following year and was later selected to attend aviation officer training in Carlsbad, New Mexico. He graduated with the rank of second lieutenant and, as a navigator, flew combat bombing missions in the western Pacific until the war ended in August 1945. Upon his release from active duty, Thomas returned to Oakland and purchased a cocktail lounge on Grand Avenue. Marital problems led to a separation and just two months after their son Tom was born, they divorced.

In 1950, Thomas was recalled to military duty for the Korean conflict. Now a first lieutenant, he navigated thirty-three combat bombing missions before returning to Ellington Air Force Base near Houston, Texas. Three days later, on November 16, 1952, while traveling at a recklessly high speed through an intersection on the Old Galveston Highway in his newly purchased sports car, Thomas collided with another vehicle killing him instantly. The other driver avoided serious injury, but a passenger in Mahoney's vehicle, reported by a local newspaper as a "pretty, young Houston model," was left in critical condition.

Thomas' body was returned to California and buried with military honors at the San Francisco National Cemetery in the Presidio.

Little Tom did not attend the service; but each Memorial Day thereafter, Patricia would drive the boy across the Bay to place flowers at his father's grave.

Thomas Patrick Mahoney III had begun life on October 3, 1947, at Providence Hospital in Oakland, located among other medical buildings on a slight prominence known to locals as Pill Hill. From there, a few miles to the west across the gray-green expanse of the bay, could be seen the celebrated hills of San Francisco and beyond that the shimmering span of the Golden Gate Bridge. The weather was clear and mild, but a storm was soon expected to bring rain in from the Pacific Ocean.

Dark clouds of another kind were forming that day thousands of miles beyond the horizon. In the Protectorate of Tonkin, French Indochina, over one thousand French Union paratroopers were poised to descend on the town of Bak-Can, near the border with China. The League for the Independence of Vietnam, called Viet Minh, were headquartered there and French colonial forces hoped to crush their seven-year-long movement in one dramatic attack. Code-named Operation Lea, another fifteen thousand French Union soldiers moved overland to encircle the Viet Minh army and block its escape.

Those at Bak-Can were stunned by the swiftness of the assault and their leader, Ho Chi Minh, eluded capture by just minutes. When paratroopers kicked in the door of his office, a still-hot cup of tea was sitting on Ho's desk beside neat stacks of correspondence awaiting his signature.[4] Ho and General Vo Nguyen Giap, the main prizes sought by the French, would slip away to safety through gaps in the French lines, along with most of their forty-thousand-person army.

Government leaders in Paris, struggling with postwar economic problems and public disenchantment about the military campaign in Indochina, knew immediately that the failure of Lea meant the end of their hold on the region. Now, consolidating their forces primarily around Hanoi, the Red River Delta and a few larger coastal cities, French forces virtually conceded the countryside and highlands to the Viet Minh. This included a small Legionnaire fort hidden deep among the rainy, jungle-entwined peaks along the Laotian border in the central Vietnam protectorate of Annam beside a coffee plantation and the sparsely inhabited village of Khe Sanh.

It would have been impossible for anyone to imagine on that October day in 1947 there could ever be a connection between the birth of a baby boy in Oakland, the subsequent escape of the Viet Minh from Bak-Can and this obscure mountain village. That sad episode was still cloaked in the future, like the ghostly fog enshrouding the mountains at Khe Sanh.

2
THE CORPS WILL
FIX THAT PROBLEM

I AM THE SECOND OLDEST of five children, four boys and a girl. My mother, Leontia (Casey) Archer, was a devout Catholic who insisted that we follow in her family's tradition and attend Saint Augustine's School in Oakland. Like the Mahoney family, some of my ancestors had emigrated from Ireland during The Great Famine in the mid-nineteenth century. Others arrived later, like my maternal grandmother who came to San Francisco as a young girl in the late 1880s. My father, Edward, hailed from a mélange of Scot, English and Welsh immigrants.

I was an excellent student throughout grammar school and loved spending time in the public libraries where I read every history book and biography I could comprehend. Bright and motivated, I took my first job at age eleven as an Oakland Tribune newspaper carrier. Then adolescence struck. By the end of my first year of high school, I had become a disciplinary problem and was barely passing academically. After my third year at Saint Mary's, I was told not to return and spent my senior year attending Oakland's Skyline High School. I enjoyed the environment of public school, but didn't improve scholastically, or otherwise, and nearly did not graduate. Not surprisingly, I was a disappointment to my father who reminded me daily about what a failure I was.

He had a right to be disappointed. Though insufferably overbearing and inconsistent, he had given me a wonderful private school educational opportunity and I squandered it. I was undisciplined and indolent, interested only in partying with my friends and getting into trouble. I had moved out of the house several times in high school, but could not make it on my own for long; once spending a few nights inside a storage locker in the underground parking garage of an apartment house—an odd foretaste of future bunker-life.

When I complained to Tom about the way my dad treated me, I received no sympathy, only a reminder of how lucky I was to have one. He often spoke of his late father with pride and affection, despite rarely, if ever, having seen him. Whether these recollections were real or constructed, it was clear to me Tom's feelings were genuine.

After graduating from high school I began work as a delivery driver for a florist shop. I enjoyed the job, had money in my pocket and never tired of the soothing fragrances of the flower arrangements. So it was with some degree of contentment that on the near-perfect, spring morning of April 17, 1967, I turned my delivery van onto Fairmount Avenue and, by chance, saw Tom Mahoney in the driveway working on his motorcycle. As I pulled to a stop, Tom walked up wiping his hands on a rag and before I could speak, blurted out that he had "to get away from Oakland" and was going to enlist in the Marine Corps. I was stunned by the impulsiveness of his decision, but even more surprised when he then asked, "Do you want to go in with me?" Without giving so much as a moment of deliberation to the notion that this might be the most important decision I would ever make in my life, one with unimaginably grave and far-reaching consequences, I replied: "Why not?"

The next day we drove together to the recruiting office in downtown Oakland where we were greeted by a robust, gunnery sergeant in blue uniform trousers and a khaki shirt with several rows of ribbons indicating he had served in Vietnam and been wounded in action. His enthusiasm and sense of pride were infectious as he rattled off the rigorous qualifications necessary to become part of that select fighting force. Yet, moments later, when I failed to complete the ten push-ups "required" for enlistment, he laughed it off for the sake of his recruitment quota, assuring me: "The Corps will fix that problem, son. You'll be knocking off a hundred of them before long." I liked the sound of that, and within a few minutes we had both signed up for the next three years.

Until the day before, I had no conscious intention of joining the Marines—quite the opposite. My father had enlisted in the Corps in 1943 and served throughout the war in the South Pacific as a water purification engineer with an artillery battalion. Most of my childhood memories contained an element of his service. As kids, my older brother, Ed, and I slept in metal, military-style bunks, under gray-green wool blankets stamped "USMC." Dad trained us to make a perfect hospital fold at each corner of our mattresses and on Saturday mornings, as eight- and nine-year-olds, we stood at attention in our pajamas as he inspected the tautness of our work by bouncing a coin on the blanket.

Most former Marines, while their pride in having served continues to grow over the years, never completely forget how irritating the frequent and excessive attention to petty details, commonly referred to as "the chicken shit," had been. Dad, however, recollected it all as a perfect experience and his memories were unassailable.

Despite a family tradition being established by my dad and Ed, who was by then a member of the Marine Corps' elite First Force Reconnaissance Company in South Vietnam, I could not picture myself in the Corps. If anything, I gravitated toward opposing ideals and resented authority. I owned all of Bob Dylan's albums with their lyrics of anger and revolution and spent my evenings on Telegraph Avenue near the University of California campus in Berkeley listening to sedition. I did not like myself and thought I did not care about living; yet characteristics traditionally representative of manhood still appealed to me and I harbored a dimly perceived need to prove I was not a failure.

Like others, I'd been drawn to Tom Mahoney by a confidence beyond his years. He required little peer approval and lacked the pretense and swagger often found in adolescents possessing less self-esteem. And, like them, I envied him without resentment. However, I didn't realize just how low my self-esteem had fallen until experiencing a surprising sense of gratefulness at Tom's confidence in me to get through boot camp with him.

My dad was delighted when I told him about our enlistment and, though I did not do it in a conscious effort to please him, his long-denied approval felt good. I am not sure how Tom's mother took the news, though I supposed that, on some level, she hoped a more structured lifestyle would help settle his growing restlessness. After graduating from high school the previous summer, our days had been filled with fun at the beaches of Santa Cruz and Lake Tahoe and frequent parties at the home of a friend, Sue Thomas, which we dubbed the "Yellow Submarine" after both the exterior color of the house and the title of a popular Beatles song by that name. Our little group's aimlessness and increasingly risky behavior was bound to get us into trouble.

On Halloween night 1966, I joined Tom and Jack Mooseau at our favorite burger hangout, The Smokehouse, on Telegraph Avenue. Jack, also a close friend of Tom's, was a stocky, fun-loving kid who I had known since we were nine-years old and was like a brother to me. It was an unusually rowdy crowd that evening with minor vandalism and scuffling between members of different groups of young men. The Berkeley police arrived, took our names, and let us go. A few days later the three of us received a warrant in the mail for our arrest and were to stand trial on charges of disturbing the peace, malicious mischief and, most incredibly, "inciting a riot." To stay out of jail, we were each required to post $100 in bail. Because I had the money available from my job, I did not have to tell my parents.

Tom did tell his mother and she was furious with us all, but particularly frustrated by her son's behavior. She arranged for us to meet with an attorney who told us his concerns. The district attorney, he said, had thrown in the "inciting a riot" charge in the hope that a conviction would help ease concerns among long-time citizens of Berkeley that something was being done about increasing political unrest and public demonstrations near campus. It was not going to be a jury trial and our judge, who had been on the bench for many years, was known to hand out harsh sentences and would likely view us as anarchists rather than middle-class kids screwing around on Halloween night.

The trial was held a few weeks later and, after all the testimony was completed, the judge ordered us to come forward and stand before him. He rebuked us for our failure to adhere to accepted standards of civilized behavior and lectured us on the dangers of political theories espousing class warfare and civil disobedience, none of which we understood. He admonished our parents (Tom's mom was the only parent present) to do a better job with us, and then banished us from the city of Berkeley for one year. If we were found there during that time, we would be brought back to him for sentencing—and spend a minimum of ninety days in the Alameda County Jail. Although it was misdirected in our case, the judge's fear about local threats to the status quo did have a basis in the growing anger and frustration about the escalating war in Vietnam.

❧ ❧

The two months between our enlistment and departure for boot camp seemed like one continuous celebration of personal freedom. With American involvement in Vietnam intensifying, Tom and I knew we would be going there, yet few in our circle of friends had been in combat and so the stories they told us were mostly exaggerated, secondhand accounts of American superiority over disorganized and cowardly guerrillas who hid in the shadows, sniping, and then running away—exactly what we wanted to hear.

We also relished their anecdotes about the difficulties of Marine boot camp and how the experience would be life changing, turning us into the confident and fearless men we longed to be. Tom and I practiced by standing at attention, eyes straight ahead, while those who had survived boot camp mimicked drill instructors screaming insults at us nose to nose.

Our reasons for enlisting in the Marines were more complex than even we knew. Despite our frequent macho protestations that we were not going to Vietnam "to help a bunch of people we didn't even know," years of Catholic education had subtly instilled in us a belief in the nobility and self-sacrificial character of social conscience. While we had convinced ourselves that we were going there only for the adventure, to test our nerve and toughness, motives subtly intermingled, and it sometimes had the feel of a heroic quest for some inexpressible ideal.

While I had not graduated from high school with Tom at Saint Mary's, I did attend the ceremony. As part of the program, the graduates sang *The Impossible Dream* from the musical *Man of La Mancha,* which had opened on Broadway the year before in 1965. The tingle of gooseflesh spreading along my arms as they reached the final stanza should have been a clue that my view of life was dangerously over-romanticized:

> *And the world will be better for this*
> *That one man, scorned and covered with scars*
> *Still strove with his last ounce of courage*
> *To reach the unreachable star.*

In addition, we were American kids who had grown up in the 1950s, loved our country and trusted our government to do the right thing. That was good enough for us. We never thought to question the necessity of the war, or balance our perspective by doing the casualty math which was exploding exponentially during the spring of 1967.

This spike in American dead and wounded was largely the result of a battle then taking place against North Vietnamese Army, or NVA (known formally as the People's Army of Vietnam) forces in a remote, mountainous corner of South Vietnam. There, U.S. Marines were attempting to dislodge nearly three thousand communist soldiers poised to capture the Khe Sanh (pronounced *Kay Sawn*) Combat Base and airfield.

On the sixth day of this battle—later called "The Hill Fights"—Marines assaulted Hill 881 South[5] where nearly four hundred NVA soldiers were waiting, aiming down prearranged lanes cut into the high grass and underbrush and holding their fire until Marines were only a few feet away. The initial barrage knocked down a dozen young men before they even knew what had happened. Stunned survivors dove for cover. Snipers in treetops picked off their primary targets—officers, radio operators and machine gunners—killing most with a single shot through the head or heart.

After seven hours of fighting, the Marines moved back down the slope leaving behind the bodies of thirty-three of their comrades, then blasted the hilltop for two days around the clock with bombs and artillery. As the Americans began their next ascent, pulling themselves up the steep gradient by grasping exposed tree roots and clumps of grass, no one complained because they were focused on revenge with bayonets fixed and a mindset of no mercy.

Ninety minutes later, upon reaching the top, they were disappointed to find that the enemy had fled before the bombardment began. Amid the splintered trees and soil pulverized to the consistency of lumpy oatmeal, the Marines began the gruesome task of locating the remains of missing comrades now horribly damaged by the explosives. It was impossible to identify most and took two days to find all visible body parts, but the smell of death hung over the hill for weeks.[6]

Immediately after the Marines occupied the hill, forty news correspondents arrived in helicopters, roaming the hilltop for more than an hour, taking photographs of the grisly scene and interviewing dazed combatants. Photos of the carnage and news stories about the viciousness of the fighting shocked the American public. Tom and I had enlisted in the Marine Corps just twelve days before and were mesmerized by the news coverage from Hill 881 South, slightly titillated, rather than frightened, in our naiveté.

That night I had a dream that Tom was killed on that very hill and, befitting the often theatric nature of an adolescent's imagination, I saw myself on my knees weeping beside his lifeless body. Upon awakening, I rationalized the dream had resulted from a combination of the powerful news accounts and my anxiety over our impending departure. I did not consider it to have any significance and so did not tell Tom about it. After all, what were the chances of him dying in the war; let alone on that particular hill?

About this time, Tom and I drove to the University of California at Davis to attend festivities surrounding their annual Picnic Day. That night, at a party in a friend's apartment near campus, I evidently insulted a hulking, drunken stranger who pinned me against a wall with the intent of beating me up. As he was cocking his right fist back to slam into my face, Tom suddenly appeared from a nearby room where he was chatting with a young woman he'd just met. He grabbed the man by the back of his shirt collar and yanked him out the front door. After some words, the two began exchanging punches.

Within minutes, the flashing red lights of a police car approached. The officer was clearly frustrated from too many such wild incidents that day and intent on quickly arresting both of them. Tom reached into his pocket and took out a copy of his orders showing a reporting date for Marine Corps boot camp just a few weeks away. The officer, impressed by his patriotism, shook Tom's hand and wished him luck before driving the other man to jail.

Law enforcement disapproval of growing antiwar activities on college campuses had worked in Tom's favor that night. If arrested, he would have violated his enlistment contract and I would have been going to boot camp alone. Yet all I could think of as I watched it unfold was how Mahoney was always there for his friends, often, like on this night, in dramatic fashion. He was larger than life, or what Jack Mooseau liked to call "a matinee idol."

Our first day of Marine Corps basic training began at the military induction center in downtown Oakland on June 6, 1967. About fifty of us were processing and spent the first hour sitting on long, highly polished wooden benches and completing numerous forms about ourselves. The remainder of the morning we underwent psychological and aptitude tests and medical examinations. Some of the draftees in our group were quite vocal about not wanting to go, trying to work up the nerve to bolt outside and join the throng of protestors picketing the building who had urged us all to "resist" as we entered that morning.

Once our processing was complete, we boarded a bus to the Oakland Airport and, after a short flight to San Diego, took a Marine Corps bus to the recruit depot where we were introduced to our drill instructors (DI). It quickly turned into a nightmarish scene of apoplectic uniformed men in "Smokey the Bear" campaign hats lurching about menacingly and bellowing commands, threats and insults at bewildered boys, often nose to nose, or with spittled lips touching our ears. Our civilian clothing and shoes disappeared in the melee, replaced by white sneakers, green utility trousers and canary yellow sweatshirts. We were then stampeded to our living quarters in galvanized metal Quonset huts.

After about four hours of sleep, we were awakened by a DI banging on a trash can lid with his swagger stick and shouting dire threats. We leapt from our racks and stood at attention. After a head count, he ordered us outside and introduced us to The Pits, rectangular areas of sand in front of each Quonset hut where we did our push-ups, counting each one in unison and loudly, always with a "Sir!" at the end. One enraged DI, not liking what he saw, ordered us to continue "Forever!" Soon our arms went numb and we were barely able to prop ourselves up on elbows to keep our faces out of the sand.

That first morning they hurried us through the mess hall with barely enough time to eat, then ran us to the barber to have our heads shaved. While waiting in line there, one DI advised us that fighting between Israel and its neighbors had broken out the day before. "You lucky maggots might not be going to Vietnam after all," he growled. "You may be heading east just in time for World War III." As it turned out, that war lasted only six days.

The next few weeks were a blur of marching, standing in lines, training classes and DI's screaming in our faces. There were endless sessions in The Pits—either as a platoon or individually—for the most insignificant infraction, often for no infraction. The Corps had pledged to tear us down and rebuild us in its image; however, it was not just a matter of pride that kept us from quitting. Because of the recruiting exigencies in the late 1960s, the Marine Corps did not accept mere failure as an excuse for sending a recruit home. Those with severe preexisting psychological and emotional problems were discharged, but borderline cases were kept and trained. Disciplinary problems and overweight recruits were recycled back through as many platoons as it took them to finally graduate.

I would soon learn that my fellow recruits were generally here for one of three reasons: they had enlisted of their own volition, they were draftees, or a criminal court ordered them to enlist in the Marine Corps in lieu of a jail sentence. The latter was a surprisingly common occurrence in the 1960s. Occasionally, one of these "sentenced" Marines would later die in Vietnam, leading to the morbid observation that, in certain legal jurisdictions of the United States, shoplifting a six-pack of beer could get you a death sentence.

From the beginning, Tom flourished in the boot camp environment and was highly successful in all phases of the training, including classroom work, physical exercises and military drills; although, like most of us "city boys," he was only average at the rifle range. On the other hand, I struggled through the first month of our two-month-long basic training. Scrawny, in poor physical condition and with a bad adolescent attitude that I'd been cultivating for years, it took some time for me to "get with the program" as my DI's constantly admonished. My moment of truth happened one afternoon in late July during pugil stick training.

A pugil stick was a mock weapon that resembled a large Q-tip with a cushion at each end, color-coded to represent the butt and blade ends of a bayoneted rifle. Bayonet fighting skills were important in the First World War, and to a lesser degree in the Second World War, yet the Corps still dedicated hours to training us in this form of combat.

That day, after the instructor showed us how to parry our opponent's attack and then do damage, we queued up on either side of an earthen quad wearing football helmets and boxing gloves for protection. Upon reaching the front of the line, we paired off against an opponent from another platoon. Excitement built as my turn approached and by the time I neared the front, I was in the throes of blood lust. When the whistle sounded, I ran toward my foe and, forgetting all the techniques I'd just been taught, kicked him in the groin. As he bent forward and fell to the ground, I slid my gloved hands down toward the bottom of the stick, holding it like a baseball bat, and began to club him mercilessly.

The instructor picked up the man's fallen pugil stick and swung it at my head, connecting solidly and sending me flying onto my back. Looking down at me, he let loose with a profanity-laced diatribe, the gist of which was for me to get out of his training area and never return. Jogging away dejectedly, I passed a small platform on which drill instructors sat enjoying the spectacle and wagering cigarettes on the contestants. My senior DI, Staff Sergeant L. L. Randolph, was staring intently at me and so I expected to soon hear the threat of some horrible punishment. Instead, he leaned in my direction and said quietly: "Nice work, son."

My chin snapped upward in pride from those unexpected words of encouragement. I immediately recognized that this episode of measured rage and utter indifference to the consequences in order to win, was the "killer instinct" he had been trying so hard to tap. At that moment Randolph knew he'd succeeded with me and I now knew I was going to make it out of boot camp—maybe even Vietnam.

The only time we rested was on Sunday afternoons when allowed to sit on overturned buckets along the company street, cleaning our rifles, shining boots or reading and writing letters. Tom was in a different squad than me, and lived in a separate hut. In the highly structured environment of Marine boot camp we had little time to speak to one another; but, on Sunday afternoons we shared rumors and information contained in our letters from home. One subject he never spoke of was the increasingly tenuous relationship he had with his high school sweetheart who had gone off to college on the East Coast.

While still in high school, as his sixteenth birthday approached, Tom was anxious to buy a motorcycle and so took a job working weekends and evenings at the Piedmont Avenue Grocery Company in Oakland. This precluded his participation in organized school sports, although he continued to exercise regularly at a private swim club, maintaining a muscular one hundred sixty pounds on his five feet eleven inch frame. Along with his blue eyes, mischievous grin and penchant for dressing well, Tom had inherited his father's fully functioning libido and taste for excitement and danger. The philosopher Kierkegaard had written that the Irish did not have the heart to immerse their male children totally when baptized, wanting to keep a little paganism in reserve, thus leaving the right arm dry "to wield a sword with it, and embrace the girls."[7] Tom epitomized such folklore.

I often teased him that he deserved a raise in pay because the grocery store's profits must have risen substantially after he was hired due to the increased patronage by so many teenage girls who came to flirt with him. One of those girls was a slender, blue-eyed blonde named Linda. She and Tom began dating and he was soon so smitten that he rarely spent time with his school chums. Linda's parents were wealthy, socially prominent residents of upscale Piedmont. And, while they seemed to have tolerated her fling with him in high school, Tom's fatherless, middle-class circumstances, which required him to work as a store clerk, was not socially acceptable to them. Linda, a grade ahead of him, graduated in 1965 and soon moved to Newport, Rhode Island to attend a private junior college for women. Tom was heartbroken.

A few weeks later, he and four friends drove up into the Oakland hills in his grandmother's new car to drink beer. While returning down the winding road at dangerously high speed, Tom lost control of the vehicle, rolling it several times before it came to a stop on its roof, now crushed down nearly to the top of the seats. Despite not wearing seat belts, no one was seriously injured. Jack Mooseau later recalled the conversation in the car just before the accident and how upset Tom was by the mounting realization that Linda's parents would never allow their relationship to continue and, perhaps for the first time in his life, he was made to feel inferior.

"Tom," Jack said, "seemed to be losing his way."

I had noticed this as well. On an afternoon in early April 1967, just a few days before we joined the Marines, I was a passenger on Tom's Honda 250cc Scrambler motorcycle along a fog-shrouded freeway through the hills of north Oakland. Traffic was light and so he decided to "let it all out" and gave the cycle full throttle on a long, downhill stretch, both of us helmetless. I forced my face forward over his right shoulder to see the speedometer, barely able to keep my eyelids from blowing shut in the onrushing wind and saw the needle was approaching one hundred miles per hour.

Later, when thinking about his father's death at high speed on a Texas highway and the rollover car crash that Tom had survived, I began to question whether his anxiousness to enlist was simply the result of a nose for adventure, or because he could not wait to look death in the eye. Something slightly ominous seemed to be at work just beneath the surface of his perpetually optimistic disposition.

Years later Jack Mooseau showed me a typical letter Tom sent him from boot camp in which he made small talk for a few paragraphs and then awkwardly inquired, "Have you heard from Linda?" While there with Tom, I presumed he'd gotten over her and moved on, and so had no idea, until much later, of the feelings he still carried for Linda and his well-concealed sense of loss.

❧ ❧

We graduated from boot camp in early August. The Archer and Mahoney families came for the ceremony and were bursting with pride. Tom not only thrived on the tempo and challenges of basic training, but also bulked up on mess hall chow. I, on the other hand, though now physically stronger and mentally tougher than on the day I arrived, and proud of what I had accomplished, barely filled out my uniform at six feet tall and one hundred forty-five pounds.

The next day we were told our occupational training assignments. Tom was to become a basic rifleman and I a field radio operator. Both of us would be stationed not far away at Camp Pendleton, though in different units several miles apart. Before going to radio school, I spent three weeks in basic infantry training and then, to my dismay, was randomly selected for a month of mess duty. By the time I was finally allowed to go home on leave, I had missed seeing Tom, who had already been there and returned.

I completed field radio school in October and then spent two weeks in advanced infantry and special weapons training. In early November, I met Tom in Oceanside, California for dinner and noticed how unusually preoccupied and somber he appeared. The seriousness of our situation was settling in. We were heading for the war and would not be home for over a year unless wounded—perhaps never. Later that evening in front of the diner we slapped each other's backs and said our goodbyes. Nothing audacious or witty came to us like we had seen in movies about our fathers' war ("Hey Mack, I'll give your regards to the Emperor"). The best I could come up with was "Keep your head down," and even that came out sounding like golf advice.

3
BAPTISM OF FIRE

TOM ARRIVED IN SOUTH VIETNAM on November 9, 1967 and joined Bravo Company, First Battalion, First Marine Regiment the following day at the recently constructed U.S. air base near Quang Tri City. After checking in with the administrative staff, Tom was sent to the supply tent to exchange his stateside utility uniform and boots for jungle-style replacements and pick up his M-16 rifle and individual combat equipment.

The next evening the men of First Battalion, who were not otherwise deployed out in the field, or engaged in other duties, celebrated the one hundred ninety-second birthday of the United States Marine Corps. Each November 10, throughout the world, Marines pause to observe the occasion as a reminder that, no matter how far flung they are, they remain a band of brothers. The ceremony includes a cake ceremoniously sliced by the traditional Mameluke sword, with the first piece presented to the oldest Marine in the command signifying respect accorded to experience and seniority. Rather than eating it, the senior Marine passes it on to the youngest, demonstrating the responsibility of veterans to teach those newer to the Corps.

While not the youngest man in the battalion, twenty-year-old Tom Mahoney was the newest. He had graduated from boot camp barely three months before and was desperate to absorb as much knowledge as he could from the combat veterans around him. Complicating this process, his unit was in an unusual state of flux. The battalion's commanding officer had just been relieved of duty and the Bravo Company commander, along with his entire First Platoon, was being sequestered at Division Headquarters in Da Nang—under investigation for murdering civilians. Tom would be part of the wholesale replacement of that platoon.

As a rifleman, he worked hard to familiarize himself with his new M-16 rifle, adjusting it to what was termed "battle-zero" in which the front and rear sights were arranged to fire accurately at short range up to point blank. This was necessary because American forces were slowly adapting to the warfare style of the North Vietnamese Army, now streaming across the border into South Vietnam, who were better equipped and trained than the soldiers of the indigenous National Front for the Liberation of South Vietnam, or Viet Cong (VC).

The NVA were especially adept in sophisticated ambushes employing a high level of preparation and fire discipline, waiting until American patrols were within a few meters of them before opening fire. This tactic limited the use of supporting artillery or air attacks from U.S. bombers and helicopters, for fear of hitting their own forces in such close proximity.

Marine rifle platoons constantly patrolled in the "bush," with only brief respites in relatively secure areas where they were provided hot food and showers and slept in a tent or hut at night. The rest of the time they were out in the field where the terrain and weather of Vietnam made their life miserable beyond description.

Whenever a patrol stopped for more than a short time, the weary Marines and corpsmen dug fox holes to avoid injury or death from the flurry of enemy mortar shells that invariably followed. Although the men were constantly exhausted from the daily labor of hiking through villages, along steep ridgelines and across boot-sucking rice paddies, sleep did not come easily, nor was it adequate for keeping their wits sharp. Even in the best conditions, when the weather was bearable, enemy pressure was light and there were fewer of the ubiquitous mosquitoes, centipedes, rats, snakes and other toxic vermin biting, stinging or slithering over them at night, they rarely managed to get more than two hours of sleep at a time due to the nightly requirements of manning ambushes, listening posts, perimeter guard watch or radio duty.

During the hot season, carrying weapons, gear and ammo, a typical infantryman could lose 20 percent of his body weight. Parasites, like leeches and hookworm were common; as were debilitating diseases such as malaria, dysentery and trench foot. In the cooler, rainy, monsoon season, they battled influenza and ailments of the lung due to mold and fungus. Casualty rates in these units due to wounds and disease ran as high as 70 percent.

The Marines shared the load of the ammunition necessary for the weapons they took on patrol, which, in addition to small arms and hand grenades, could include heavy belts of machine gun bullets, mortar shells and mines. They possessed few personal items, since any additional weight magnified the difficulty of the march. While other U.S. military personnel also engaged in high risk occupations during the Vietnam War, including those in aviation, none lived a more wretched and precarious existence than the men of a Marine rifle platoon in the field.

Along with the physical ordeal, there was a persistent fear of injury, death or capture. The elusiveness of the enemy was particularly frustrating. Marines rarely knew of their presence until a booby trap explosion maimed or killed some of them, or a sudden ambush erupted on an exposed flank with murderous rifle and machine gun fire and a shower of hand- and rocket-propelled grenades. For this reason, they bore a nagging concern that they might not meet the challenge, later described by combat veteran and author Tim O'Brien as, "the common secret of cowardice barely restrained, the instinct to run or freeze or hide." In some respects, he wrote, it was probably the most difficult burden of all "for it could never be put down... they were too frightened to be cowards."[8]

Tom Mahoney entered this hellish world just eleven days after arriving in Vietnam, when Bravo Company moved fifteen miles northwest to a place called Con Thien, a muddy, treeless high spot in otherwise flat terrain, hugging the Demilitarized Zone (DMZ). Early missionaries had named it Nui Con Thien, or "Mount of Angels;" however, it was the *least* heavenly place in all of South Vietnam.

The NVA had launched several fierce ground attacks against the camp since early 1967, and, over the course of the ensuing sixteen months, nearly ten thousand Marines and corpsmen would be killed or wounded at Con Thien and in the area just to the south and east of it called Leatherneck Square. Throughout the summer and early autumn of 1967, scores of enemy artillery shells, mortars and rockets pounded the camp each day. There were few days without any incoming, and on some days the number was frightfully high. During one eight-day span in September, over three thousand rounds landed on the little camp. Marine artillery proved ineffective in knocking out these guns and mortars because the NVA kept them well hidden in caves and camouflaged pits, often located north of the DMZ. American fighter/bombers trying to destroy them were frequently hampered by low rain clouds.

High altitude, saturation bombing was soon deemed the best way to deal with the situation. Air Force B-52 Stratofortress bombers, originally designed as a major component of the United States' nuclear warfare capability, would now be used as conventional bombers over South Vietnam and Laos. Code named "Arc Light," a typical mission consisted of two sets of three bombers arriving ten minutes apart and passing over a target area approximately one mile long by one-half-mile wide. Each plane dropped fifty tons of high-explosives from an altitude of over thirty thousand feet, with almost no warning to those in the target area. In the month of September 1967, the U.S. directed nine hundred Arc Light bombing missions in the defense of Con Thien, yet unrelenting enemy shelling of the camp continued.

Because of this constant, deadly enemy artillery bombardment, Marines began referring to Con Thien as "The Meatgrinder" or "The Barrel" (as in the phrase, "Our turn in The Barrel"). American units were rotated in and out on a monthly basis due to the high number of physical casualties and mental health issues associated with the unremitting anxiety of not being safe from death anywhere in the camp at any time.

On November 20, 1967, Tom Mahoney and his battalion arrived for their turn in the barrel, and it did not go unnoticed by the NVA who greeted Bravo Company's sector with over one hundred rounds of mortar and artillery fire before the day was over.[9] Before arriving at Con Thien, the battalion's four companies were required to be close to full strength. This meant three platoons of forty-six Marines and Navy medical corpsmen, divided into three squads of approximately thirteen men, plus various command and weapons personnel and the company headquarters and support contingent. Ideally, each company would consist of about one hundred eighty men, but in reality, Marine combat units in South Vietnam were lucky to be operating at 80 percent of full strength at any given time.

Tom's first taste of combat was on December 15 when Bravo was ambushed by several hundred NVA soldiers while patrolling just a mile northwest of the camp. The sudden eruption of gunfire sent the Americans scrambling for cover. As enemy heavy machine gun bullets scythed through the tall grass above their heads, Tom and the others hurriedly dug shallow foxholes and tried their best to return fire as mortar shells and grenades began to explode among them. After being pinned down for over an hour, one hundred fifty more Marines arrived to assist, and quickly came under attack. Finally, with the aid of tanks, supporting artillery and air strikes, the Marines were able to extricate themselves by nightfall, carrying out thirty-seven dead and wounded. An officer later wrote "the enemy's excellent fire discipline and tenacity, indicated a large and well-organized unit."[10]

By the time his battalion departed Con Thien just before Christmas, Tom was settling into First Platoon and still unscathed. His thoughts about this first battle are lost to us, but knowing Tom, I'm sure he considered it a thrilling adrenalin rush and was hankering for more. He would not have to wait long. Bravo Company was now scarred by combat and the scandal of murdered civilians and, as they stood guard at an airport just south of the city called Hué (pronounced *Whey*), few could imagine they would soon be pushed to their limits in one of the most savage battles of the Vietnam War.

4
KHE SANH

MY ADVANCED INFANTRY TRAINING ended about two weeks after Tom and I exchanged goodbyes in front of the diner in Oceanside. The instructors had led us through mock ambushes, patrols and defensive perimeter situations, regularly inserting the morose disclaimer that even the best-trained Marines ended up dead. By the time they had walked us back along the paths of our training patrols, pointing out all the deadly devices and ambush cues we'd missed, my adolescent daydreams of heroics on the battlefield were significantly eroded.

I landed at the Da Nang airfield on the morning of December 6, 1967, and was soon walking with the other new guys past a line of servicemen going home, mostly Marines, waiting to board the plane we'd just arrived on. A few sang out the traditional "You'll be sor-r-r-e-e," and other exaggerated expressions of mock condolence, but most stood mutely, their sidelong glances containing a look of mild disappointment, as if they had expected us to be wiser. They were, as a San Francisco poet once described, hearing "the distant roaring of our futures."[11] A few gazed more strangely, their heavy lids hiding something I did not yet recognize, a weariness, a torpor, a disturbing lack of interest.

We were driven to the in-country flight terminal in another part of the sprawling air base in a bus with metal screens welded over the windows to deflect hand grenades. I had orders for Khe Sanh and after checking in, waited about an hour for my flight; spending most of that time on the floor, leaning on my bag and talking nervously with others, all the while feeling jumpy inside—wanting to go, and not wanting to go, in alternating waves of excitement and dread. I was soon bathed in sweat from a combination of anxiety and unfamiliarity with tropical humidity, which made me light-headed, heightening the sensation that I was being swept along by some irresistible current toward an unknown fate.

I finally boarded a C-123, twin-engine, cargo plane loaded with pallets of C-rations and mortar ammunition. Within fifteen minutes, the plane was airborne and heading north. My seat was on the left side near a small window from which I could view the stunning countryside as it passed below.

Central Vietnam at the latitude of Khe Sanh is a slender neck only forty miles wide with wildly varying terrain. Along the South China Sea, wide stretches of sand dunes and tidal estuaries gave way to a fertile rice growing plain. Further to the west, foothills slowly rise at first, then abruptly turn into the lofty, rugged, and largely impenetrable Annamite Mountains. There, towering peaks are cloaked in rainforests, with tall stands of teak and mahogany forming an upper canopy above a secondary covering of smaller trees closer to the ground. Moving along the trails beneath this thick lid of vegetation, the days are a perpetual twilight, and nights are pitch black.

From October to May, the northeast monsoon sweeping in off the ocean makes Khe Sanh the rainiest place in Vietnam. As our plane beat its way through the last few miles of dark, leaden clouds, a gap suddenly opened up, not much larger than the plane itself, and we plunged through it in a steep left bank. Below me, amid rags of mist, Khe Sanh Combat Base suddenly appeared as a mile-long, rust-colored scrape in the damp, green vegetation. Our landing on the newly upgraded runway was smooth and the plane rolled to a stop near the center of the base.

My first impression of Khe Sanh was its smell, as if someone had just turned over a large, wet rock—the moldy stench of sodden decay. As I walked from the airstrip down the main road, I noticed wisps of greasy black smoke rising from metal tubs, and my nose was assaulted by the revolting mixture of burning diesel fuel and human waste. It was my introduction to the favored manner of eliminating the contents of our latrines ("heads" or "crappers" in the vernacular of the Marines) and I reflexively thrust an index finger against my nose to keep from gagging.

After asking directions, I was soon slogging along a muddy road toward the Twenty-sixth Marine Regimental Headquarters Company area. Once the paperwork was completed, a clerk directed me to my living quarters, a large tent near the east end of the runway next to the base's main ammunition dump.

The next day I went to the company supply office and received my individual combat gear, M-16 rifle, new jungle boots and a jungle uniform, which I hoped would stop me from looking so conspicuously new to the place. A Marine in my tent convinced me that I needed to check in at the morgue to be measured for my body bag. When I naively showed up there an hour later to be fitted, the sergeant had a good, long, derisive laugh at my expense. Except for similar harmless pranks, most members of my unit were friendly and helpful.

Two days later, a sergeant led some of us new men out past the east end of the runway in order to become familiar with our M-16 rifles. It was the first time I had used an M-16, having trained only with the M-14 and M-1. As we fired a few hundred rounds across the runway, I remember thinking how incredibly beautiful the countryside was. The pinnacle of Hill 1015 to the north was covered in dense, verdant rain forest of hues I did not even know existed. Its lower slopes broadened slightly into a plain of yellowish-green elephant grass, in places, over six feet high. Near the Rao Quan River gorge, the slope disappeared in a thick tangle of vine and bamboo. In the tranquil magnificence of that afternoon, it would have been difficult to picture an enemy camped on top of that mountain, vigilantly observing our every move though high-powered binoculars. More impossible to believe was that a few weeks later the very place I was now standing would be in enemy hands.

I was assigned to work in the underground regimental Combat Operations Center, called the COC (pronounced *see-oh-see*). This large, cement bunker near the center of the base was constructed in October 1965 to store ammunition, but was soon converted to a command center when the NVA began shelling the place three months later.

As a radio operator with the Tactical Air Control Party, or "air team," my new duties included coordinating close air support bombers and medevac and resupply choppers throughout the area. I worked alongside fire-direction officers and radio operators from our artillery unit, the First Battalion, Thirteenth Marines, in advising those aircraft where "friendly" artillery fire was being aimed so they could steer clear of it and not be knocked down in midair by one of our own rounds. As enemy activity around the base increased, our outgoing artillery fire did as well, and keeping track of it all became nearly impossible. Helicopter pilots increasingly complained of "close calls" and I was always conscious of the fact that a disaster could happen on my watch, regardless of my best efforts, and I would likely be blamed.

When not on radio watch, I kept busy with labor projects around the base and tried to learn what I could from the experienced hands. Some of them had been there since just after the grueling Hill Fights that Tom and I had watched so intently on television eight months before. These men still would not sleep in tents, but rather in small underground bunkers with sandbagged roofs, knowing the enemy would be back again someday with artillery and assault forces to capture the combat base.

The NVA Central Command in Hanoi had long intended to take the combat base and were poised to do so in May 1967. However, their inability to hold the high ground to the west, forced them to scrub the plan. Marine commanders during the Hill Fights were well aware the combat base was the prize, concluding that if the NVA had successfully defended the hills for just a few more days, their 325C Division in nearby Laos would have passed another two thousand soldiers through them to capture the airfield and base—perhaps altering the course of the war.

I soon learned that I was part of a calculated buildup of forces there because American intelligence reports recently determined that the NVA were again planning to seize the combat base, though they had not identified exactly *when*. Many high ranking Marine officers, seeing little practical value in defending Khe Sanh, were also wondering *why* they should make a stand at a location so favorable to the enemy.

The Marines had first splashed ashore at Da Nang in 1965 and set to work trying to secure the populated coastal regions by conducting aggressive operations against the Viet Cong. The aim was to provide security for harried villagers, and win them over by providing rudimentary healthcare and other government services. The Marines joined with local militias to form Combined Action Platoons and within two years there would be nearly eighty such units implementing a strategy designed to force communist guerrillas from the villages and keep them separated from the local population.

Without a pliant peasantry to inform, feed and reinforce the thousands of North Vietnamese soldiers who had infiltrated into the mountains west of the population centers, they would have to either transport massive amounts of food down jungle trails to sustain themselves, or send soldiers into coastal villages to seize from poor peasants the rice they needed to survive. As Marine leaders saw it, the presence of effective combined action units would force the NVA to prosecute the war on terms much more favorable to the Americans and South Vietnamese. The only problem was that General William C. Westmoreland did not trust the loyalty of the South Vietnamese people or the competency of the Marines.

Westmoreland headed the Military Assistance Command-Vietnam (MACV) headquartered in Saigon, making him commander of all American forces in South Vietnam. Tall, lantern-jawed, the imperious spawn of South Carolina aristocracy dating back to the American Revolution, Westmoreland's presence exuded command and experience; although, as a field-grade artillery officer during the Second World War and Korea, he had virtually no familiarly with front line combat. He later became a peacetime protégé of General

Maxwell Taylor, another former artillery commander, who as Chair of the Joint Chiefs of Staff and private presidential advisor, would be directly responsible for Westmoreland's appointment as head of MACV.

Taylor would later be described by historians, such as (Lieutenant General) H.R. McMaster in his book *Dereliction of Duty,* as so blindly loyal to President Johnson that he intentionally distorted the recommendations of the Joint Chiefs on how to conduct the war in order to poison relations between them and the civilian leadership, thus strengthening Secretary of Defense Robert McNamara's hand in steering the strategy as he saw fit. Taylor and Westmoreland shared the belief that the Vietnamese people, after having endured long periods of foreign occupations over the centuries, were strongly xenophobic and that "sometimes the only way to establish control is remove the people and destroy the village."[12]

Both men had learned their craft later in the Second World War when Allies began emulating the strategy of conquering German and Japanese forces by frequently and intentionally targeting civilians for massive bombardment, killing hundreds of thousands in an effort to break the will of these two nations to continue the fight.

The path to victory, Westmoreland said, was to force the enemy to the negotiating table by using America's superior firepower to kill them in numbers unacceptable to the government in Hanoi.

In October 1965, Henry Kissinger, director of the Harvard Defense Studies Program, who as Secretary of State eight years later would negotiate the peace accords that ended American involvement in the war, met with General Westmoreland in Saigon. Later that evening Kissinger wrote in his diary:

> A great deal of military planning assumes that the opponent is stupid and that he will fight the kind of war for which one is best prepared. However… the essence of guerrilla warfare is never to fight the kind of war your opponent expects. We must not become prisoners now of a large-unit mentality[13]

Marine generals, drawing on decades of experience gained during similar deployments in places like the Philippines and the Dominican Republic, also disagreed with Westmoreland's approach. Spearheaded by Lieutenant General Victor Krulak, commander of the Fleet Marine Force-Pacific, they hoped to correct his misconceptions about the Vietnamese people and their history.

Krulak, at five-feet, four-inches tall and born in Denver, Colorado to Jewish immigrants from Russia, did not have Westmoreland's stately physical appearance or pedigree, but proved to be a remarkable visionary since graduating in 1934 from the U.S. Naval Academy, and would later personally lead troops into combat in the South Pacific during the Second World War. Historian Neil Sheehan wrote that Krulak's intellect and honesty gave him "the distinction of becoming an American military leader who understood the minds of the men in Hanoi."[14] While he had, during the early years of U.S involvement in Vietnam, agreed with Westmoreland's predecessor, General Paul D. Harkins, that U.S. and South Vietnamese forces were winning the war against the Viet Cong, Krulak now called for sweeping social and economic changes in the south, including land reform and a pacification strategy designed to win over the support of the Vietnamese peasantry. Even with this in place, victory could not be achieved if the flow of war materiel into North Vietnam's seaports was not stopped by mining the harbors and bombing the docks. President Johnson, fearing damage to Russian or Chinese vessels there might broaden the conflict, refused to consider such action.

From the early 1960s, ideological rifts and occasional military clashes along their common borders, kept tensions high between the Soviet Union and the People's Republic of China, the world's two most powerful communist nations. Because North Vietnam was dependent on both countries for military supplies, yet wary of their geopolitical designs, leaders in Hanoi were engaged in a perpetual diplomatic balancing act. While the Soviet Union and the United States were using Vietnam as a proxy for carrying out their ongoing Cold War power struggle, the People's Republic of China, which shared a border with North Vietnam, was in throes of severe, internal instability called The Great Proletarian Cultural Revolution. As such, President Johnson worried that further provocations against them would result in a disastrous scenario similar to what had happened in 1950, when over a hundred thousand Chinese soldiers suddenly moved against U.S. and NATO forces in Korea.

In late 1966, General Westmoreland demanded that the Marines move away from protecting the civilian population and attack NVA units hiding in well-fortified encampments amid the jungle-clad mountains along the country's border with Laos near Khe Sanh. Krulak rushed to Vietnam to meet with him. The Khe Sanh airstrip and base, he told Westmoreland, could not be defended without stationing hundreds of Marines on several hills overlooking it from a distance of between two and five miles, and would require a major helicopter commitment because these outposts could not be supported overland. He reminded Westmoreland that because the Khe Sanh valley had the worst weather in all of South Vietnam, visibility for air operations and other tactical actions would be problematic for six months of the year.

Westmoreland had a different view. Reinforcing this isolated airfield, he said, was critical to blocking enemy movement into South Vietnam and should be maintained as a future jumping-off point for invading NVA supply dumps in Laos. More importantly, it was a perfect venue to lure thousands of communist soldiers into the open and annihilate them with the enormous firepower at his disposal.

Krulak persisted. Holding Khe Sanh would not deter the North Vietnamese from infiltrating into the south, as they had proven convincingly they could do without roads such as Highway 9, the main route extending from Laos through Khe Sanh to the sea. And a war of attrition would fail because it played precisely into the enemy's plan. The communists were seeking to attract U.S. forces into violent, close-quarters combat which tended to diminish the advantage in supporting arms. The north could replace troops faster, and with less negative political consequences at home than could the Americans. It was, Krulak said, "the mathematics of futility"[15] in which Hanoi would count on high American casualties to erode the national will.

General Westmoreland remained adamant, and so in September 1966 the Marines reluctantly acquiesced to his demand, permanently stationing units at the Khe Sanh camp. The commander of the Third Marine Division immediately warned that at Khe Sanh the NVA were going to wait until the weather closes in and then "jump on us."[16] Another, Marine Brigadier General Lowell English, a tough combat veteran of places like Guadalcanal and Iwo Jima, called Khe Sanh "a trap" and chafed at the insistence by Westmoreland to "expend absolutely unreasonable amounts of men and materiel" to defend the place. "When you're at Khe Sanh," English said, "you're not really anywhere. You could lose it and you really haven't lost a damn thing."[17]

In May 1967, the Twenty-sixth Marine Regiment arrived there and throughout the summer fought bloody skirmishes with the enemy in the surrounding hills. The NVA frequently shelled the combat base in retaliation for these incursions, but by late August things quieted down. Marine patrols continued to roam the area throughout the rest of the summer and fall and, while the enemy remained elusive, no one doubted they were out there and planning something big.

As I was settling into life at Khe Sanh in December of that year, part of our evening routine was listening on the radio to Trinh Thi Ngo, aka "Hanoi Hannah." Broadcasting a nightly program in English out of North Vietnam, Hannah would, between the music of shrill Vietnamese female sopranos, marching bands and an occasional contemporary rock song, dispense propaganda in a clipped, though oddly coquettish, monotone. On New Year's Eve I listened as she played *Auld Lang Syne*, dedicating it to the "men of the Twenty-sixth Regiment," and informing us that North Vietnam's president, Ho Chi Minh, would be celebrating the Tet holiday in the Khe Sanh mess hall. We made our usual obscene comments about her, but the personal nature of this threat left us slightly uneasy. We had good reason to feel that way.

General Westmoreland anticipated that the upcoming battle for Khe Sanh would be the greatest of the war. And, while costly in American lives, he believed it would be far more disastrous for the North Vietnamese[18] who he planned to "drown" in an unprecedented cascade of bombs, fittingly code-named "Operation Niagara." Westmoreland sent General Philip Davidson to the combat base to personally discuss the enemy build up with the Twenty-sixth Marines' new regimental commander, Colonel David E. Lownds. A dismayed Davidson reported back that the place was not ready to survive such an attack, with most of the men, fuel and ammunition still aboveground and unprotected, and "a general lack of preparation to withstand heavy concentrations of artillery and mortar fire."[19]

There is no question we were ill-prepared, but the reason was not entirely our fault. In preparation for what he hoped would be the war's defining battle, Westmoreland ordered the airstrip upgraded to accommodate larger cargo planes and so it was closed from August 1967 until late October. With the runway shut down, the base was resupplied by helicopter and parachute drops. Priority for space onboard resupply choppers and airdrop aircraft went to the airfield enhancement project. By the time work was completed, the winter monsoon blew in with its usual blanketing fog and steady, cold rain, greatly reducing air operations. Paradoxically, it was this effort to improve the resupply capability of Khe Sanh that prevented the arrival of materiel to strengthen our bunkers to withstand the artillery, rocket and mortar attacks we knew were coming.

Local materials proved inadequate, especially around the hill outposts where the remaining trees were so full of shrapnel from the Hill Fights that they broke chainsaws and axes when the Americans tried to harvest them for bunker building. On November 10, 1967, the Marine Corps Birthday, Colonel Lownds flew through a driving rain to Hill 881 South, encouraging his men there to dig in as securely as they could. "We here at Khe Sanh," he told them, "will be remembered in our American history books."[20]

In the waning days of 1967, Marine patrols from the combat base and hill outposts aggressively swept the area to the south and west, but found little evidence of an NVA presence. General Westmoreland suspected the Marines were intentionally avoiding the enemy in order to claim they were not there in the numbers he believed, and that the poor defensive posture of the base was yet another manifestation of Marine resistance to his plans for Khe Sanh. Accordingly, he ordered the entire First Air Cavalry Division to be moved from central South Vietnam so they could quickly reinforce Khe Sanh should the need arise. By the end of January 1968, 40 percent of all U.S. infantry and armor battalions in South Vietnam were positioned within one hundred miles of Khe Sanh.

While publicly downplaying the significance of this move, Westmoreland actually had little respect for the fighting capabilities of Marines, explaining his concerns in a communiqué to the Army Chief of Staff that "the tactical professionalism" of the Marines fell "far short of the standards that should be demanded by our armed forces;" adding that he had brought so many of U.S. Army forces north because he felt "insecure with the situation in Quang Tri Province, in view of my knowledge of their shortcomings."[21]

❧ ❧

I was unaware of this inter-service strife while learning my duties at Khe Sanh Combat Base. As a new guy, I was often given the least desirable late night radio duty in the big map room of the COC, occasionally alongside another new arrival, Steve Orr. I first met Steve in field radio school at Camp Pendleton during the fall of 1967 and immediately disliked him. An overactive, baby-faced, nineteen-year old Alabaman, who had lived the last few years in California, Steve enjoyed the nightlife in Oceanside and visiting his girlfriend two hundred miles away in Santa Barbara, and so was always short of cash. To remedy this, he carried a deck of playing cards with him at all times, producing it whenever he picked up the scent of an unwary Marine with a few dollars in his pocket; or turned huckster, peddling clothes and personal items in the barracks. He and I received orders for Vietnam at the same time and sat beside one another on the long plane ride to Asia. Upon arriving at Khe Sanh, we were assigned to the same platoon. From that point on I recognized that Fate had ordained us to be friends and we have remained so for a lifetime.

While the two of us were on radio watch late one night in early January, Colonel Lownds came into the room, dropped into his lawn chair and lit a cigar. Lownds began studying the big wall map, absently twirling one end of his handlebar mustache. Suddenly, as if in the midst of a revelation, he muttered, "We're slowly getting surrounded."

I glanced sidelong at Steve and rolled my eyes in an effort to mask my anxiety. Twenty-three-years earlier as a young lieutenant, Lownds had been wounded during ferocious battles on Saipan and Iwo Jima and so had no illusions about how bad things could get. I, on the other hand, had not yet even heard the sound of hostile gunfire and so could not imagine how bad things were about to become. Still, for months afterward, during the worst of times when we needed a good laugh at the absurdity of our situation, Steve and I would lampoon the Colonel by twirling our imaginary mustaches and grimly pronouncing: "We're slowly getting surrounded."

The NVA's 304th Division arrived in late 1967 and set up a command post about fifteen miles southwest of the Khe Sanh Combat Base. Their expectations about the coming battle were so high that they brought with them bundles of English-language pamphlets for the instruction of the hundreds of American captives they anticipated taking.

Tension grew at the combat base as we waited and watched. In mid-January 1968, a Marine reconnaissance (recon) team patrolling six miles to the west of us surprised and shot two NVA soldiers sitting alongside a trail, then quickly found themselves surrounded. In the ensuing firefight, two Marines were killed and it would be well after nightfall before the team was able to extricate themselves and their dead.

News of this encounter distressed the North Vietnamese high command more than it did the Americans. Their original plan had been to secretly move adequate forces into the area and then launch simultaneous devastating assaults against the combat base and its outposts in early February. But, because the Americans were now tipped off to their presence, the date of the attacks would have to be moved up before U.S. forces could react in sufficient numbers to disrupt them. They decided upon January 20—just five days away—setting off frantic movements of soldiers, ammunition and food to forward staging areas.[22]

They set up artillery firebases in a broad arc to the south and west, most just out of range of American artillery.[23] During the last week of 1967, the majority of the NVA's 325-C Division arrived at the front. Two of their regiments were returning after having fought against Marines in the Hill Fights the previous spring and "felt ready and excited about the upcoming campaign."[24]

On the eve of the battle, the NVA had a force of about 27,000 in position. Of them, 9,000 were infantry riflemen, half of whom were armed with assault rifles, the remainder carrying older weapons, and nearly four hundred with rocket-propelled grenade (RPG) launchers. Crew-served weapons included more than one thousand five hundred light- and heavy-machine guns, forty recoilless rifles and one hundred eighty mortar tubes.[25] It was the one of the largest and best supported attack forces ever fielded by the Vietnamese, and, as it tightened the noose around the scattered and out-numbered Americans at Khe Sanh, seemed invincible.

5
THEY'RE EVERYWHERE

AT FIRST LIGHT on January 20, 1968, Marines on Hill 881 South set out on a patrol to learn the strength of enemy forces nearby, unaware that this was the date selected by the NVA High Command to begin the general attack. Less than a mile into their march the Americans ran into hundreds of enemy soldiers coming the other way to capture their hill. Before becoming encircled and trapped, the Marines fought their way back up to the safety of their defensive positions.

At 3:30 a.m. the following morning, about five hundred NVA soldiers attacked Hill 861 overlooking the combat base, intent on recapturing it after having been driven from there by Marines during the Hill Fights seven months before. Being intimately familiar with that terrain, the NVA quickly breached the barbed wire and engaged the American defenders in bitter, often hand-to-hand, combat.

They held some units in reserve in an area considered safe from Marine cannons at the combat base, intending to use these forces to finish off the defenders on Hill 861. But, because Marines on nearby Hill 881 South had ruined the enemy plan for a surprise attack against them, they were now free to use their artillery and mortars in helping defend Hill 861, firing over two thousand rounds directly into that "safe area." This, coupled with the valiant stand of the out-numbered Marines in the trenches of Hill 861 that dark morning, drove the attackers into retreat.

If the Marines on Hill 881 South had not accidentally crossed paths the day before with the large enemy force advancing to capture their position, their hill may have been lost, and Hill 861, not ben-efitting from that timely artillery support, may have fallen too. Had that happened, the NVA would have once again owned that high ground directly overlooking the airstrip at Khe Sanh Combat Base. It was a close call, requiring a stroke of luck for the Americans and the inability, or unwillingness, of NVA commanders in the field to anticipate that scenario of artillery support and call off the doomed attack on 861.

❧ ❧

Nine days before this fighting, I had been ordered, along with another Marine from my communications platoon, to assist the lone radio operator at the combined action company in Khe Sanh village. With Colonel Lownds' recent comment about the base "slowly getting surrounded" still fresh in my mind, I quickly wrote my parents because I had no idea when, or if, I was ever getting back. I was scared. Our little convoy crept to the village over two miles of badly rutted road, arriving in the late morning at our destination, the Huong Hoa District Headquarters. The compound consisted of several French colonial-style buildings housing the South Vietnamese government's official presence in that part of Quang Tri Province. Khe Sanh village was the largest population center in the area, with about thirteen hundred Vietnamese inhabiting the place along with a handful of French and American civilians. In addition, approximately twenty thousand Montagnards, mostly of the Bru tribe, lived in the vicinity. For centuries these indigenous peoples had lived an isolated and primitive existence within the Annamite mountain chain, which extended from China south to the low foothills near Cambodia and by 1968 numbered about two million.

The north side of the district headquarters compound, along Highway 9, was guarded by U.S. Marines and Bru militiamen, and the south side by two platoons of regional Vietnamese forces, with four U.S. Army advisors. The radio bunker where I stood my nightly watch was directly behind the headquarters building and about twenty meters from the barbed wire fence forming the west side of the compound. Topped by a corrugated metal roof and some sand-bags, only half of this bunker was below ground.

Because we did not have a secure, encrypted means of communication, we knew little of what was going on outside the village. My hometown football team, the Oakland Raiders, had been crushed in Super Bowl II and even that information came to me in succinct, unauthorized transmissions over the tactical radio network from my friends at the base who had Armed Forces Radio reception. The last of these messages that day to me (radio call sign *Mutter*) came from Steve Orr (*Intrigue*): "Mutter this is Intrigue. Final. Packers 33, Raiders 14. Sorry, buddy. Intrigue out."

Despite Hills 861 and 881 South being only three to four miles from the village, I did not know about the fighting there on January 20. However, by late that afternoon we were advised that a large NVA force would soon be attacking us. After breaking that bad news, the various intelligence community people and South Vietnamese government officials at the district headquarters quickly bundled up whatever classified material and equipment they had and sped off in their vehicles before dark to the safety of the combat base. The rest of us assembled at the edge of the LZ just outside the compound to test fire our weapons, including our lone mortar. I was surprised by how calmly we went about our business that evening, fully cognizant that hundreds, maybe thousands, of enemy troops were rapidly closing in on our tiny force of about thirty Americans and one hundred forty indigenous soldiers and militia.

I began my radio watch at 6:00 p.m. and transmitted hourly situation reports to the base, first checking to make sure I had several magazines of ammunition for my M-16, grenades and spare batteries for the radio. At approximately 5:30 a.m. on January 21, a radio transmission from the combat base put all forces in the area on red alert. Minutes later we were under attack in an earsplitting din of chattering semi-automatic rifles, the rapid knocking of machine guns, jarring detonations of rocket-propelled grenades and the deep, reverberating crunch of exploding mortar shells. At times, the sound shifted away and then back, like waves on a beach. At other times, one side of the compound would abruptly go silent for a few seconds—long enough for me to nervously wonder if the defenders there had been overwhelmed.

Moments before the attack I had left the bunker to wake up the Marine commander, Lieutenant Thomas Stamper, an easy-going, thirty-three-year-old former enlisted man who had arrived just two weeks before. I would quickly come to respect him for his calmness and optimism during the ensuing fight. About five minutes after the assault began, Stamper made it safely through the gunfire to my radio bunker and ordered me to call in our prearranged artillery fire missions, designed to explode in the air about twenty-five feet directly above us, creating a sizzling spray of jagged shrapnel, deadly to anyone caught in the open. It seemed to take forever, but soon the first of those shells burst overhead, like thunder reverberating in a narrow canyon. Through the small rifle port in the bunker wall, I could see the white-orange explosion flashes against the morning gloom. It seemed to go on for a long time. I never wanted it to end.

Once the artillery finally stopped, it was deathly quiet for several minutes. Hundreds of shells had burst in the air above us killing or wounding most of our exposed attackers. Sporadic enemy small arms and machine gun fire eventually resumed, along with an occasional flurry of mortar rounds, but with nothing of its previous intensity. At first light, I was able to see just how close we had come to being completely overrun. Enemy dead littered the ground right up to our fighting positions. Some of the surviving NVA soldiers now dug in close to our barbed wire and continued sniping at us.

Despite our successful defense of the district headquarters compound that morning, the NVA had taken the rest of the village. A relief force, which in normal times would have taken less than an hour to walk to us from the combat base, halted just outside the little town, warned by a Montagnard about an impending ambush.[26] Colonel Lownds soon recalled them to the base.

Because we were already so low on ammunition by then, I believed that without reinforcements or resupply we would not make it through the coming night. If the NVA had enough soldiers in the village to have blocked that company-sized rescue effort, they would certainly overrun us with ease. A surge of anger gripped me. Marines never left other Marines behind. You risked your life to save your buddy—that was the code. I stood by the radio bench stiff and silent, trying to come to terms with the potential consequences of this abandonment.

Upon learning the Marine relief force had withdrawn, the commander of the Special Forces unit radioed his headquarters about sixty miles away in Quang Tri. Several U.S. Army helicopters, carrying Army of the Republic of Vietnam (ARVN) volunteers led by an American advisor, attempted to reach our compound that evening. As they landed a half mile away, near an abandoned French fort, the choppers were mauled by enemy ground fire and RPGs. Four U.S. Army soldiers were killed and the bulk of the ARVNs either died or were captured. Most of the helicopters returned safely to Quang Tri.

When news reached us that the relief force was annihilated, I sat down on the earthen floor of the bunker with my back resting against the radio bench. Through the narrow rifle port in the bunker wall the setting sun cast a ray upon my face. Watching dust motes swirling in that warm beam of light, I suddenly felt an unexpected sense of peace, as though some enormous weight was lifted. I envisioned my family and friends, and how they would react to word of my death, and the absence of a body to bury. I pictured each for just a moment, as if checking them off some private list in my heart, including Tom Mahoney, who I knew would be distraught. I hoped he would make it home safely and warn others about such meaningless endings. Once done, I was resigned to my fate.

We held on through the night largely because several aircraft took shifts circling overhead dropping flares to provide illumination which deterred the enemy from attacking again. A specially equipped flare ship, nicknamed "*Spooky,*" arrived around midnight with its several electrically-fired Gatling guns capable of hosing down an area with thousands of bullets per minute. Stamper and I climbed on top of the radio bunker, staying pressed against the corrugated roof because of snipers. We directed *Spooky,* in whispers, to fire on an area about a mile to the south. This was the direction from which we believed the main NVA force had arrived and might still be using to stage reinforcements.

Later, Stamper went to his living quarters, fetched a bottle of Johnnie Walker Red Label scotch, and braved the persistent sniper fire to check in with his Marine's along the trench line, giving each man a swallow from the bottle before telling them the bad news that they had better attach bayonets onto their rifle barrels because we would soon be out of ammunition. My buddies on the radio at the combat base, sensing my disillusionment and despair at being abandoned (probably from the sullenness in my voice), made quick, surreptitious calls to me with words of encouragement throughout the night.

I worked hard to keep in constant communication with our flare ships, but about 3:00 a.m., now without sleep for over thirty hours, I nodded off, allowing a plane to drift off station. Darkness enveloped the compound causing the enemy close by to intensify their gunfire in preparation for another assault. The clatter of that snapped me awake and I ran with my radio outside into the trench line and eventually guided the plane back over us. By sunrise, our attackers had withdrawn and most of the defenders of the village, along with most of the civilian population, walked to the combat base unmolested by the enemy.

I found room on a Marine helicopter that had landed near our compound and, as we flew toward Khe Sanh base, it appeared the place was enshrouded in fog. I soon realized it was smoke, and from my vantage point it seemed half the combat base was missing. I had trouble at first comprehending the extent of the devastation, but would soon learn that incoming enemy shells had touched off the main ammunition dump, where over eleven thousand artillery and mortar shells along with other lethal ordnance, were stacked in a series of open pits. In a kind of chain reaction, our own ammunition rained down on the base, starting fires and creating numerous additional casualties.

The NVA occupied the District Headquarters the day after we abandoned it, a significant propaganda coup since it was the first time a seat of governmental authority had been captured by communist forces within the borders of South Vietnam. Yet the most immediate benefits for them was that they now had "a forward food depot," important because their supply chain from the rear area was not yet in place.[27] And, now just two miles from the combat base, they had sanctuary from U.S. artillery and bombs as they hid among the hundreds of civilians who had not been allowed into the base that morning and walked back to their homes in the village.

The second battle of Khe Sanh that General Westmoreland planned and hoped for had begun. He was confident in his ability to hold the combat base, and, at the same time, kill the enemy by the thousands with an unparalleled concentration of bombing and artillery. During the preceding week, he had reinforced Khe Sanh with three additional battalions, bringing the number of American and South Vietnamese defenders, at both the combat base and the outposts, to about six thousand men. Westmoreland knew American and ARVN casualties in the coming battle would be high. A graphic indication of that was provided two days after the initial attacks, when four large boxes arrived by cargo plane, each stenciled "5th Graves Registration Team, Khe Sanh," containing two tons of body bags.[28]

The NVA did not use bomber or attack aircraft against Khe Sanh, as was widely rumored they might, but their artillery was effective and constant with a range of up to nineteen miles. The largest Marine artillery pieces had a range of only nine.[29] So while their shells could reach us, we could not hit them back. Efforts by the Americans to destroy these guns with aerial bombardment were largely ineffective not only due to the weather, but because the NVA deployed them in caves and pits with extreme secrecy, often miles apart. Khe Sanh Combat Base were soon receiving hundreds of artillery rounds each day—some days exceeding a thousand.

The northerners maximized the effectiveness of this artillery by creating observation posts on high ground to spot the impact of their shells, assess damage and casualties, and identify new targets of opportunity, such as men congregating in the open. We defenders soon tuned into the rhythm of the incoming barrages and planned our travels around the base in short dashes from one piece of cover to another, lest enemy observers spot us standing in one place too long.

A few days after the initial attack on the base, twenty-seven-year-old Army Captain Mark Swearengen, from Monroe City, Missouri, arrived at Khe Sanh and was assigned to the COC as a forward fire support coordinator for the long-range, 175mm guns located a dozen miles east at Camp Carroll. Swearengen later recalled with a chuckle his first evening there, meeting with Marine Captain Kent Steen in the cramped, fire support coordination center. Swearengen, notebook in hand and pencil poised, anxiously waited for a detailed briefing on the disposition of enemy forces. Steen, the gifted, twenty-six-year-old Floridian responsible for prioritizing enemy targets now tightly encircling the combat base, paused for a few moments not knowing where to begin. Finally, exhaling a long sigh of exasperation, Steen swept his hand in a broad circle over the map he used to plot artillery fire and said simply: "They're everywhere."

6
SURVIVING HUÉ

IN THE SUMMER OF 1966 life could not have been better for twenty-two-year-old Frank Ahearn. Recently hired as an engineer to help build elevated highways through New Orleans, he was making more money than he ever imagined. As a bachelor, in his arctic white, four-door, 1963 Cadillac Sedan DeVille, he would cruise the French Quarter and other exciting parts of The Big Easy at night looking for fun. Then one day Frank visited his mailbox in the upscale, singles apartment complex where he lived, and that all changed. His draft notice had arrived.

Rather than waiting to be drafted as an enlisted man, Frank attempted to enroll in Navy flight training. He qualified, but there was a six-month waiting list for the next opening, during which he would not be protected from the draft. The Navy recruiter suggested he go downstairs to the Marine Corps office. There Frank negotiated a relatively short three-year military obligation to become a Marine officer, not fully comprehending that he had just made one of the most dangerous professional choices a young man in America could ask for in 1966.

In January 1967 Frank departed for Officer Candidate School (OCS) at Quantico, Virginia. His platoon consisted of about fifty candidates in a single cold, damp squad bay who, Frank later explained, were a broad mixture "of Ivy League spoiled brats, college fraternity types, mamma's boys, jocks, pseudo-intellectuals, a few southern hillbillies and several whiners." He described himself as a conservative Midwesterner, careful to think before reacting, not trendy like some from the West Coast, nor steeped in military traditions like some of his East Coast and Southern-bred peers.[30] Frank hadn't known privilege while growing up, but learned self-sufficiency early on—a quality that would serve him well.

Francis Blake Ahearn Jr., was born in Saint Louis, Missouri on December 22, 1943. His father, a caring, responsible and talented man, worked long hours at his day job while attending night school at Washington University, eventually earning a degree in architecture. With such an ambitious role model, young Frank rarely failed to complete a task, and, on the rare occasion he did not, his father was quick to remind him that there were "no excuses" in life. He did not allow himself any, and wanted his son to share this strong sense of personal responsibility.

Frank's mother was ill much of her adult life and died when he was fourteen. His father died ten months later of a heart attack. Now, at age fifteen, Frank and his six orphaned younger siblings were split between relatives and foster homes. He was fortunate to be raised by an aunt and uncle who provided him with a nurturing home life. After graduating from high school, Frank was accepted to the Saint Louis University Institute of Technology. Juggling a full time job and with studies, as his father had, Frank excelled, graduating in 1965 as the Outstanding Civil Engineering Student of his class.

By the end of the tough, ten-week OCS program, physical attrition and voluntary drop-outs had reduced Frank's platoon to thirty-two men from the original fifty. After a short visit home, he returned to Quantico for twenty-two weeks of The Basic School. Unlike OCS, there was no harassment, the classes were conducted professionally and the men were housed, two or three together, in comfortable dormitory rooms. Despite enjoying the atmosphere, Frank had decided by then that he did not want to make the military a career. "I'm glad there are qualified and dedicated people who like the mission and lifestyle of the military," he later said, "but I was in it because my country was at war and the law at that time stated I was supposed to serve in the military."

He was among about five hundred in his class who were commissioned as second lieutenants in August 1967. By the first anniversary of their graduation, thirty-three of them would have been killed in action. Frank requested assignment as an infantry officer, but was instead sent to a ten-week course in Psychological Operations at the Special Warfare School, Fort Bragg, North Carolina. There, he attended Vietnamese language classes and enjoyed learning about the culture from the native Vietnamese instructors. The other courses were interesting and informative, but Frank left there believing that "the best psychological operator in the world was a Marine and his rifle."

He enjoyed Christmas in Saint Louis and arrived in South Vietnam on the morning of January 10, 1968, a lanky, easygoing, intelligent twenty-four-year-old "eager to commence battle with the Viet Cong." Later that day he joined Bravo Company, First Marine Regiment, reporting in to the commander, First Lieutenant Gordon Matthews, a gruff, burly, former enlisted man, who immediately gave Frank command of First Platoon.

With nearly fifteen years of relative peace having passed since the Korean War, most Marine company- and platoon-level officers in Vietnam lacked combat experience and, by 1968, their high attrition rate in battle further diminished the pool of junior officers. Frank felt particularly vulnerable because his earlier assignment to the psychological operations course had deprived him of some advanced infantry training courses received by others in command of rifle platoons. "It was good I met my platoon at night," Frank recalled, "so they could not see how nervous I was."

Tom Mahoney and the others in First Platoon had recently returned from intense fighting at Con Thein and were not fooled by the darkness as to just how green this second lieutenant was. So it was with some relief by all that their next assignment was the relatively safe duty of providing security for a section of the Phu Bai airport, eight miles south of Hué. They would not have to wait long to learn if Frank would be up to the challenge of leading them into combat. It was two weeks before the Vietnamese lunar New Year celebration of Tet, and tens of thousands of communist fighters were already quietly moving into position to launch surprise attacks against American and South Vietnamese forces across the country, a plan designed by Hanoi's bellicose, militant ruling faction to quickly end the war by forcing the Americans to the bargaining table.

As lowly enlisted men, neither Tom Mahoney nor I had any idea what was going on within those halls of power. The North Vietnamese regulars being sent south in growing numbers to kill us were also pawns in a high-stakes political game that was playing out in the communist north, a game so secretive that no one, neither General Westmoreland or President Johnson, had an idea of what was to come.

The ascendant militant faction, led by Party First Secretary Le Duan, was concerned that relentless American bombing of the north, coupled with recent hard fighting in the hills around Khe Sanh between U.S. Marines and crack NVA battalions, would soon drive a consensus of the Politburo to sue for a negotiated peace. To prevent that, in July 1967 Le Duan ordered the arrest of hundreds of moderates, military officers and intelligentsia, pushing the venerable Ho Chi Minh and General Vo Nguyen Giap aside in what was later called the Revisionist Anti-Party Affair. While it was a common belief by those in the western world that the struggle for national liberation was fought by a unified leadership and patriotic volunteers from both the north and south, historian Lien-Hang T. Nguyen points out that "in reality, Le Duan constructed a national security state that devoted all of its resources to war and labeled any resistance to its policies as treason."[31]

With moderates now out of the way, Le Duan set in motion his plan for a broad conventional military offensive that would strike hundreds of targets in South Vietnam. He believed the south was ripe for change and would erupt in a popular uprising at the sight of communist forces in the streets of their cities. In reality, it was a fantasy concocted by him with little evidence to support it. While a launch date for the campaign against Khe Sanh had to be moved up to January 20 after NVA preparations there were discovered by the Marines, the broader nationwide offensive was to begin ten days later, on January 31, the first feast day of Tet, during a holiday cease-fire declared by the Americans and South Vietnamese.

A prominent target of this offensive was South Vietnam's third largest city, Hué, with a population of approximately 140,000. Located about fifty miles south of the DMZ, it was actually two distinct towns separated by the Song Huong (Perfume River). On the river's northwest bank was the one hundred fifty-year-old Citadel, a massive fortress enclosed by a moat and masonry walls twenty-feet high and sixty-feet thick extending for over a mile on each side. In addition to the tightly clustered houses of the tens of thousands of residents who lived within its walls, the Citadel held the Imperial City, a walled compound one-and-one half miles in circumference where emperors of the Nguyen Dynasty had resided until 1945. The New City, on the southeast side of the river, was smaller than the Citadel and consisted primarily of university and government office buildings and colonial-style residential districts.

As the cultural, spiritual and educational center of Vietnam, Hué had remained largely insulated from the war. The city's religious and academic leaders emphasized traditional Vietnamese values and generally mistrusted both the communist government in Hanoi and the U.S.-supported regime in Saigon. But Hue's strategic importance as a key stop along the critical north-south National Highway 1 and the nation's principal railroad line, trumped the best nonaligned efforts of the city's civic and religious leaders.

Hué had a sizable military presence, including the ARVN First Infantry Division in the Citadel, and American advisors at the MACV-Forward headquarters compound in the New City. Still, North Vietnamese military strategists saw it as an obtainable objective since the bulk of American and South Vietnamese forces were concentrated miles to the north along the DMZ.

By January 30, 1968, thousands of visitors had converged on Hué to celebrate Tet. Mingling with the holiday crowds were hundreds of communist infiltrators disguised as peasants or ARVN, their own uniforms and weapons previously concealed at strategic points around the city. Hiding three miles west, two NVA regiments, about 7,500 soldiers, underwent a final inspection of their gear and then "ate a special meal of dumplings, Tet cakes, dried meat, and glutinous rice mixed with sugar."[32]

The next morning communist forces unleashed the nationwide offensive. At Hué, an NVA regiment attacked the Citadel and maneuvered to capture the ARVN headquarters and airfield. However, the ARVN commander, sensing something was afoot, had recalled his troops from their holiday leave just hours before the attack—likely saving his division. Another NVA regiment moved into the New City to attack the U.S. MACV-Forward compound, university and government offices, and release Viet Cong sympathizers from jail. By mid-morning, communist forces had seized large areas on both sides of the river and the flag of the National Liberation Front waved above the Citadel.

American forces in the New City, far less prepared than their ARVN counterparts, scrounged street maps from a local gas station and police headquarters to begin cobbling together a defense. Communications disruptions carried out by communist troops concealed the enormity of the attack from the outside world for several critical hours. As such, the First Marine Division's forward headquarters, eight miles south in Phu Bai, blithely ordered only two rifle companies, about four hundred men, to be trucked to the city limits with orders to proceed on foot to the MACV-Forward compound. As the Marines entered Hué, accompanied by four tanks, they ran a gauntlet of enemy gunfire from surrounding buildings for about a half mile to the U.S. compound.

One of the Marine companies then attempted to enter the Citadel on the opposite side of the river, but was turned back by murderous gunfire from atop the fortress walls, the Americans sustaining high casualties as they fought their way back across the bridge. A few nights later, NVA sappers blew up the bridge to prevent further incursions.

On February 4, now five days after the battle had begun, Bravo Company was ordered to Hué. For the entire eight miles to the city's edge, the highway was clogged with thousands of civilian refugees streaming in the opposite direction, carrying whatever possessions they could grab as the fighting quickly swept through their neighborhoods. The shock and terror on their faces, particularly graphic on the children, created growing anxiety among the Marines, who still did not understand the gravity of the fighting they were heading into.

As the men of Bravo walked the last half mile to their destination on the Perfume River through narrow streets amid constant sniper and rocket fire from windows and rooftops hiding an invisible enemy, they quickly recognized that they had no idea how to go about fighting back. Tom Mahoney and his friend, Lance Corporal Mark Milburn, entered the city together. Mark, a nineteen-year old from Lomita, California, later recalled the surreal nature of this urban fighting and how totally untrained they were for it. "We set up in vacant houses," he said. "We knew nothing about anything."[33] First Platoon consisted of fewer than thirty men and its most experienced senior enlisted man was temporarily out of the country for training. With less than three weeks in Vietnam and little advanced infantry training, Second Lieutenant Frank Ahearn tried not to let the challenge overwhelm him. He later recalled that as darkness fell along the Perfume River it was cold and damp and smelled of dead bodies. "I spent the night in a beautiful villa overlooking the river," Frank said. "But didn't sleep well at all."[34]

Two days later, Bravo's commanding officer, Lieutenant Gordon Matthews, was killed by a sniper while leading a recovery effort to help Marines trapped in an NVA killing zone near the city's sports stadium. Captain Robert Black, the sinewy, energetic twenty-seven-year old battalion intelligence officer was given command.

Robert Atticks Black, Jr. was born into a family with a century-long tradition of military service. Most recently, his father, a U.S. Naval Academy graduate, class of 1935, served with Marine fighter and bomber squadrons on Guadalcanal in the early days of the Second World War and went on to have a fine career in the Corps, retiring as a Colonel. Robert, after overcoming polio early in life, graduated from high school in Honolulu, then attended the U.S. Naval Academy where, in 1963, he received a bachelor's degree in engineering. A skilled fencer and 1964 Olympic trials semifinalist in foil, Black served shipboard for fleet exercises in the Mediterranean, studied Vietnamese at the Defense Language Institute in California and arrived in Vietnam in the fall of 1967, joining the battalion at Con Thien in late November.

American and South Vietnamese forces, now in constant combat in Hué, were expending all types of ammunition at ten times the normal rate. Immediate and constant resupply was critical, but dependable helicopter support was hampered by low-lying rain clouds and accurate enemy antiaircraft fire. Upon arriving, Bravo was given the assignment of securing a half mile of waterfront along the southeast bank of the Perfume River, including the crucial military boat ramp. Once accomplished, Navy landing craft were soon arriving with badly needed ammunition and supplies from ships in the South China Sea, but not without cost. As they slowly plied the river and narrow ship channel for the eleven miles from the sea, these vessels were hammered by mortar and heavy machine gun fire. Despite their gunboat escorts, many vessels sustained significant damage and three were totally destroyed.

The men of Bravo were then ordered to retake a portion of the New City to the northeast. It was a daunting task for any full strength, properly reinforced Marine infantry company; however, only two of the company's three platoons had entered Hué. To augment its strength, Captain Black created a provisional platoon consisting of clerks, cooks, bakers and other support personnel. Later, he added a second platoon comprised of scout/snipers and vehicle mechanics, led by a gunnery sergeant from the battalion's intelligence unit. These two makeshift units fought each day alongside combat veterans of the First and Second Platoons, acquitting themselves well and reinforcing the old adage that every Marine is first, and foremost, a rifleman.

Bravo drove on each day, first through city buildings, then through a suburban area of detached, traditional Vietnamese and French colonial-style villas, and finally into more humble rural hamlets and paddy lands. "The troops had to switch mental gears automatically with each change of surroundings," Black later wrote. The presence of civilians complicated this process.[35]

Frank Ahearn later elaborated on this: "At Hué the message to civilians was clear, get out or we will assume you are working with the VC." Over a hundred thousand civilian refugees fled the city at the beginning of the fighting, but some remained. "I had no animosity toward civilians," Frank said. "But my job was to get my Marines back alive. If one of my men was injured or killed by a booby trap and nearby civilians allowed it to happen, they bore some responsibility. We didn't start shooting them up indiscriminately, or anything like that—but there would be consequences."[36]

Now down to just nineteen men, Frank's platoon was ordered to capture an enemy-held village along a bank of the Van Duong River, a tough assignment because it could only be approached from one direction, across three hundred meters of open rice paddy, broken only by a single, four-foot high pagoda in the center. He positioned one squad to lay down suppressive fire, held another in reserve and used the third to make the assault. Frank joined the attackers as they moved forward, keeping them on line until they reached the pagoda. Pausing to reload, they then lined up again and began the final assault, all the while exposed to heavy automatic weapons fire and RPGs. As they reached the edge of the village, the enemy defenders fled.

Captain Black, watching from his command post in an abandoned farm house, observed with amusement that because Frank had not received the usual training as an infantry officer, or even the opportunity to practice with his unit, he had to improvise. "Frank was just thrown into battle," Black said. "That assault found him putting troops on line like Redcoats in the French and Indian wars."[37]

Two days later, Tom Mahoney and his platoon mates were angered when ordered to pull back from the area they had just fought so hard to secure. Frank, too, was frustrated, but understood. First Platoon was now woefully undermanned, going on two to three hours of sleep each night, filthy and exhibiting symptoms of battle fatigue. In addition, Frank said, the platoon was receiving numerous green replacements "which meant you had to watch out for those FNG's [f—king new guys] in addition to the enemy."

It was about that time that Frank first noticed Tom Mahoney's ability and composure under fire and, despite Tom having less than three months of experience in Vietnam, selected him as leader of a four-man fire team. His squad leader later recalled how quickly Tom grew into this new role, "always looking out for those he led through the difficult house-to-house fighting and doing a great job."[38]

After less than forty-eight hours of rest, the platoon was ordered to retake the same village. There they clashed with about a dozen NVA soldiers who they soon had trapped along the river bank. Suddenly mortar shells began to explode among the Marines. Frank, his corpsman, and six others were wounded. He knew immediately it was "friendly fire," and called frantically for it to cease. Fortunately, weather conditions at that moment permitted helicopters to land and remove the more seriously wounded. In the confusion, the NVA soldiers escaped. Frank was furious about this blunder that had further decimated his platoon. After having his wound treated at a nearby aid station, he rejoined his men that night, taking roll. Of the thirty who entered Hué a week before, Tom Mahoney was one of only nine who had not been killed or seriously wounded.

A week later, as other Marines and ARVN soldiers were moving through the Citadel in their final sweep, U.S. Army forces captured a large enemy supply depot just a few miles to the west. Now, cut off from provisions and reinforcements, the remaining NVA and VC forces withdrew from the city on February 23.

Just three weeks earlier, they had caught the American and South Vietnamese by surprise and were confident in their ability to hold the city. However, they seem to have become victims of their own pre-offensive propaganda, both in Hué and around the country, bewildered when the vast majority of citizens failed to view them as liberators and assist in their efforts. Le Duan's grand expectation of a popular uprising never materialized.

Lasting twenty-six days, the battle of Hué was the longest and bloodiest of the Tet Offensive. Americans lost two hundred sixteen killed (one hundred forty-two Marines) and 1,364 wounded in action (about 1,100 Marines). South Vietnamese Army losses were

three hundred eighty-four killed and 1,830 wounded and an estimated 3,000-5,000 NVA and VC were killed or wounded. Of the
pre-Offensive civilian population of 140,000, over 5,800 were killed,
most executed by the communists, and 116,000 left homeless.

For the Marines at Hué, the absence of preparation and slow reaction by their superiors, made the courage, sacrifice and resourcefulness
of these under-equipped, outnumbered, emotionally and physically
exhausted men so remarkable. Army Sergeant John Olsson, a photographer for *Stars and Stripes,* who covered every major battle in
1968, including Khe Sanh, would later say that "Nothing compared
to Hué." He went on to describe the stress of house-to-house fighting, the frequent inability to save the wounded because helicopters
could not get through the rain clouds and antiaircraft fire, the lack of
dependable radio contact, and what seemed to be the Marines' constant predicament of being pinned down by enemy gunfire.

Olsson once watched a Catholic chaplain giving Last Rites to the
dead and then offering to provide the sacrament to any others who
wanted it, not only the wounded—but even those who were as yet
unscathed! [39] With the exception of the battle for Seoul during the
Korean War, Hué was the largest urban battle the Marines had ever
fought. Frank Ahearn sardonically commented years later: "If I'd
known I was making Marine Corps history, I would have paid more
attention."

After Hué city was officially declared secure, Bravo swept a flank
of the Perfume River all the way to a South Vietnamese naval base
near the coast. Except for a minor firefight at a ruined monastery,
they met no resistance. "The enemy," Frank recalled, "just seemed
to vanish into thin air." In early April, the battalion moved west to
LZ Stud on the upper reaches of the Quang Tri River and prepared
to relieve the defenders of Khe Sanh. There, Frank's "First Herd," as
the men self-deprecatingly called themselves, enjoyed relatively easy
duty running a few patrols, cleaning their gear and finally getting a
chance to sleep.

Checking on his men one afternoon, Frank found Tom Mahoney
in a tent cleaning his rifle in preparation for their upcoming mission

to Khe Sanh and asked him how things were going. Tom flashed his engaging smile and replied that all was just fine. Frank then asked him if he liked the Marine Corps, and Tom said he did. The lieutenant then suggested that Tom consider applying to Officer Candidate School. "I had seen Mahoney in combat," Frank later said, "and he seemed to already have that knowledge about him that a young lieutenant might have. Mahoney said he would think about it and so I simply left it at that."

The next day Frank was approached by Tom's squad leader, Corporal Ken Fernandes, a tall, athletic, nineteen-year-old from tiny, Newman, Illinois. Clearly irritated, Ken asked the lieutenant what he had "done to Mahoney?" Frank replied that he had mentioned to Tom the possibility of going to OCS when his tour in Vietnam was up. "That must have triggered a significant change in his attitude," he recalled. "Because Ken said Tom was now going around acting superior and on his high horse." Frank apologized.

It took a few days of guard duty and night patrols, Frank later explained, in order to "get Tom back to being a normal, miserable, neglected, and overworked combat Marine, but Ken did it." Frank, who had been recently promoted to First Lieutenant, concluded that his elevated rank had not made him any smarter and that he should discontinue "career counseling."

"My job," he said, "was just to get them back alive."[40]

7
THE SIEGE

BY LATE JANUARY 1968, military and political leaders in Washington were growing increasingly apprehensive about what was unfolding at Khe Sanh. Despite the enormous amount of American firepower unleashed around the combat base, the enemy seemed stronger than ever. General Earle Wheeler, Chairman of the Joint Chiefs, raised the issue with General Westmoreland of whether tactical nuclear weapons should be used if the situation became more desperate. Both men knew such a plan had already been drawn up, code-named "Operation Fracture Jaw." Westmoreland replied that while such action would probably be unnecessary, "small tactical nuclear weapons would be the way to tell Hanoi something."[41] Those of us at the combat base were hearing rumors that special gun sites had been secretly delivered to our artillery battalion for firing nuclear-tipped shells. Like most rumors, this proved to be untrue; but remained a source of anxiety to those of us living there who felt nothing good could come from such an experiment.

American intelligence analysts studying radio intercepts, identi-fied an unusually high volume of traffic emanating from the tiny village of Sar Lit in Laos, about twenty-five miles northwest of Khe Sanh. The area was known for its unusual geologic spires and deep natural caves, and the Americans were now convinced it was the location of the headquarters for the entire Khe Sanh campaign. They were correct. On January 30, scores of B-52 bombers struck Sar Lit destroying the complex. A memorandum sent by General Westmo-reland to the U.S. Ambassador in Laos speculated that the shattered headquarters might "conceivably be manned by Giap, or at least his representative."[42]

Like Westmoreland, those of us then at Khe Sanh were hoping that the fifty-six-year-old General Vo Nguyen Giap, who was rumored to be personally commanding the Khe Sanh front, had been caught in that attack. Giap was a national hero who had engineered and led the siege and capture of another isolated Khe Sanh-like fortification fourteen years earlier at Dien Bien Phu, bringing about the defeat of French colonial forces in Vietnam. Giap, however, was not involved in planning or leading the Khe Sanh campaign. What few knew at the time, including U.S. intelligence sources, was that, with most of his staff now in jail as a result of the Revisionist Anti-Party Affair the previous July, Defense Minister Giap had traveled to Eastern Europe in September 1967, ostensibly for medical treatment. He did not return to Hanoi until the day after the Tet Offensive was launched, just in time to join the NVA High Command in agonizing over the devastating security failure at Sar Lit.

The resulting breakdown of communications across the campaign front, coming at a time when the NVA were anticipating great success rolling up additional American outposts around Khe Sanh, slowed their momentum. Two days after surviving the bombing of his headquarters at Sar Lit, General Tran Quy Hai, commanding the Khe Sanh campaign, received a landline telephone call at his new operations center from the Chief of the General Staff in Hanoi demanding to know why his forces were not pressing the attack more vigorously in order to draw U.S. reinforcements in, thus away from the countrywide offensive. This complaint spurred Hai to action.

At 4:00 a.m. on the morning of February 5, several hundred NVA soldiers attacked Hill 861 Alpha, a newly fortified knoll adjacent to Hill 861, about two miles from the combat base. Heavy fog and no moonlight made it so dark that one literally could not see a hand held up in front of a face. The enemy swarmed among the defenders in hand-to-hand fighting. By dawn, the outnumbered Marines had somehow pushed the attackers off the hill. One hundred nine NVA soldiers and seven Americans were killed.

Before that attack, Captain Mirza "Harry" Baig, a thirty-six-year-old target intelligence officer in the regimental operations center, had been studying information from acoustic and seismic sensors previously placed by air drops in "strings" along approaches to the base and some of the outposts. He identified over one thousand five hundred enemy troops, possibly a combination of infantry and porters, on the move in the direction of Hill 881 South. Baig correctly pinpointed their avenue of attack and, as they began their assault, enveloped them in a murderous box of artillery fire. Audio sensors recorded anguished cries of NVA soldiers retreating in terror from the walls of exploding shells. Hill 881 South was spared.

However, because of inadequate strings of sensors on the approaches to Hill 861 Alpha, the captain did not detect, until too late, that part of the advancing force had split off and moved against that position. As such, Baig had not prepared a plan for using artillery fire to block enemy attack there. Once NVA assault troops had gotten too close to the Marines, artillery support was no longer an option and the defenders had to drive them back with just what they had on the hill. Captain Baig, ever the perfectionist, never fully forgave himself for being outfoxed by the enemy that morning. It would prove to be a rare occurrence.

I worked within a few feet of Baig throughout the siege and found him to be one of the most interesting people I have ever known. A peculiar Marine, he had been born to Muslim parents in pre-independence India and educated in England, where his father, Osman, had attended Sandhurst before becoming a general in the British Indian Army and later a high ranking Pakistani diplomat. Young Mirza grew up in an atmosphere of power and privilege and later recalled regular visits to his boyhood home by his father's friend, Mohandas Gandhi. He eventually moved to the United States and joined the Marines as an enlisted man, attaining the rank of sergeant before being selected as an officer candidate.

At Khe Sanh, his immaculate utility uniform and gear, which included a curved Kukri short sword in scabbard, and a small, blue Boy Scout backpack, coupled with his British accent and refined bearing, always seemed to me so out of place in the shabbiness and muck of the base and the coarseness and bluster of we enlisted Marines surrounding him.

Baig later wrote that he had based his planning, procedures and doctrines in fighting the NVA not only on his counterintelligence and artillery experiences, but on the writings of General Giap. Giap, like Baig, was a student of eighteenth-century siege warfare and First World War artillery tactics and techniques. "I found this information invaluable at Khe Sanh," Baig said.[43]

The day after the failed attack on Hill 861 Alpha, the NVA's Ninth Regiment, more than two thousand troops, was ordered to advance on Khe Sanh Combat Base and be prepared to attack not only we defenders, but the hundreds of reinforcements they expected would soon be arriving by helicopter. As the daylight march moved forward in a nearly mile-long column beside a stream, the Second Battalion was completely engulfed in an Arc Light targeted by Baig.

The regiment's First and Third Battalions, marching behind them, were not hit in the initial strike, but when they rushed forward to assist the casualties, a second wave of B-52s arrived overhead and hundreds of bombs exploded among them. "Flames and smoke filled the air," the Third Battalion commander later wrote. "Dead and wounded soldiers lay strewn through the trees and bushes on both sides of the stream." The regiment sustained hundreds, perhaps over one thousand, casualties. While the exact number is unknown, records in Hanoi indicate that over two hundred were killed in the Second Battalion, alone, and large quantities of weapons and equipment destroyed.[44] The loss of so many of their comrades had an immediate impact on the morale of the survivors. "A number of soldiers deserted, or shot themselves so they could be taken to the rear," a regimental history later recorded, "but others wanted to directly attack the Americans in order to get revenge for their unit."[45]

Just hours after this devastating loss, another NVA battalion attacked and captured the U.S. Special Forces camp at Lang Vei using Soviet-built tanks, flamethrowers and supporting artillery fire from nearby Laos. Captain William Dabney, a handsome, six-feet-four-inch, Canadian-born, former enlisted man, and son-in-law of

Marine Corps legend Lieutenant General Lewis B. "Chesty" Puller, was commanding the Marines on Hill 881 South, three miles north of Lang Vei, but was in no position to help. He later summed up the hopelessness of the Lang Vei predicament, observing there was nobody in overall command there and thus no comprehensive plan of defense. Some of the units did not even answer to General Westmoreland, but were commanded directly from the Pentagon or by the CIA, adding: "It wouldn't have mattered anyway. [They] were not going to hold off twenty thousand men who have artillery and tanks! They should never have been there."[46]

For Colonel Lownds, Dabney said, "it was a foregone conclusion there was going to be a tragedy. I believe he saw it coming, but he lacked the authority to do anything." Indeed, Lang Vei's usefulness in preventing the NVA from vehicular traffic along Highway 9 was quickly becoming a non-issue because they were building a significant truck road just a few miles south of, and parallel to, that highway. Ironically, it was by way of that new road that they had gotten their tanks into position to launch the surprise attack on that camp.

The fighting at Lang Vei was costly for both sides. Indigenous forces suffered three hundred nine killed, sixty-four wounded, and one hundred twenty-two captured. Of the twenty-four American defenders, seven were killed in action and three taken prisoner. The remaining U.S. survivors, almost all of whom were wounded, were rescued later that day by a helicopter-borne U.S. Army reaction force. The battle marked the first use of tanks by the NVA within South Vietnam. They later claimed to have lost ninety soldiers killed and two hundred twenty wounded.

No sooner had Lang Vei fallen, when a reinforced Marine platoon guarding a knoll a few hundred meters west of the combat base came under intense mortar attack followed by a broad infantry assault. The defenders were quickly overrun. Of the sixty-four Americans on the hill, twenty-four died and another twenty-nine were wounded. These were incredibly desperate days for the defenders of Khe Sanh. With the fall of the Hoang Hoa district headquarters and Lang Vei and ferocious attacks on nearby hills, it now seemed the momentum generated by these two NVA divisions, with their tanks and artillery, might not be stopped. Soon an unmistakable sense of doom was evident on the faces and in the conversations of everyone. By the end of that first week in February, it was like the cold, gloomy Khe Sanh fog had crept down into the corridors of the COC and hung over all our heads.

Then, inexplicably, the NVA adopted a passive approach to the fighting, changing their focus from attack to encirclement. The Second Battalion, Ninth Regiment, wanting revenge, but still frantically rebuilding their ranks after the ravages of the Arc Light strike days before, positioned themselves as close to our defensive perimeter at the combat base as possible, hoping to avoid a repeat of that costly bombing. They quickly dug an elaborate system of trenches and bunkers opposite our lines. A deputy political officer from their division headquarters soon visited these men telling them that because they were now so close to the base, the Americans "would become fearful and demoralized."[47]

Far from being demoralized, the Marines at the combat base were straining for an opportunity to run them off. On February 25, a platoon from Bravo Company, Twenty-sixth Marines, was sent to reconnoiter an area to the south. The patrol walked into a well-concealed, battalion-sized, ambush and was nearly wiped out. As the survivors were returning to the combat base, Bravo commander Captain Ken Pipes requested an additional rifle company to break through the NVA blocking positions in order to recover the dead and wounded. His request was denied.

Colonel Lownds now faced the most difficult decision a commander has to make, one that violates the most profound principle held by Marines: Never leave your own behind. In an encrypted message that day to the Third Marine Division, Lownds said it would require "a minimum of two companies and probably a battalion," to recover the missing against such a large enemy force, an impossible risk considering the perilously weak defensive posture in which it would leave the combat base.

In addition to abandoning these men out on the field of battle, Lownds had to make the painful decision to use artillery, bombs and napalm on these now-identified enemy positions so close to the combat base. If not directly contributing to the death or injury of Americans still alive out there, it would, at the very least, destroy the remains of the dead. As evening approached, Pipes reported the platoon commander had been killed, twenty-one others were wounded and twenty were missing and presumed dead. This incident would later be referred to in Khe Sanh lore as "The Ghost Patrol." Word of the successful ambush of the Marine patrol, which their political officers spun as a major American "counterattack," boosted the flagging morale of the NVA soldiers encircling Khe Sanh. Three days later, a helicopter carrying twenty-three Marines and Navy corpsmen was shot down by NVA antiaircraft fire while attempting to get into the combat base through heavy rain. There were no survivors. The new enemy tactic of patiently waiting for opportunities to kill Americans outside the combat base seemed to be working.

Despite the massive firepower Americans were bringing to bear on the NVA, the noose around the base was tightening. The enemy's continuous and accurate artillery fire, coupled with low clouds and fog, closed the airfield to all but a few landings from fixed-wing aircraft. Those that tried, ran a gauntlet of antiaircraft fire on the way in and out. Once on the runway, mortar and artillery rounds chased them along. Several aircraft were shot down, including a U.S. Air Force C-123 on March 6, killing all forty-nine people onboard, many Marines and corpsmen returning from prior medical evacuations. Following that tragedy, the airstrip was closed to all fixed-wing aircraft, and we now received our supplies by way of parachute drops and helicopters. With two hundred forty-eight Americans now killed and over a thousand wounded, it had been a harrowing first thirty days for the defenders of Khe Sanh, and it was not yet even half over.

Major General John Tolson, commanding the First Air Cavalry Division, was disgusted when he first flew to Khe Sanh to discuss the upcoming relief operation. "It was the most depressing, demoralizing place I ever visited," he said. "Strewn with rubble, dud rounds and damaged equipment, and with the troops living a life more similar to rats than human beings."[48]

In fact, tens of thousands of rats shared the combat base with us, often ranging outside our defensive perimeter to feed on the carnage and carrying infected fleas back into our bunkers, compelling our medical staff to inoculate us all against plague. Rabies, transmitted by rat bites, was also a major source of concern. A Marine I knew awoke one night to find a cat-size rat sitting on his chest, chewing the food residue off his lower lip. As the siege wore on, the number of rat bites and associated medical treatments for rabies soared and constituted a widespread health problem, and so a tactical problem as well.

Water was scarce and, as a consequence of rationing, we Marines exhibited varying degrees of cleanliness. Typically, I washed myself with a damp rag, one part of the body each day over a three to four day cycle, shaving about once a week. Except to briefly wash my feet every few days, I never removed my boots for nearly three months, even to sleep, in case I had to make a quick exit. When our combat utility uniforms became so filthy, smelly and tattered that we could no longer stand being in them, which was usually about every three to four weeks, we would go to the medical units and scrounge through piles of discarded clothing from those who had died or been treated for wounds or illness and medevaced out. I recall how elated I was one morning in early March when I discovered trousers and a shirt with almost no blood stains.

The enemy clung to the combat base, confident that we would be reluctant to bomb them for fear of harming nearby American and ARVN forces. That luxury ended the day after The Ghost Patrol was lost, when Captain Baig was finally granted permission to target Arc

Light strikes within the procedural "danger close" restriction of three thousand meters from friendly ground forces.

On February 26, intelligence sources reported the enemy massing their assault troops and tanks among the civilians at Khe Sanh village for one last, big push to take the combat base. Baig ordered an Arc Light on the little town the following day. While the mission undoubtedly preempted any plans the enemy had, it was later estimated that as many as a thousand civilian Montagnard "human shields" were killed that day. Until that bombing of Khe Sanh village, the NVA had maintained a plan to "liberate" Khe Sanh base using four thousand crack soldiers attacking across a relatively short distance from the south and southwest, assisted by tanks and artillery.[49] Had Baig not received permission in late February to relax the rules of engagement for Arc Light missions, they may have been successful.

Others agreed Baig's importance to the survival of Khe Sanh could not be overstated. Captain Kent Steen, who worked closely with him in devising many of the customized joint air and artillery "time-on-target" missions, later wrote that while the Marine Corps attracts "strongly put-together people, Harry was clearly of another genius. I was more aware than most how near [tenuous] a thing our survival was. The rest of us were probably interchangeable; Harry was one of a kind."[50]

After the devastating Arc Light mission on Khe Sanh village, the NVA General Staff ordered thousands of its troops away from Khe Sanh to the Central Highlands. Most of us at the combat base were unaware of this change, and so throughout the first part of March waited for the final massive assault by the NVA, many of whom were still hunkering down just outside our defensive wire and anxious to oblige.

One of my air team responsibilities was to retrieve aerial reconnaissance photos of enemy positions encircling us. Each morning at sunrise, a single-engine Cessna would fly low over the base's main east-west road and drop a canvas satchel out of the plane's door. I always volunteered for this duty of standing out on the road and popping a smoke grenade to mark the drop spot, despite the risk, because the bag usually included goodies for me from the pilot: a warm can of soda pop, some candy bars and occasionally a copy of *Playboy* magazine. As soon as the satchel hit the ground, I would grab it and race back underground just ahead of NVA gunners homing in on my smoke.

These pictures typically showed the progress of the NVA trench lines as they crept closer to us each night. Exact copies were often shown to President Johnson as he fretted about Khe Sanh in the basement Situation Room of the White House. It occurred to me later that if the can of carbonated soda pop in the bag had ever exploded on impact, it likely would have ruined the quality of these tactically vital eight by ten inch, black-and-white, glossy photos; and mused about how one might explain to the President why the besieged commander at Khe Sanh didn't get his copies.

In an effort to show that progress was being made at Khe Sanh, General Westmoreland's staff inundated President Johnson with such data. Their daily reports included a variety of claims about "confirmed" and "probable" enemy killed, as well as an obsession with Bomb Damage Assessment, in which they even tallied Yards of Trenchline Destroyed. Colonel James Wesley Hammond Jr., a Marine combat veteran in both Korea and Vietnam, later observed that "a trench is a hole in the ground and a bomb makes a hole in the ground. Does a bomb in a trench destroy it or enlarge it? But they felt it was a significant figure when presented in the White House."[51]

By mid-March, enemy probes against the base decreased, but the incoming did not. During the afternoon and evening of March 23, the NVA pounded us unrelentingly with over thirteen hundred rounds of artillery—one of the most terrifying days of my life. For hours, enemy gunners walked the artillery rounds the length of the base, from west to east. A few minutes would pass, and then it would start all over again. Each time the shelling turned back toward us, the suspense became maddening. We began to recognize a pattern developing and soon we were able to count the number of rounds coming toward our bunker and predict which one in the sequence was going to be the closest. When we knew that shell was on the way, we would all clench our teeth and stick fingers in our ears. It seemed like forever before it landed. Finally, it would—barely missing us—and we were spared for a few more minutes.

After numerous salvos, each noticeably closer to our hole than the previous one, we were sure the next round would be it. I remember looking around in the dim light of the bunker. Everyone was tense. Some had that far-away look of deep concentration. On some, lips moved fitfully in silent prayer. Some, like me, searched the faces of the others for answers, but there were none.

Then it struck. It was not quite a direct hit because the roof did not collapse, but it could not have been closer. There was absolutely no sound. We were inside the explosion. A vacuum instantly sucked dust, loose paper and other light objects out the bunker's hatchway. A painful pressure pushed on my eardrums. Then, as swiftly as it had happened, it was over and, miraculously, we had been spared from the concussive effects of such near misses that we had heard so much about.

The siege "officially" ended on April 5, but with approximately seven thousand North Vietnamese soldiers still in the vicinity of Khe Sanh, that event was more media hoopla than real.

The Tet Offensive proved to be a series of tactical victories for U.S. forces, but a strategic defeat because of how it was perceived by the American public. Extensive film coverage brought harrowing scenes of the war into American homes via television, most notably of stunned American soldiers fighting inside the U.S. Embassy compound in Saigon and a South Vietnamese policeman executing a trussed-up Viet Cong soldier with a pistol shot to the head. Viewers also followed Marines each day through the hell of Hué city and diving for cover from incoming shells at Khe Sanh. It was no surprise a majority of Americans were coming to the conclusion that, despite the commitment of half a million American troops, thousands of aircraft and mountains of supplies, the enemy seemed to be holding their own and—more significantly—could go anywhere they chose to in South Vietnam.

The existence of thousands of northern soldiers now in the south also undercut one of the main reasons given by American strategic planners to hold the base at Khe Sanh: that blocking Highway 9 would thwart just such an invasion. The message of antiwar activists now seemed more legitimate than that of the government. Influential media voices, like highly respected TV journalist Walter Cronkite, publicly abandoned their beliefs that the war was winnable. Even a usually dependable conservative organ, *The Wall Street Journal,* ran an editorial warning Americans who still supported the war that "the whole Vietnam effort may be doomed."[52]

Tet and the fighting at Khe Sanh also ended Lyndon Johnson's aspiration of becoming the second longest-serving president in U.S. history. On March 31, while the siege was still underway, Johnson announced he would not seek reelection, ordered a halt to the bombing of North Vietnam above the twentieth parallel, and offered to open negotiations to end the war, which Hanoi accepted "in principle" four days later.

A month before, Secretary of Defense Robert S. McNamara, chief architect of the war, had stepped down. Unknown to the American public, McNamara had sent a private memo to the President the previous November saying he no longer had confidence in America's ability to win. McNamara would publicly continue to support the war and defend his earlier decisions, rather than own up to his mistake. The President, bitter over this and other defections by key advisors, pressed on. Historian George Herring saw this not so much as personal courage, but a stubbornness to avoid admitting failure: "He had invested his personal prestige to a degree that made it impossible for him to back off."[53]

American and South Vietnamese troops had no doubt that the bombing halt in the north would not only increase the flow of materiel and fighters coming south, but also lift the morale of the NVA and VC. More importantly, these events began to erode the confidence and effectiveness of U.S. combat forces as the reality set in that, going forward, we were pawns in a deadly game of negotiated compromise to end the fighting—and no one wanted to be the last to die in a lost cause.

8
SAVING FACE

PLANNING FOR THE OVERLAND RELIEF of Khe Sanh had begun in January 1968 as a response to President Johnson's anxiety about losing the place to the North Vietnamese. The result was a resource-intensive, 30,000-person scheme, labeled Operation Pegasus, under the operational control of the U.S. Army's First Air Cavalry Division. Engineers built a new camp and airstrip, called LZ Stud, ten miles east of Khe Sanh for staging the relief operation.

The whole idea of Pegasus exasperated the Marines who had not wanted to hold Khe Sanh in the first place and then were criticized for their lack of preparation by those who sent them there. Most of all, the Marines were appalled by the implication of a rescue. By late March, NVA troop strength around Khe Sanh had noticeably declined and most Army and Marine generals felt the operation was an unnecessary expenditure of resources badly needed elsewhere in the country.

With Pegasus, the sky above Khe Sanh was filled with an incredible number of U.S. Army helicopters, like endless flights of geese migrating in every direction. I had never seen the giant wasp-like Sikorsky Skycrane or the Huey Cobra, bristling with guns and rocket pods, which seemed to me like something from the future, especially compared to what the Marine Corps had. I was suddenly sickened by the thought of how many nights on the air team radio I'd listened as wounded men died in the hills around us for want of adequate helicopter support.

American Army and ARVN units quickly leapfrogged along Highway 9, south and southwest of the base, blasting a series of helicopter landing zones and establishing temporary artillery firebases in a largely unsuccessful attempt to entrap retreating battalions of the 304th Division. The old French fort was finally recaptured after a two-day battle. To the east, engineers repaired the roadway and bridges from LZ Stud, allowing vehicles to reach the combat base by land for the first time in over a year.

Colonel Bruce F. Meyers assumed command of the Twenty-sixth Marine Regiment on April 12. A small formation of officers stood at attention just a few meters east of the COC bunker to witness what Meyers later called "a very brief change of command ceremony." The skies were clear that day, so they knew enemy artillery observers would quickly see the congregation and fire upon it.

Meyers stood at attention before Lownds and stated, "I relieve you, Sir."

Lownds replied, "I stand relieved, Sir."

Lownds then passed the flagstaff containing the regimental colors to Meyers, the formation was promptly dismissed and all participants quickstepped to the nearby command bunker just as a flurry of mortar shells exploded in the area they had just vacated.[54]

As Marines pushed out from the base and its outposts they encountered stiff resistance from the NVA. On Hill 700, about two miles to the northwest, two companies, about three hundred men, ran into a large entrenched NVA force, suffering high casualties. A week later, on Easter Sunday morning, Captain Dabney's men moved off Hill 881 South to attack a ridgeline to the north from which the enemy had launched many of their rockets at the combat base.

The men were surprised to discover how atrophied their muscles had become from months of inactivity, reaching the top by mid-afternoon, but not before six Marines were killed and twenty-one wounded. The NVA suffered one hundred six dead and several prisoners were taken. Before returning to Hill 881 South, a Marine signaled the victory by fastening an American flag to a burned tree limb. The next morning the flag was gone. This would be the final engagement of Operation Pegasus, and the Marines once again assumed direct responsibility for Khe Sanh area.

Marine Lieutenant General Robert Cushman and Army Lieutenant General William B. Rosson had been petitioning the MACV to cease operations and abandon Khe Sanh Base as soon as the siege was lifted. Their plan was to replace those fixed fortifications with a mobile helicopter capability out of LZ Stud, recently renamed Camp Vandergrift. This would allow the Marines a continued presence in northwestern Quang Tri Province, but comfortably beyond the range of enemy artillery batteries in Laos. Camp Vandergrift was also not subject to Khe Sanh's terrible weather and so was easier to supply and reinforce. In early-April, the two generals received what they believed was approval from General Westmoreland.

On April 15, General Rosson hosted a conference with his subordinate commanders at his headquarters at Phu Bai to finalize the plan and issue orders for the immediate abandonment of the base. He invited General Cushman, and Cushman, as a courtesy, invited his superior officer General Westmoreland. General Rosson later recalled that he had just finished outlining the plan when "to Cushman's and my own surprise and embarrassment" Westmoreland stated that units at Khe Sanh Combat Base and its outposts would continue to "comb the area" indefinitely. Any decision to curtail these activities, or dismantle the combat base, would have to "wait for other developments."[55]

Foremost among the "other developments" was Westmoreland's imminent promotion to U.S. Army Chief of Staff in Washington, D.C. He would later write that he had basically agreed with Rosson's plan, "but not its timing." Yet General Rosson remained puzzled: "In essence, I either misunderstood General Westmoreland's approval, or he had second thoughts."

Prior to this meeting, Major General Rathvon Tompkins, commanding the Third Marine Division, was advised the plan to abandon Khe Sanh would be carried out immediately and so sent his assistant division commander, Brigadier General Jacob Glick, there with orders to close down the combat base. "I went up there with a minimum staff and instructions to hold on without mounting any operations," Glick said. However, "the rules changed" after what he believed to be Westmoreland's reversal of his earlier decision.[56]

The following day, as a result of Westmoreland's vague instruction to "comb the area," Marines began patrolling the northeast slope of Hill 689, two miles southwest of the combat base, and came under fire from well-camouflaged NVA positions, taking heavy casualties. After hours of costly fighting, magnified by a series of disastrous tactical decisions by the battalion's commanding officer, the Marines finally moved back off the hill leaving the bodies of over thirty Americans behind. It would be six days before they were able to recover them, finding all but three.[57] The final casualty count from that fighting on Hill 689 was thirty-eight Marines and three Navy corpsmen killed and thirty-two others wounded. While the *official* blame for this debacle was directed toward battalion and regimental officers, others believed the Marines were doomed by an indecisive General Westmoreland, who had provided fuzzy operational objectives to his incredulous subordinates at the conference in Phu Bai just days before.

During the siege months from late January through the end of March, about four hundred Americans were killed at, and around, Khe Sanh and nearly three thousand were wounded.[58] General Westmoreland's primary reason for accepting such losses was to block NVA forces from attacking South Vietnam's more populated regions. Yet, during the recent Tet Offensive, the NVA had joined the VC by the tens of thousands in attacking over one hundred cities and towns without the aid of Highway 9 through Khe Sanh, or other primary roads into the country. Even in the midst of the siege, the NVA moved over a thousand soldiers between the Khe Sanh battlefield and the fighting at Hue, in less than two days, and totally unnoticed by the Americans.

Others, including several Marine Corps generals, had made repeated efforts to convince Westmoreland that occupying Khe Sanh would not impede the NVA from attacking cities in South Vietnam, but actually assist them by tying down thousands of American and ARVN soldiers at this remote location, rather than employing them more efficiently elsewhere in the country against the communist offensive. Though Westmoreland's pride would not allow him to admit this was true, his subsequent actions revealed he knew it to be a source of embarrassment.

In the first days of April, media correspondents from around the world, who had come in droves to witness, document, and in some ways create, the high drama of American boys besieged at a modern-day Alamo, now disappeared. As such, most of the world would never know that, in a largely pointless effort to salvage U.S. prestige, nearly six hundred more Americans would be killed and thousands more wounded while trying to hang on at Khe Sanh for as long as they could in a stalling tactic designed to avoid the negative political fallout that would come with abandoning that admittedly untenable place to the enemy.

This needless loss and suffering had less to do less with the NVA doing their homework, than it did the indifference of a lame-duck President, who had just announced his abdication as a candidate in the coming election, and the soon-departing General William Westmoreland, whose overriding ambition to choreograph a flattering place in history required him to create a "decent interval" for face-saving purposes in an effort to disguise his conspicuous strategic blunders now exposed by the Tet Offensive and the decision to defend Khe Sanh.

᛭ ᚱ

On April 16, Tom Mahoney, along with the rest of Bravo Company, arrived at the combat base by truck convoy. Surprisingly there was no effort made by the enemy to stop them along the ten miles of narrow, winding road. Once inside the base, Tom hoped to have time to find me, but a chopper was waiting to immediately transport his platoon up to Hill 950, the steep-sided peak towering over the base on the north.

Two days later, the day I thought would never come, the Twenty-sixth Marines left Khe Sanh. The night before, as I laid in my bunker staring into the pitch darkness, a profound sadness engulfed me. I had, long ago, stopped imagining life beyond Khe Sanh, and, in a strange way, I did not want to leave. For many of us, the routine of daily life, as dangerous as it was, made Khe Sanh our home and aroused our territorial instincts. As long as we remained there prepared to fight, the enemy would never prevail. To us, Khe Sanh was not just a cluster of tiny, toothpick flags on President Johnson's now-celebrated sand table terrain model, but a terrible, tangible thing, purchased with the lives of our friends. I had arrived on a cool, rainy afternoon in late autumn and was now leaving on a warm, spring morning. Burrowed for so long into the red clay of Khe Sanh, the seasons had become irrelevant.

I left my bunker for the last time on the morning of April 18, and remembered that it had been exactly one year ago that Tom and I signed our enlistment papers at the recruiting office in downtown Oakland. Since that day when we set out to "prove ourselves," the awful face of war had surpassed anything I could have imagined. Rather than turning out to be some noble test of guile and endurance, where the better man won, it quickly dissolved into an endless burden of dread in knowing that death was an indiscriminate, mocking thing over which we had almost no control.

On the truck bound for our embarkation point at the far west end of the base, I stood up facing forward holding on to a railing above the cab and watched as Marines from Tom's battalion trudged along both sides of the road in the opposite direction. Mortar shells exploded just ahead. It was dreamlike to see the black plumes of explosives and dust, but not hear it over the howling truck motor. A half-minute later, as we passed the point of impact, a Marine was lying face down on the side of the road, not moving. I wondered if it might be Tom, and was surprised by my level of concern for his safety. He had already survived some of the worst fighting of the war at Con Thien and Hué; yet, I couldn't shake this sense that Khe Sanh would grind down all those who came to take our place.

The landing zone was a large, uncomfortably flat space, with little cover from the incoming, but our chopper touched down within a few minutes and I raced aboard with a dozen others. We then ascended to about two thousand feet and went into a holding pattern over the base waiting for the lift-off of a second chopper.

As we circled, I had an opportunity to view the countryside and was stunned by the extent of destruction. No longer the verdant jungle and hills I had marveled at five months before when first flying into the base, it was now a moonscape of interlocking artillery and bomb craters in every direction as far as I could see. I could not easily find where the village had been, but eventually located it, a spattering of chalky smudges along a lifeless swath of pulverized red volcanic earth beside a crazily meandering stream.

My eyes followed the course of shell-pitted Highway 9 off to the west where the Co Roc Massif, an immense escarpment rising up from the Xe Pone River was now visible, still concealing many of the formidable artillery pieces that had made our days so miserable. Beyond that was a broad, flat, nearly unbroken plateau running west across Laos into the mist. I tried to burn these images into my mind, not for tactical reasons, but because I sensed that I would someday need to assure myself it had all been real.

During the previous eleven weeks we had been driven underground by thousands of incoming shells slamming into the narrow confines of the combat base. I wondered what it was going to be like to live on the surface once again, no longer walking in the guarded "Khe Sanh crouch" or being unceasingly attentive for the murmurs of those distant guns. At that moment, I could no longer recall what life had been like without the undeniable possibility that every moment might be my last; and was worried that the relentless psychological trauma had made me crazy and I just didn't realize it yet because everyone around me was crazy, too.

Our chopper landed at the Quang Tri airfield about thirty minutes later and we galloped off into the bright sunlight and a euphoric sense of relief. Here people sauntered leisurely from place to place in clean clothes without flak jackets and helmets, living in tents or huts. Many of them stopped to gawk at us—filthy, emaciated, and slightly dazed—as if we were ghosts.

Trucks were nearby to transport us to an area where tents and cots were already set up and waiting. I showered for the first time in over three months, the clean, cool water turning into a gritty, maroon puddle around my feet. In our new jungle uniforms and boots, we were led to a mess hall and tasted our first freshly cooked meal since January. The menu, which included beefsteaks and all the cold milk we could drink, quickly sent many of us out the door to vomit, our digestive systems needing time to adjust to such rich food after months of bland C-rations. Our hosts provided everything they could think of to make us comfortable, but before lying down on soft, canvass cots that night, many of us dug shallow foxholes just outside the tents.

Within a week, I departed for five days of R&R. My destination was Singapore, a safe, cosmopolitan city, whose modern business district reminded me a little of Montgomery Street in San Francisco. My hotel room was clean, with all the modern conveniences. I slept under sheets for the first time in five months and took hot showers whenever I felt like it. I immediately purchased civilian clothes and spent as much time as I could outdoors, enjoying the sunlight and fresh air, hoping to shed the last vestiges of my Khe Sanh-induced agoraphobia. I telephoned my family and talked to each of them. In a time before modern telecommunications, this call took over an hour for the various telephone operators to complete the international connection and would be the only time in thirteen months that I spoke to anyone in the United States. When my time came to return to Vietnam, I was ready to face the next eight months I had left on my tour of duty.

❧ ❧

I received a letter from Tom a few weeks after I left Khe Sanh telling me that he'd caught a helicopter down from Hill 950 to the combat base on April 19, the day after I departed, in hopes of us getting to meet for a few hours. He went on in a positive tone, mentioning that we might still run into each other while in Vietnam, or, at least, have a great time the following New Year's Eve, when we would both be back home. Despite the fact that Tom and I were rarely more than forty miles from each other while in Vietnam, our mail would have to travel to the Fleet Post Office in San Francisco and back—over twelve thousand miles. This usually took about two weeks and thus limited the number of times we corresponded. In his letter, Tom told of how his platoon commander had recently suggested he consider becoming an officer. He was clearly proud of the compliment it implied and excited at the prospect of going to OCS. I later recognized that Tom had finally found in Frank Ahearn a father figure he admired and wished to emulate, and a lieutenant like the dad he never knew.

I wrote back deriding him good-naturedly about wanting to become "a lifer," though I secretly envied him for seriously considering a career—in anything—because it meant he had accepted responsibility for whatever success he might achieve in life. This was a level of maturity and confidence that had, as yet, eluded me.

Frank Ahearn later recalled life on Hill 950 for First Platoon was quiet most days, shrouded in morning fog after which they saw "more monkeys than NVA" in the jungle around them. This did not surprise him: "I firmly believed that we had won the war after the Tet offensive and Hué city and we were just marking time until the VC and NVA gave up."[59] In early May, Bravo moved to Hill 881 South.

Although frequent shelling of the combat base continued throughout the latter half of April and early May, contact with the enemy slowed dramatically. The NVA had shifted focus thirty-five miles to the east, where they were moving in the tens of thousands across the DMZ in an effort to capture the big U.S. military base and airfield at Dong Ha. In four weeks of fierce, often close-quarters combat, American and ARVN forces killed over three thousand communist fighters, many by air strikes due to the unusually brazen nature of their daylight attacks. The cost to the allies was also high with over four hundred killed and fifteen hundred wounded.

In conjunction with this prolonged fighting around Dong Ha, communist forces began a second phase of the general offensive, called the "Mini-Tet" by Americans, striking over one hundred objectives throughout South Vietnam, including Saigon again, and Kham Duc, an isolated American camp similar to Khe Sanh, deep in the mountains west of Da Nang. Intelligence information about an enemy buildup near Kham Duc prompted General Westmoreland to begin upgrading the airstrip and fortifying the defenses as he had at Khe Sanh late the previous year. Once again, the General was convinced he could destroy a numerically superior enemy with an intense artillery and bombing campaign. However, when the 2,500 NVA soldiers moving on Kham Duc swiftly overran surrounding outposts and took the high ground above the airfield, Westmoreland reluctantly ordered the evacuation of all military and civilian inhabitants. Two days after surrendering it, sixty B-52 bombers destroyed the camp.

While quickly abandoning Kham Duc as a lost cause, Westmoreland was still not willing to do the same at Khe Sanh—despite continuing entreaties by many of his subordinate generals. The government in Hanoi realized this and sought to ratchet up pressure on U.S. negotiators now meeting with North Vietnamese representatives in Paris. To that end, they moved more assault troops back into the Khe Sanh area in May with the intention of capturing the combat base, now protected by far fewer Americans than during the siege. Intelligence reports prompted official warnings to the Marines at Khe Sanh of the high probability of imminent attack by several thousand enemy soldiers.

9
THE THIRD BATTLE
OF KHE SANH

ON THE NIGHT OF MAY 4, 1968, four hundred NVA soldiers assaulted LZ Peanuts, an artillery firebase being guarded by elements of the U.S. Army's First Air Cavalry Division, two miles southwest of Khe Sanh Combat Base. Peanuts had been established to suppress artillery coming from the Co Roc Massif in Laos, and was doing an effective job. Before the fighting was over that night, twenty-one U.S. soldiers were dead and nearly all others wounded. The Americans abandoned the firebase, allowing the northerners again to put uncontested artillery fire on the combat base and its outposts from their batteries within the sanctuary of Laos.

Trucks carrying away stockpiled supplies from the Khe Sanh Combat Base were now making regular trips to Camp Vandergrift and the increased traffic was not lost on the NVA. In mid-May they attacked a convoy a mile southeast of the base. More bloody skirmishes over the next few days made it clear that the NVA was trying to regain control of Highway 9. Casualties mounted on both sides as the Marines finally captured the enemy stronghold on Hill 689, where forty Americans had died in the attempt just a month before.

As this was taking place, about two hundred NVA infantrymen attacked a patrol less than a mile south of the combat base, literally a few minutes' walk from the front gate. When the Americans counterattacked they were repelled by enemy soldiers occupying the same fighting positions they had used to ambush The Ghost Patrol two months earlier.

Reserve forces from the combat base joined in a renewed assault on the entrenched enemy, but were again stopped. As the Marines fell back to better defensive positions, a shrill, whistle signal from an NVA officer brought his soldiers swarming out of their bunkers in pursuit of the Americans. Just then, more reinforcements arrived from the base and, along with air support in the form of napalm, forced the NVA to retreat south across Highway 9. A Marine company commander later reported that the enemy combatants appeared to have just arrived from a rear area in Laos with fresh haircuts, clean uniforms and brand new rifles and gear. By then, two NVA regiments, about three thousand soldiers, had moved into the area. A defector advised the Americans at the combat base that they would soon be overrun "as Dien Bien Phu had been." [60]

In late May, nearly six hundred Marines clashed with hundreds of NVA near the Rao Quan Bridge on Highway 9, two miles southeast of the combat base, with the Americans finally capturing a bunker complex after scores of dead and wounded on both sides. One company then moved about a mile and a half to the southwest, occupying a position the locals knew as Bang Hill, called Foxtrot Ridge by the Marines. At 3:00 a.m. the following morning, NVA infantrymen charged up the slope from the north on a wide front, blazing away with small arms and machine gun fire and launching scores of RPG's. They quickly penetrated the Marine defensive perimeter, driving, a platoon from its fighting holes and overrunning the company's mortar position. The survivors withdrew, establishing a hasty position on a nearby knoll, and fought on.

The NVA then called in heavy artillery and soon dozens of 130mm shells crashed into the Marine positions. American air support arrived in the form of flare ships and *Spooky*, but concentrated enemy antiaircraft fire forced them to stay at too high an altitude to be effective. The battle raged within the company's original perimeter for another two hours, with the attackers repeatedly being driven back, regrouping and again storming the Marines. The assault finally stalled after a U.S. fighter-bomber managed to get in close enough to obliterate a column of NVA reinforcements with napalm. By the time additional Marines arrived, the defenders had suffered thirteen dead and forty-four wounded. Two hundred thirty NVA bodies were left behind.[61]

This commitment of an entire NVA battalion against a Marine company, and the ferocity of the fighting, indicated the importance the High Command in Hanoi placed on wiping out the Marines on Foxtrot Ridge. Once eliminating those Americans, they planned to immediately go after the combat base, hoping the Marines would hurriedly abandon the place "leaving behind their heavy equipment."[62]

At 4:00 a.m. on May 31, Memorial Day in the United States, another North Vietnamese battalion again tried to push the Marines off Foxtrot Ridge, attacking from four directions, and once again aided by coordinated fire from their artillery and mortars. Four miles to the northwest, Bravo Company, which just the day before had been replaced on Hill 881 South and flown to an area near the combat base, was immediately ordered to march overland to the aid of those beleaguered Marines.

After going about two miles, they stopped at the foot of a two hundred-foot-high hill, called Chop Non by the locals, near where the main road from the combat base intersected with Highway 9. Because of the hill's obvious tactical value sitting above the crossroad, and the density of the trees and undergrowth on it for hiding ambushers, the Marines were apprehensive about moving forward. Lance Corporal Steve Busby, a rifleman in Second Platoon, hailed from Chico, California and had enlisted at seventeen. He later recalled: "We drew straws to see which fire team would first assault the hill. My team drew third, a good draw."[63]

The Second Platoon commander, Lieutenant Gerry Rohlich, of Madison, Wisconsin, had just celebrated his twenty-fourth birthday. He had joined Bravo at Con Thien in December 1967, replacing a badly wounded officer, and subsequently led his men through the bitter combat at Hué. However, Rohlich, and the others, were about to experience the costliest single day of fighting Bravo Company would undergo in the war. Frank later said, "The Second Platoon ran smack into a dug-in company of NVA and were just about decimated."

The ensuing battle in the tall grass was vicious, often hand-to-hand, and lasted several hours. Frank led Mahoney and the others forward on a flank to help, but were soon pinned down for nearly an hour by a strategically placed NVA machine gun. Eventually, Corporal Tom Northrop, a squad leader in First Platoon, was able to maneuver into position to knock out the gun, a daring feat that would earn him a Silver Star Medal. Raised in upstate New York, twenty-three year old Northrop had been pulled from the fighting in Hué city the previous February to attend his father's funeral and just returned to the unit a few weeks before.

By the time he and the others reached the Marines of Second Platoon it was too late. "All we could do," Frank later said, "was suppress enemy fire and get the dead bodies out of there." Despite such gunfire from the nearly invisible enemy, he and his men removed as many bodies as they could find and then pulled back to allow bombers to work the hillside. The air support arrived in the form of older, South Vietnamese propeller aircraft, slowly pounding the NVA positions with bombs and napalm.

Frank's First Platoon then moved back up to recover more Marine dead, still facing enemy resistance, though now primarily in the form of grenades being thrown at them from enemy soldiers hidden in small, shoulder-deep, protective pits covered by a camouflaged lids, that the Marines called "spider holes" from similar structures constructed by "trapdoor spiders," common to the grassy, training areas of Camp Pendleton. Northrop recalled some of the Marine bodies were now so badly burned by the napalm they could not be lifted without coming apart and so were carefully rolled onto ponchos before being carried off the hill.

American tanks soon arrived, Steve Busby remembered, "flying Confederate flags and machine gunned a couple of NVA that tried to give up with white flags." However, Texan Lance Corporal Luis Perez grabbed one prisoner just as the tankers were about to shoot him. Tom Northrop would retain a grim recollection of that captive, telling how after returning from the hill to Frank's location with another burned Marine body, he saw five or six other dead Marines lying face up. One of them was a young machine gunner he knew from First Platoon. "I still see that kid's face," Tom Northrop would later recall. "Nearby was a POW and we were so pissed off we wanted to blow him away, because it looked like he was smiling."[64]

During the fighting, Tom Mahoney's friend Mark Milburn threw a grenade toward the hidden enemy at almost the same moment an NVA soldier threw one at him. Upon hearing the "thud" of that grenade landing beside his head, Mark quickly rolled backwards from it. "Fortunately, it took a few seconds to go off," he later said. "I was far enough away to where I got only shrapnel wounds and was bleeding from my ears and nose due to the concussion." Though stunned, Mark was able to help carry other badly wounded men off the hill. "The next thing I remember is a tank being there and people loading us wounded on it." He was medevaced out to a hospital and, this being his third serious wound in Vietnam, was now qualified to return home. "They basically kicked the shit out of us," he said. "I never saw anyone again."[65]

Still up on the hill was NVA political cell leader Nguyen Van Pham, who, along with thirty-six others in his platoon, had taken positions on the hill the night before amid the trees and tall grass with orders to prevent Americans from reinforcing those on Foxtrot Ridge.[66] As Bravo's Second Platoon moved to within a few meters of Pham's location he still had not received a command from his superiors to open fire, but started shooting anyway, killing two Marines.

American artillery shells then began arriving, Pham later said, and soon aircraft dropped napalm, burning him and leaving a large permanent scar on the top of his head. During a break in the fighting he came out of his bunker "to collect weapons and saw many dead soldiers," both Vietnamese and American. Still lacking communication with his battalion headquarters, Pham failed to receive an order to retreat. Later, as the tanks moved away with the Marines following, he stood up and fired two B-40 rocket-propelled grenades at the group, later saying, "I saw a large explosion, but did not know if the tank was damaged, or if any U.S. troops were killed." After carrying some wounded comrades into his bunker, Pham fell unconscious.

That night, "transportation and reconnaissance troops" from his battalion found him when they returned for bodies and weapons and he was taken to a field hospital about two miles away.

Though Bravo was unable to complete its mission of reaching Foxtrot Ridge, the Americans there held on, but not before another dozen were killed in the fighting. When the remnants of Bravo arrived back at their camp near the combat base that evening, after suffering thirteen killed and thirty-one wounded, Tom Northrop remembered, "one Marine had a transistor radio and we listened to the Indy 500 for a little while." Others took the day's events less tranquilly. According to Steve Busby, two Marines were medevaced to the rear the next day for rabies inoculations due to rat bites, after having intentionally smeared peanut butter on their hands the night before.

Despite the horror of that day, Tom Mahoney remained unharmed and seemingly unfazed; still, as his Irish ancestors would have said, "living a charmed life." It later occurred to me how strange it was that, of all the bad places he and I were throughout South Vietnam, our worst single day of combat—me at the district headquarters compound in the village and Tom at Chop Non Hill—was less than a mile apart. Such was the continuous and intense nature of the war at Khe Sanh.

A week before this costly Memorial Day fight, President Johnson awarded the Presidential Unit Citation to those who defended the place during the siege. As a national TV audience tuned into the ceremony from the White House Cabinet Room, most believed the war at Khe Sanh was over. The President spent the first two minutes of his five-minute speech placing the decision to defend the combat base squarely in the lap of General Westmoreland, and another minute exhorting Hanoi to speed up the peace negotiations now underway in Paris. He ended by reinforcing the public perception about victory at Khe Sanh, stating "unable to conquer, the enemy withdrew." Secretary of the Navy Paul Ignatius then read the text of the unit citation, part of which said that at Khe Sanh "enemy forces were denied the military and psychological victory they so desperately sought."

As these glowing assessments of U.S. success were being recited, now seven weeks after the battle had *officially* ended, Americans were still being killed and wounded in the hundreds, at times just outside the gate of the Khe Sanh Combat Base, in a desperate fight to prevent it from being captured by thousands of NVA soldiers still in the area.

As May ended, aerial photography revealed the new road that northern forces were building now extended fifteen miles into South Vietnam. When additional intelligence from operatives in eastern Laos reported that several NVA tank battalions were awaiting its completion to attack in the general direction of Hué, Marines were ordered to disrupt the road construction.[67]

On June 2, 1968, with just one day to rest after losing over forty men during the fighting on Chop Non Hill, Bravo Company joined other First Battalion units being choppered to LZ Robin, a newly prepared landing zone on a steep hill five miles southeast of the combat base. Upon arriving, they attacked north hoping to drive the enemy into American blocking positions along Highway 9. That advance met its only significant resistance when Frank, Tom Mahoney and others assaulted and overran an NVA bunker complex just before reaching the highway.

Two days later, at another new position, LZ Loon, two miles west of Robin, four hundred enemy soldiers crashed through the Marine's barbed wire. After a two-hour battle, in which the defenders called in artillery, attack aircraft and helicopter gunships, the NVA broke contact leaving one hundred fifty-four dead. However, unceasing enemy mortar and artillery fire, coupled with concentrated automatic weapons fire and RPGs from high ground nearby, made Loon untenable. Helicopters began lifting the Marines back to LZ Robin the following day. As the last chopper pulled out,

North Vietnamese antiaircraft fire brought it down in flames, killing most onboard. Of the one hundred eighty Marines who had defended LZ Loon over the last three days, only sixty survived. The bodies of at least twenty-two of those killed had to be left behind, though retrieved several weeks later during a quick, clandestine visit by another Marine unit.[68]

Despite the heavy losses at Loon, Marines launched the second phase of the plan on June 6. Called Operation Robin South, its mission was to destroy as much of the new jungle road as possible. For several days they advanced along the well-constructed roadway blasting apart bridges and culverts and destroying abandoned underground living quarters, hospitals, kitchens and a wealth of construction equipment and tools.

A few miles to the north, Marine units engaged in several fierce firefights, suffering over forty killed and scores wounded. Hundreds more NVA soldiers battled Americans on a hill near abandoned LZ Loon, penetrating the defensive lines and occupying several of the Marine positions, including the company's command bunker. The Marines counterattacked three hours later, driving the enemy off and using helicopter gunships to keep them from regrouping. The Americans lost sixteen dead and fifty-eight wounded. As they began to bury the two hundred ten enemy bodies left behind, some, who were feigning death, popped up and fired at them. In spite of such deadly deception, the Marines showed remarkable self-restraint by bringing back eleven prisoners.

The staggering number of casualties suffered by the North Vietnamese that day appeared only to whet their appetite. The next morning at 2:00 a.m., they struck LZ Torch, a fire support base recently established near their jungle road, breaking through the barbed wire and into the encampment. Under the light of flares, Marine gunners leveled the tubes of their cannons and slammed round after round of "Beehive" ammunition into the attacking North Vietnamese. The thousands of spiky, flechettes proved too much for them and they fell back leaving twenty-eight dead. Fourteen Americans died in the assault. Three days later, they again attacked a company of Marines near the road. After four hours of tough fighting, the NVA retreated leaving one hundred thirty-one bodies. American casualties included eleven killed and thirty wounded. Operation Robin South ended the following day.

From early April until the end of June, U.S. casualties around Khe Sanh now exceeded the number of those suffered during the siege—and it was not over yet.

10

THE UNMISTAKABLE FEELING OF LOSS

BRAVO COMPANY ENDED its sweep north to Highway 9 from LZ Robin on June 10 and was helilifted back to Hill 881 South and its now familiar treeless stretch of cement-colored rock carved into a maze of trenches, sandbagged dugouts, circular mortar emplacements and countless, slowly eroding bomb and shell craters. This narrow, eight-hundred-meter-long outpost consisted of two knolls with a slight depression, or "saddle," in between. The easternmost high ground was technically Hill 881 South and the western, about five hundred meters away, sometimes referred to by Marines as Hill 881 Alpha, was actually Hill 865. To avoid confusion, Hill 865 will henceforth be referred to as the western sector of Hill 881 South.

Traditionally guarded by a reinforced company of over two hundred men, the two knolls were now being held by only half that number, Bravo still awaiting adequate replacements for the forty Marines killed and wounded at Chop Non just ten days before. Captain Black's headquarters and support unit, along with two infantry platoons, manned the main position on Hill 881 South, while Lieutenant Frank Ahearn's platoon, at half strength with only twenty-three men including Tom Mahoney, was responsible for defending the western sector. Combined, they did not have enough men to guard the saddle at night. "When we'd go into dusk lockdown," Captain Black later said, "it created a 'no man's land' in between. The western sector was totally isolated."

For the rest of June, Tom joined the others in First Platoon standing guard duty or out in hidden "listening posts" at night, and patrolling around the hill during the day. During these patrols the men were often so exhausted that when ordered to halt, some were asleep as soon as they hit the ground. The heat was wretched and their only relief was the occasional cloudburst from an afternoon thunderstorm. "Our utilities smelled of dried blood from helping out the wounded," Frank said. "We stunk and we were always tired. And, of course, there was always the constant threat of death."

Before the war made Khe Sanh one of deadliest places on earth, it was often spoken of as a "Garden of Eden." Monkeys, deer, feral pigs and birds flourished and elephants roamed the river valleys. The forest was abundant with wild fruit, nuts and berries. The governmental district there was aptly named Huong Hoa—"fragrant flowers." However, undergrowth in these mountains was dense and foot travel difficult due to vines, thorn trees and fields of razor sharp grass. Vipers, pythons and tigers lurked in the dense mahogany groves and thickets of bamboo.

Lance Corporal Jim Hayden, the son of a firefighter from tiny Sumner, Washington, was at Khe Sanh that summer and later wrote about the agony of patrolling those mountains, often ingesting eighteen salt replacement pills a day, most swallowed without water. "I can't describe the hell your brain goes through under that blazing sun," he said, "and how the sweat tortures the millions of little razor cuts on your arms from the elephant grass."[69]

❧ ❦

The earlier siege of Khe Sanh had captured the attention of the American public like no other battle before in the war. During February and March 1968, nearly twenty-five percent of news reports shown on evening television about the Vietnam War were devoted to the situation there, and, in the case of CBS News, over fifty percent. In many ways Khe Sanh had become a victim of its own notoriety. The best way to keep it from continuing to cause a negative impact on public support for the war was to make it go away.

So when four NVA regiments, assisted by heavy artillery, returned in May 1968 for another try at capturing the combat base, it was apparent to most American military leaders that things there remained much the same as they had been during both the 1967 Hill Fights and the siege months. For the Johnson Administration, abandoning Khe Sanh was a thorny political issue. "I believe we have a serious problem," said National Security Advisor Walt W. Rostow. "Perhaps of substance, certainly of public relations."[70]

By late May, the combat base already had the feel of a ghost town. Jim Hayden described the place in a letter to his parents saying it resembled Con Thien with its trenches and bunkers, "but at Con Thien we ran it like a garrison. There were police calls [clean up] and certain cleanliness rules." By comparison, Khe Sanh was "a veritable dump." The trenches were clogged with discarded C-ration cans and newspapers two months old, Jim wrote:

> And every type of round and projectile for every type of
> weapon is lying around without much scrutiny and nothing
> outside is left without shrapnel holes. Wrecked equipment
> is strewn everywhere and when the wind blows and parts
> of the wrecked equipment clang, it gives the place an eerie,
> deserted air.[71]

The demolition of the base, called Operation Charlie, began in June with Marine infantrymen and engineers ordered to move or destroy anything of possible use to the enemy. Daily truck convoys traveled the ten miles from Khe Sanh to Vandergrift laden with stockpiles of supplies, broken equipment and salvaged building materials for use in the ongoing construction of that new camp. Mechanics dismantled damaged vehicles and aircraft, moving or burying the parts to prevent them from being used in displays of enemy propaganda. The same Navy Seabee unit that had upgraded the airstrip just nine months before, now returned to tear up the matting (although much of it still remained in place on the day the base was abandoned).

Work details destroyed hundreds of bunkers, slitting open countless sandbags as the ubiquitous rats scurried in droves from the collapsing structures. It was a hazardous job due to the abundance of unexploded ordnance, and one unlucky Marine, swinging his entrenching tool to rip open a bunker wall, struck an unexploded mortar round, killing him and wounding four others. Scores of damaged wooden structures were burned and three miles of concertina barbed wire was bulldozed into the trench lines for burial. During the final few days, Marines set booby trap explosives and sprinkled chemical irritant agents to discourage the enemy from digging through the ruins.

It was physically demanding work, often ten-hours a day under the broiling, summer sun, made worse because as they filled in the trenches and bunkers, the Americans were also destroying whatever cover they had on the flat surface of the base, a situation not lost on the NVA waiting nearby. Sniper, mortar and artillery fire increased with deadly effects. On some days, as many as one hundred fifty shells fell on the base, many causing casualties. A single incoming round on June 29 wounded twelve exposed Marines.

The former regimental COC bunker, where I had worked each night, was packed with six hundred pounds of TNT and the subsequent explosion left nothing but a giant crater in the sunbaked, red crust. The NVA knew the exact location of that command bunker as early as their initial mortar attack on January 3, 1966, and had tried to knock it out hundreds of times over the next two and a half years with an array of guns, large mortars and rockets. Remarkably, the only significant damage they did was on January 22, 1968, when a rocket blew off a corner of the bunker roof and cracked some interior walls. A direct hit above the big map room, with a large, delay-fused artillery round would probably have killed most of the regimental command officers and interrupted the coordinated defense of the base and outposts for quite some time. It was hard to understand why the enemy did not better exploit this knowledge.

I was in the bunker one night in early February 1968 when a large artillery shell from Co Roc barely missed the COC; but, jolted the place so violently that cement dust knocked down from the ceiling filled the rooms as if with smoke. Webbed-gear and helmets shook loose from pegs on the wall and coffee cups danced off desk tops.

Colonel Lownds had no doubt the enemy knew exactly where the COC was located; and from the beginning of the siege was having a new regimental command center constructed near the runway, just west of the Logistical Support Area. This bunker was touted as being much more artillery-resistant than our current one, but we all dreaded moving there; not only because we felt lucky in our current position, but also because this new bunker was adjacent to the airfield, long dubbed "The Mortar Magnet."

Late one afternoon in early March, we were ordered to pack up our equipment and move that evening under cover of darkness. Then, incredibly, the landline telephone rang bringing word that a large enemy artillery shell had just punched through a wall of the new COC bunker and destroyed it. Enemy observers on high ground above the combat base had been watching the construction project with interest for many weeks and probably guessed that it was now occupied. One day early, their impetuousness likely saved my life and that of most of the regimental staff. We unpacked and stayed in the old COC until the day our regiment left—never sustaining a direct hit. It took the Marines, themselves, to destroy that bunker three months later.

The U.S. military high command in Saigon was careful to keep the abandonment of the combat base quiet, but on June 27 in a *Baltimore Sun* story, correspondent John S. Carroll told of having boarded a helicopter on a slow news day and happened to fly over Khe Sanh where it was apparent to him that the combat base had nearly disappeared. An irate MACV suspended Carroll's press credentials for six months.

A spokesperson in Hanoi, spring boarding off the international attention given to the Carroll piece, claimed the American retreat from Khe Sanh was their "gravest tactical and strategic defeat." Units around the base were warned by division headquarters that the enemy might soon attack to lend credibility to these claims. At dawn on July 1, four days after the news story broke, five hundred NVA soldiers launched a full-scale assault on a Marine company near the old French fort. The fighting continued until late afternoon, with the Americans later reporting over two hundred dead North Vietnamese.

Like many Americans who survived Khe Sanh, I spent years thereafter vilifying Carroll as a scoundrel for exposing my friend Tom Mahoney and his fellow Marines to unnecessary risk by telling the world of Khe Sanh's abandonment. But, in reality, the NVA were already determined to make the Marines' last days there a living hell.

The final convoy departed just past midnight in the opening minutes of July 6, 1968, carrying with it the last remains of Khe Sanh Combat Base. As the trucks slowly progressed in the darkness along Highway 9, engineers moved behind them removing the tactical bridges they had installed during Operation Pegasus two months before. Jim Hayden, among the last Marines off the base, later said: "I will never forget walking out of Khe Sanh that night down Highway 9 and the unmistakable feeling of loss somehow."[72] Within a few days, the flag of the National Liberation Front flag was waving in the breeze on a pole beside the abandoned airfield.[73]

I received a letter from Tom in mid-June which he had mailed earlier that month. Despite the viciousness of the Memorial Day fighting and the misery of patrolling the steep ridgelines around Khe Sanh in the oppressive heat, he remained upbeat about his situation and still had a taste for military life and its challenges. His positive attitude was appreciated by those around him.

Bravo's artillery forward observer, Lance Corporal Ken Campbell, a tall, lean, Philadelphian had, like Tom, attended Catholic schools, developed a penchant for risky behavior and joined the Marines at age nineteen with no loftier aspiration than to test his courage and prove his "manhood" by the standards of the day.[7] Ken was impressed by Tom's engaging personality and refined sense of responsibility. The two became friends and would have long conversations during night watches. Once, on Hill 950, Tom's alertness helped Ken knock out two enemy guns that had been pounding Khe Sanh Base with impunity.

Frank Ahearn recalled that even after all Tom had been through he remained remarkably unaffected:

> I could always count on Tom Mahoney. A good Marine, unselfish, with sandy hair and a good build. Like all Marines from California, he was cocky, well trained, and quite a bit up on the issues involved with the Vietnamese war. He had recently shown me a picture of his girl back home and she was a beautiful young woman, blond hair, blue eyes, and that look of high expectations that so marked young ladies from that age.

Still, Frank occasionally worried about his impetuous nature: "Tom was a little rambunctious, very experimental and wasn't ever afraid of anything. Yet, all in all, I thought that he was going to come through Viet Nam just fine. I was wrong."[75]

11
JULY 6, 1968

JUST BEFORE BRAVO COMPANY arrived at Khe Sanh in mid-April, Captain Black was told at a battalion briefing that they were to act as though they intended to operate from there "until Hell froze over."[76] Ten weeks later, on July 1, 1968, Black received word that the combat base and hill outposts, with the exception of the radio relay site on Hill 950, were to be abandoned and that nothing of value should be left to the enemy. Over the next two days, they destroyed most of the bunkers on Hill 881 South and were, as Frank recalled, "sleeping out under the stars." They were still there on the evening of July 4th, joining with those on the other hills in sending up red and white pop flares, rifle tracers and whatever other colorful ordnance they could spare.

With the destruction of the combat base now complete, the absence of daily demolition explosions reverberating up the ravines unnerved those still on the hills. More disturbing, was the sudden realization that American artillery was no longer nearby to support them in case of an attack. Adding to that anxiety, the men of Bravo were told that they must remain on the hill for at least one additional night because all helicopters in the area were needed to support a problem that had arisen on nearby Hill 689.

Because the terrain on 689 allowed the enemy to approach close to the defensive wire unseen, the Marines there were forced to patrol continuously just outside their perimeter to avoid surprise attacks. On July 5, a patrol searching for the body of a Marine killed four days earlier, was ambushed by the NVA just below the northwest trench line. As was too often the case at Khe Sanh, the enemy was lying in wait, this time with mortars, automatic weapons and a heavy machine gun on a nearby knoll aimed directly at the killing zone around the Marine's body, and tunneled in so deeply it could not be spotted. Any Marine or corpsman who tried to enter the zone to retrieve him would appear in the gun's sights. Despite this impossibly difficult and deadly situation, the Marines pressed on until nightfall forced them to quit, still without the body they had originally gone after—and leaving ten more dead Americans behind.

By the time Frank learned of this dilemma he was already fuming over the decision to abandon Khe Sanh: "When they started blowing up the ammo at Khe Sanh base I became upset and despondent. Why were we giving up the most important site in the whole war? Then we had several 'hurry-up-and-wait' days after we caved in the bunkers and prepared to depart the hill forever."[77]

Frank's frustration at the lack of helicopters to take them away was further aggravated when he was told by his radio operator, who had been anxiously monitoring conversations between aircraft for any indication of when they might be lifted off the hill, that one pilot had spoken about making a special trip to deliver a refrigerated, chocolate cake to Marine Captain Chuck Robb from his wife, Lynda, the eldest daughter of President Johnson. Robb's birthday had been ten days earlier and he was stationed over one hundred miles south of Khe Sanh, so the radio operator must have either heard pilots now working the Khe Sanh evacuation chatting about that previous mission, or was receiving an atmospheric radio signal "bounce" from elsewhere (not uncommon with the FM radio equipment we were then using).

The sense of utter isolation on the hills around Khe Sanh was most keenly felt in the lack of information about what was going on elsewhere. Even mail from home took weeks to arrive. Anxious for a connection to the outside, the men relied on rumors to supplant what they did not know. If a story was believable, it was believed. If believed, and with nothing to refute it, rumor became indistinguishable from fact and, in such fretful combat conditions, carried the same emotional impact. The cake story, Frank said, was the final straw: "I was totally demoralized and convinced that we had been betrayed."

He was not alone in his despondency. This same sense of dejection upon first learning of Khe Sanh's abandonment was shared by the thousands of American troops who had fought there. Because it had been a well-kept secret, the news stunned a majority of us. We were disturbed by other events earlier in the year, particularly President Johnson's decision not to run for reelection—announced just before the Khe Sanh siege was lifted, which seemed to many of us like the act of a disappointed coach quitting his team in mid-game. It made us feel that our hard work and sacrifices were pointless, and worse, that the deaths of so many of our comrades, victims of apparent political choreography and indecisiveness on the part of our leaders, was morally unforgivable.

Yet nothing compared to the sick, personal sensation of betrayal we all felt at the news that Khe Sanh was to be handed over to the enemy. I can still recall exactly where I was standing at Phu Bai when I read the short article about it buried in the back of *Stars & Stripes*, and the mocking sting of treachery like a slap to the face.

With the warmth of the rising sun on July 6, 1968, a light fog began dissolving along the ridgeline of Hill 881 South. Captain Black hoped the evacuation choppers would arrive before the mist completely burned off, providing a bit more safety from both mortar and antiaircraft fire. But now surveying the situation, he was overcome by "a bad feeling about that day" and decided to switch the evacuation of the hill from his main position, to an LZ in the western sector.

He had struggled with that decision because, just a few days before, a Marine patrol near there had surprised two NVA soldiers studying the First Platoon position. Before they could kill or capture them, the duo dropped off the northern lip of the ridgeline and disappeared. Black weighed that encounter against his knowledge that, unlike his main position on the hill, the western sector had not been mortared during Bravo's time there and so was likely the safest LZ from which to lift out the entire company. Upon his order, Lieutenant Gerry Rohlich led his Second Platoon across the saddle to that sector and settled into a large, bomb crater that Frank was now using as his platoon command post.

Like the others, Tom Mahoney awoke that morning expecting this was to be his last day on the hill. To earn his $202.70 a month, of which $65 was "hostile fire pay," he'd survived the bitterest fighting of the war and in the worst places like, Con Thien, Hué and now Khe Sanh. Barring the unforeseen, and with a little more luck, he had only five months left to go in Vietnam.

Tom, his squad leader Ken Fernandes later said, "always had a lot on his mind, because he was constantly concerned about the safety of those with him,"[78] but that morning he seemed unusually preoccupied. In addition to his simmering resentment at having to help in the abandonment of Khe Sanh, Tom had just received a "Dear John" letter from his girlfriend, cruelly breaking all ties with him because of his involvement in the war. Worried, Ken took him aside:

> Tom was just very despondent about the letter he received from home and was now acting like he didn't seem to care about anything. I tried my best to make light of the situation, saying that in a few months he'd be going home and the situation would all be worked out. He just gave a little smirk, as if he understood where I was coming from. As we ended our conversation, he looked at me and said that I had been a good squad leader and thanked me for listening.[79]

Not long after this conversation, at about 2:00 p.m., Frank was sitting in his bomb-crater command post, along with Lieutenant Rohlich and his men, when a distressed Ken Fernandes ran up to tell him that a sentry had just observed Tom leave the safety of the barbed wire perimeter, ostensibly to relieve himself. He, and several others near the gate, then heard Tom shout for help, followed by the distinctive sound of an enemy AK-47 assault rifle being fired—then nothing.

Frank jumped up and headed in the direction of the gate. He had gone only a few yards when an enemy mortar shell exploded in the crater, badly wounding at least a dozen men, including Lieutenant Rohlich and his corpsman. Frank immediately returned to assist the wounded, ordering Ken to search the hilltop to be sure Tom was actually gone. He then radioed Captain Black about both Tom's predicament and the terrible toll the mortar round had just inflicted on Second Platoon. Black immediately realized that the enemy now had the western sector targeted for mortar fire and so ordered Second Platoon to begin moving their wounded back to an LZ closer to his main position.

Just then, Ken returned to tell Frank that he could not locate Tom within the perimeter. The two men ran to the guard post at the far end of the sector and learned that Tom had passed that position about ten minutes before, his subsequent cry for help coming from just beyond the gate. Ken went out to investigate, came under fire from enemy troops hiding in the grass, and safely crawled back to inform Frank that he'd gotten far enough out to see fresh blood on the trail just beyond the barbed wire. Frank then ordered Ken to take charge of moving all those wounded by the mortar attack over to the LZ to be medevaced.

Captain Black arrived and was momentarily speechless at how the situation had so rapidly deteriorated. A shaken Frank believed he was about to be relieved of command for not having exercised better control over his men. "I could see the desperation in the captain's face," he recalled. "I was mad, sick, angry, and really wanted to get the body back and maybe kill some NVA in the process." Black told Frank to make an effort to recover Tom, but not to "overinvest" and lose any more men, as was occurring over on Hill 689, where rescuers quickly became victims. He suggested they use a CS tear gas launcher to help cover their movements.

Frank asked for volunteers and Privates First Class Bruce Bird, Richard Delucie and Private Wayne Sherwin stepped up. The men set out through the zigzag gate path to the outer opening in the barbed wire. From the trench line behind them, other Marines discharged a CS canister, creating a cloud of gas that soon covered a football-field-size area down the slope. Marine machine guns began raking the area where they suspected the NVA were hiding, while others tossed grenades. The gas-masked rescue team then moved forward under this covering fire.

Just outside the gate they found a pool of bubbly blood and evidence that Tom had relieved himself, then saw him about thirty feet away, lying face down, his head pointing downslope and partially hidden in the grass. Richard Delucie was the first to move toward the body and, as he got within ten feet, automatic weapons fire erupted from a concealed enemy position, wounding him in the foot. The others pulled him back up the hill and then made another attempt, this time with Bruce Bird leading.

Bruce, a twenty-four year old from North Plainfield, New Jersey, who was already bleeding from a shrapnel wound to the arm inflicted just minutes before from the mortar explosion on the hilltop, began moving forward in a tight crouch to within a few feet of Tom when a bullet struck him in the neck. Frank and Wayne Sherwin went to his aid and dragged him back to safety.

The CS gas weapon, acquired by Bravo while improvising tactics during house-to-house fighting in Hué, was not as effective in the open air. Tom Northrop recalled that the wind was moving the gas in the wrong direction and, halfway through discharging, the canister fell over on its side sending Marines without masks racing down the partially collapsed trenchline to get away from it. When the gas finally cleared, he brought his squad back and saw Bruce Bird laying near the trench covered in blood. "There was a lot of confusion," Northrop recalled.[80]

The enemy now began lobbing grenades and mortar shells up into the American position on the hilltop. Despite this, Frank made another attempt to retrieve Tom, this time with Wayne and Lance Corporal Allen V. Williams. Earlier that afternoon, Allen, a tall, twenty-year-old from New York City, and a close friend of Tom's, had been trying to nap in a foxhole when he was snapped out of half sleep by a familiar voice shouting, "Oh my God, help me!" Then shots. "I knew immediately what had happened," he later said, "and jumped up and ran yelling Tommy's name, screaming for him and others started screaming for him."[81]

After Bruce was wounded, the rescue effort was stalled by effective enemy fire. The Marines had gotten exasperatingly close to the body before being driven back. Captain Black realized that unless fire from their positions was suppressed by supporting arms, "anyone approaching Mahoney's body would be drilled in the same manner as Delucie and Bird."

Bravo had expended all their mortar ammunition in anticipation of quickly moving off the hill, and there was no longer Marine artillery at the now-abandoned combat base. Neither, could Captain Black call in the long-range 175mm guns at Camp Carroll because of a bad gun-target line and a "danger close" safety restriction of less than twenty-five meters from friendlies. He would have preferred helicopter gunships, with their machine guns and rockets, to assist his men in locating and shooting up the ambushers; however all gunships in the area were involved in lifting the rest of the battalion to Hill 689 to help with the recovery of American bodies now outside the wire there and under similar ambush conditions. On the radio, Black pleaded for the use of just a single gunship for ten minutes. His request was denied.

Soon a pair of Marine fighter-bombers came on station. A target a few meters downhill from Tom's body was marked with smoke by an airborne controller in a Cessna. The pilot did not actually see the NVA soldiers, but was surmising their location in relation to Tom's body. The plane then returned to the sky above Hill 689, leaving Bravo's forward air controller on the hill to direct the bombing run. Frank and the other rescuers backed off to let bombers do their work. Because of their proximity to the Marines on the hilltop, the delivery of the bombs had to be extremely accurate, so the controller chose a relatively safe bomb run line tangential to the hill. The two hundred, fifty-pound bombs exploded close to the smoke marker and, upon departing, one of the planes did a victory roll just as Frank and his men prepared to make another attempt to recover the body.

By now Captain Black had returned to his command post at the main position and was able to observe the slow progress of Second Platoon's wounded still being transported across the saddle toward him and the enemy mortar shells exploding around them periodically. Transport helicopters began to arrive and, amid some sporadic mortar fire now aimed at the LZ, Black organized the evacuation, scheduling First Platoon to board last to give them more time. Captain Black then received a radio call from the battalion operations officer, Captain James P. McHenry, ordering him to immediately prepare the last of his troops to move off the hill because more helicopters had just been freed up and now were on the way. Black asked for "any possible delay" to allow Frank and his men to reach Tom's body.

Before McHenry could reply, another voice came up on the radio, Black later said, "and really laid into me for not being ready to lift out." That voice belonged to Colonel Robert Barrow (later the twenty-seventh Commandant of the Marine Corps), commanding the Ninth Marine Regiment who, as a result of the almost daily succession of such changes at Khe Sanh during those chaotic final days, had just been given temporary command of all forces in the area.

"Barrow," Black recalled, "punctuated his transmission liberally with expletives and said to break contact, just get on the choppers and forget about everything else. Since he chose to do this on the company net [radio network], virtually every Marine knew what he had done and in a manner that made him look the fool."[82] He was not so much offended at being publicly chewed out in this fashion by a regimental commander, as he was fuming at the affront to his sense of justice by his superior officers who had, for the entire afternoon, refused his urgent requests for "the gunship we needed to get Mahoney out." Despite Barrow's order, Black radioed Frank to continue his efforts, "but get it done quickly." Joining the lieutenant in this final attempt were Allen Williams and Wayne Sherwin, from the previous try, and a new volunteer, Private First Class Richard A. Patten.

Once leaving the trail, the elephant grass was short and slick, so rather than working their way down in a switchback motion, the men slid straight down on their backs. "I could see Tommy lying about ten meters down the hill," Allen Williams recalled, "and I started calling out his name through the grass in hopes that the sound of my voice might help him regain consciousness."

Because neither side could now identify exactly where the others were, they stopped shooting and started exchanging hand grenades. Allen was hit in the right arm by grenade fragments and, though not a deep wound, the limb went numb. "The frustration nearly drove me crazy," he recalled. "I tried pulling the pins out of grenades and throwing them with one hand, but it didn't work and so I pulled pins for the other guys to throw. There were many grenades thrown."[83]

The NVA soldiers opposing them in this late afternoon grenade duel were not in that particular location by accident, but had carefully chosen the site because it put them at the gate the Marines would most likely choose to begin a march overland to Hill 689. If the Americans were, instead, to be helilifted out, the team was now beneath the path helicopters traditionally used when approaching and departing the westernmost of the four landing zones on the hill and might easily be shot down.

Leading them was squad leader and combat veteran Nguyen Van Luong. Luong had been raised in Phu Tho Province, dropped out of high school six years earlier to join the army and now held the rank of warrant officer. When his unit arrived at Khe Sanh in March, he was a deputy platoon leader, but high attrition in the unit soon relegated him to squad leader. When he took over the squad in May it consisted of sixteen men; however, constant combat had now reduced that number to only five.[84]

On the night of July 5, Luong and his men quietly worked their way up the slope through several barbed wire barriers to within thirty meters of the Marines, then spent the hours before dawn digging and camouflaging their fighting holes. While going about this business they could "clearly hear the voices of the Americans and smell cigarette smoke from the bunkers." At sunrise, they moved into these concealed positions and tried to get some sleep.

The *History of the 246th Regiment* graphically describes what happened next:

> At 1400 on the following day [July 6, 1968], we saw one
> American walking outside the entrance to the outpost. His
> face was red and his eyes were blue like a mean animal. He
> was looking toward Mr. Luong's team. The sounds of AK
> weapons roared immediately, and the American fell. Mr.
> Luong and Mr. [Tran Ngoc] Long jumped out of their
> positions and dragged the American's body down. They
> placed the body in front of them to create an ambush for
> the other Americans coming out of their bunkers. [85]

Now, several hours into the skirmish, Frank received the radioed order from Captain Black that he had been dreading: "Stand down" and immediately move back to the main position in order to leave the hill. He was sure they would soon be able to maneuver close enough to the body to pull it away and so begged for just a few more minutes. Black replied that the order came from "higher up" and he no longer had any leeway in the situation. What neither men knew at the time was that Captain McHenry, who was in his first day on the job as battalion operations officer, had obtained "a promise from higher headquarters that a recon insert would attempt to recover the body in a day or two."[86] Frank reluctantly ordered his men back and, gathering up all the gear they could carry, crossed the saddle to the main position as darkness was falling.

As the chopper lifted off a few minutes later, Frank stared out an open porthole in an unsuccessful attempt to glimpse Tom one more time. His thoughts then went back to earlier in the day when he had returned to the bomb crater to assist the wounded and saw that the mortar shell had exploded on the exact sandbag where he had been sitting. In going to look for Tom, Frank had avoided certain death by mere seconds. "Tom Mahoney," he would later state with calm conviction, "saved my life."

Many in Bravo Company expressed a similar belief that Tom's inexplicable behavior had saved them by inadvertently tipping them off to the presence of enemy troops waiting nearby. "An entire platoon, or more, would have been lost," Captain Black later said. "Tom's irrational action in reality saved Bravo Company from being severely hurt as we lifted off the hill. Many of us knew that, even if we didn't realize it at the moment." Indeed, Luong's team was in a perfect spot to do just that because the helicopters would have only been a few feet off of the ground and traveling very slowly when passing over them. Such a tragic scenario had occurred four weeks earlier, and just a few miles away, when dozens of Americans were killed and wounded after their helicopter was shot down at close range as it lifted off during the abandonment of LZ Loon.

Tom Mahoney has the sad distinction of being the last American to die on that infamous mountain outpost. The place had been wrested fifteen months earlier from an entrenched North Vietnamese battalion in a bloody four-day battle that resulted in scores of dead and wounded, and was held at great additional cost of life as the linchpin to Khe Sanh's survival. As the rhythmic popping of the helicopter blades receded into that July night, the agony of Hill 881 South finally came to an end.

December 1954, Tom Mahoney in third grade, age seven, bareheaded, back row, center. (*Courtesy of Bob Morgan*)

Tom's high school graduation yearbook photo, 1966.

South Lake Tahoe, California August 1966. (L-R) Author, our friend
Katie Frame and Tom. *(Courtesy of Sue Thomas and Jack Mooseau)*

Tom during our first week of boot camp, June 1967.

Boot camp graduation August 1967. (L-R back row standing) Brian Archer, author, Patricia Mahoney, Tom's sister Claudia, Sue Archer, Tom, Edward Archer. (L-R seated) Leontia Archer, Ruby Waterman, Kevin Archer.

Khe Sanh Combat Base, March 1968. (*Courtesy of Jim Singer*)

Regimental "brain trust": Colonel David Lownds at center
leaning over map, Captain Kent Steen behind him with hand on
forehead. Captain Mirza Baig, wearing glasses, is to Lownds' left.
(With permission from David Douglas Duncan)

Colonel Lownds in lawn chair in the Khe Sanh
command center, February 1968.

Steve Orr lampooning Colonel Lownds by twirling an imaginary
handlebar mustache, Khe Sanh, February 1968.

Author in bunker at Khe Sanh, February 1968.
(Courtesy of Raul Orozco)

Tom Mahoney at LZ Stud, March 1968.
(Courtesy of Claudia Harris)

Lieutenant Frank Ahearn after Khe Sanh, 1968.
(Courtesy of Frank Ahearn)

Operation Pegasus, near Khe Sanh Combat Base, April 1968.
(L-R) Lieutenant Frank Ahearn, Lieutenant Edward "Bo"
Stollenwerck and Captain Robert Black.
(Courtesy of Edward Stollenwerck)

Tom Northrop near Khe Sanh base just hours after Memorial Day
battle on Chop Non Hill, May 31, 1968. *(Courtesy of Tom Northrop)*

On Hill 881 South, western sector, January 1968.
(Courtesy of Michael Reath)

Hill 881 South, western sector as seen from the main position, April
1968. (Note the enemy mortar shell exploding near the top.)

(L-R) Richard Delucie, Bruce Bird and Ernie Vaughn, May 1968 near Khe Sanh. *(Courtesy of Ernie Vaughn)*

Ken Fernandes, Hill 881 South, June 1968.
(Courtesy of Ken Fernandes)

Hill 881 South main position as seen from western sector, July 1968.
(Courtesy of Steve Busby)

Steve Busby, near Khe Sanh Combat Base, May 1968.
(Courtesy of Steve Busby)

Allen Williams near Khe Sanh Combat Base, May 1968.
(Courtesy of Allen Williams)

Ken Campbell, Hill 689, July 10, 1968.
(Courtesy of Ken Campbell)

```
                    COMPANY "B"
            1ST Battalion, 1ST Marines
            1ST Marine Division (Rein) MC
            FPO, San Francisco, California
```

                                        12 July 1968

Mrs. Patricia Mahoney

Dear Mrs. Mahoney:

It is difficult for me to express the regrets and sorrow felt by the
Marines in the company and myself over the recent death of your son,
Lance Corporal Thomas P. Mahoney III, U. S. Marine Corps, on 6 July
1968, in Quang Tri Province, Republic of Vietnam.

As you know Thomas was assigned as a rifleman in our first platoon.
During the afternoon of 6 July 1968, the company was in defensive
position and was engaged by the enemy. During the ensuing battle,
Thomas was mortally wounded by enemy rifle fire.

It may comfort you to know that a special mass will be said for Thomas
at our Sunday service, which will be attended by his many friends.

Thomas was a sincere hard working young man who impressed everyone
with his eager manner and courteous demeanor. He took great pride in
doing every job well and constantly displayed those qualities of eager-
ness and self-reliance that gained him the respect of his seniors and
contemporaries alike. Although I realize that words can do little to
console you at a time such as this, I hope the knowledge that we share
your sorrow will help alleviate the suffering caused by your great
loss.

Thomas' personal effects are being prepared for shipment and will be
forwarded to you in the near future.

If you feel that in any way I can be of assistance to you, please feel
free to write.

                            Sincerely yours,

                            R. A. BLACK, JR.
                        Captain, U. S. Marine Corps
                                Commanding

Letter of condolence from Captain Robert
Black to Patricia Mahoney, July 1968.

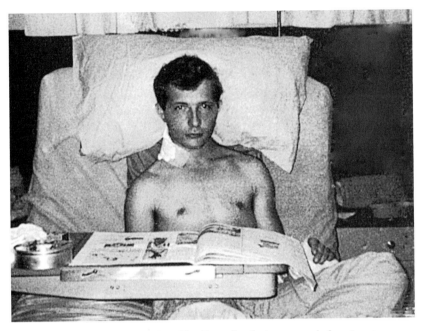

Bruce Bird in hospital at Phu Bai after being wounded trying to
reach Tom, July 1968. *(Courtesy of Bruce Bird)*

(L-R) Claudia, Jack Mooseau and Patricia Mahoney at the
Mahoney home just days before the author's visit after returning
from Vietnam, December 1968. *(Courtesy of Jack Mooseau)*

12
LAST STAND AT HILL 689

LATER THAT NIGHT before brief, merciful, sleep engulfed the men who had tried so hard to reach Tom's body, each struggled with the same questions: Why did he leave the safety of the hilltop that afternoon? If it was merely to relieve himself, why didn't he just use the "head" on the hilltop, which had been left intact during the dismantling of other structures?

Everyone on Hill 881 South had been aware of what was happening over on Hill 689 that day; how the NVA had ambushed Marines just outside the perimeter, placing the bodies in prepared kill zones awaiting others to retrieve them. In addition, Tom had to have been aware that, a few days before, a First Platoon patrol had chased off two NVA reconnaissance soldiers standing near where he was later killed. Just as puzzling, why would a seasoned combat veteran venture out into enemy territory without a weapon?

Years later, Ken Campbell recalled that "the day Mahoney took that walk, his friend told me that he had been depressed because of a recent Dear John letter and he suspected that Tom was 'inviting suicide.'" Ken felt there may have been some truth in that "because to go outside the wire without your rifle just did not make sense."[87]

Allen Williams concurred, later saying, "Tommy never let me see the 'Dear John' letter, but we all knew about it and he was very distraught for days. After he got that letter, he was in bad shape. Very bad shape. He was just not thinking clearly. He was hurt, really hurt."[88] Such behavior was entirely out of character for him Allen said:

Tommy was a decent human being who always wanted to do the right thing and always seemed to succeed. He always stayed awake on watch. He always knew the right thing to say and do. I never heard him say a bad word about anyone, and he got along with everyone. Tommy had that way with everything he did.

His fellow Marines agreed. By all accounts, Tom was probably the least careless member of the platoon, and although Frank knew him to be fearless and often "rambunctious and experimental" in combat situations, Tom was not negligent, and the last person they would expect to take such an unnecessary risk.

"I don't think Mahoney was trying to commit suicide," Frank would later say. "We had not patrolled for days while waiting to evacuate the hill. We were just sitting ducks." He was of the opinion that, while Tom could stoically endure "the pain of war," he was also a sentimental-type, and perhaps that was his Achilles heel. Savvy and battle-hardened, he may have gotten careless for a moment—undone by "a broken heart."

While Frank's take on this might sound overly romanticized, it sprang from the terrible anguish he endured as a boy, watching his mother die a slow death as his father struggled mightily to pay her medical bills and encourage her not to give up. The elder Ahearn, a responsible, intelligent man who adored his children, could no longer find the will to go on without her and would die in his sleep ten months later, orphaning Frank and his six younger siblings. "He loved her very much," Frank said of his father. "The cause of death was attributed to a heart attack, but I knew it was actually a broken heart."[89]

As he examined the events of the day on the five-minute flight from Hill 881 South to Hill 689, Frank was inconsolable: "I didn't bring back Mahoney's body and was allowed 'no excuses' like my father had taught me. The Marine Corps has high standards for this and I didn't meet them. I believed I had let everyone down who ever trusted me. Words cannot describe my feeling of hopelessness and loss that day and for many years thereafter."

Others had a higher opinion of Frank than he did of himself. Ken Campbell later wrote to him saying, "Tom Mahoney was a good guy. I know you tried hard that bad day to get him back. You should take comfort that you did your best… and the rest of us knew and appreciated it." Tom Northrop, who had been Mahoney's squad leader for a time, emphatically seconded Campbell's sentiment, recalling Tom "as probably the most well-liked brother in our platoon" and Ahearn as "the best damn line officer a Marine could have."

"When I try to think back and remember certain things that happened during my tour," Northrop added, "very little comes back. But, July 6, 1968, will always be on my mind."[90]

Many decades later, Marine General James "Mad Dog" Mattis observed that, "some platoons are worth as much as a company because of the social energy of their leaders." He must have been thinking of men like Lieutenant Frank Ahearn.

Some in Bravo could not endure another minute of the strain and danger. One man confided to me years later that while helping the wounded on Hill 881 South, he had stayed onboard a chopper bound directly for a hospital in a safe area to the east. Though not injured himself, he was covered with so much blood from those he had carried that no one would question him until he was too far away from Khe Sanh for it to matter. He made this decision to avoid going to Hill 689, where it was obvious the battalion was preparing to make a last stand and he believed he'd run out of luck. His platoon had been badly mauled a few weeks before on Memorial Day and the subsequent anxiety of trying to defend Hill 881 South with so few people added to his emotional damage. The peculiar circumstances of Tom's death, coupled with the simultaneous mortar attack wounding over a dozen Marines and a corpsman, was the final straw. His story reminded me that each of us had a breaking point. He reached his on July 6, 1968. We will never know if Tom Mahoney did so that afternoon as well.

Frank was so exhausted by the time he arrived on Hill 689 that he slid into the first hole he could find, an old bomb crater, to get some rest. As his eyes adjusted to the dark interior he noticed an unexploded NVA satchel charge (a canvass bag filled with dynamite), but was too tired to move and so curled up beside it and fell into a deep sleep.

Earlier that day, Lieutenant Colonel Archie Van Winkle, commander of the First Battalion, First Marine Regiment, moved the remainder of his troops, including his headquarters staff, to Hill 689 in order to deal with the dire situation; setting up a command post in a deep, cave-like hole hastily dug below the northeast rim of the hill. Van Winkle, who received the Medal of Honor as a staff sergeant platoon leader in Korea, had taken command of the battalion just the month before when the previous commander was shot down in a helicopter near the site of Khe Sanh village, leaving him gravely injured while two others died in the crash.

Due to unrelenting attrition since late May, Van Winkle's command was now a "battalion" in name only, closer in troop strength to just two companies, about five hundred men, rather than the customary twelve hundred. The NVA knew that the senior Marine officer had moved his command post to Hill 689 and were anxious to achieve maximum propaganda value by annihilating this last American battalion at Khe Sanh. Major General Raymond Davis, commanding the Third Marine Division, added some media bluster by announcing, "We are going to move off the hill, but not until we have defeated the North Vietnamese," failing to mention there was now no other option left for the isolated and outnumbered Marines but to hold.

Bravo got busy digging defensive positions on the southeast side of the hill and Captain Black, who arrived after dark, immediately ordered a radar-guided bombing strike on his old command post to keep the enemy from using what was left of it. The bombs, he recalled, were on target and "that mountaintop lit up." Charlie Company set up in the center of the fortification, reinforcing badly depleted Delta. Alpha Company covertly moved into position just outside the northwest defensive perimeter to protect the flank and rear of the hill. This put them just above the killing zone where Marine bodies were located from NVA ambushes days earlier, the stench of death nauseating them throughout the night.

Alpha was led by Lieutenant Ray L. Smith, who had reassumed temporary command just that day, after having also led the company through the terrible fighting in Hue four months before. He and Frank had been classmates at Officers Candidate School where Frank had quickly taken notice of this focused, young, Oklahoman's natural leadership abilities. Originally an enlisted Marine, Smith had so impressed his superiors in boot camp that he was immediately tabbed as officer material and sent to Quantico (he would retire in 1999 as a major general). When Frank had suggested to Tom Mahoney three months earlier that he consider becoming an officer, it was, Frank later said, because "Tom's calm, but deliberate, and focused demeanor reminded me of a young Ray Smith."

The following night, July 7, scores of NVA soldiers moved across the ravine from the northwest some calling out of the darkness in English phrases, like "friendly corpsman" and "friendlies coming in," to deceive the defenders into thinking wounded comrades were finally making their way back to safety.[91] This ruse allowed the enemy to approach within a few meters before bursting through the perimeter barbed wire and flowing to the right and left down the Americans' trench lines. The attackers quickly overwhelmed fighting positions and bunkers, but their effort to capture the crest of the mountaintop, and the battalion command post, was stalled by Charlie and Delta Companies tenaciously defending the interior of the fortification.

Some attackers, attempting to sneak onto the northwest ridgeline, were surprised and driven back by the waiting Alpha Company. Lieutenant Smith then led a counterattack back into the main position, killing the surprised invaders and retaking captured bunkers and trenches. So as not to be mistaken for the English-speaking NVA who had deceived the hill's defenders earlier, Smith's men were told to sing the Marine Corps hymn to identify them as actual "friendlies" coming back into the defensive perimeter.[92]

Bravo Company was ordered to provide a platoon at once to assist in the counterattack, granting Frank his wish from the day before when, in the throes of despair after losing Tom, he bitterly hoped to "maybe kill some NVA." Those who witnessed his audacious charge down the trench line ahead of his troops, firing point blank into the stunned enemy, never forgot. Ernie Vaughn, a twenty-year-old Lance Corporal from Keokuk, Iowa, was right behind Frank and later recalled: "The NVA were everywhere and Lieutenant Ahearn traded his .45 caliber pistol with me for my M-16 to increase his fire power." They soon came upon a Marine bunker now occupied by the enemy. "Lieutenant Ahearn fired a LAW [Light Anti-Tank Weapon] into it," Vaughn said, "and when we went over to check, there were several dead NVA [the later official count was six] laying there. I wanted their flag, which they were intending to raise above the hill in victory, but the lieutenant told me to leave it because it could be booby trapped."[93]

Throughout the night, the Americans waited for the NVA's heavy artillery to pulverize their positions on the hill, as they had done a few weeks earlier at LZ Loon and Foxtrot Ridge. Many were later incredulous that they passed up on the opportunity to so easily destroy the Marine battalion with unrelenting artillery fire, rather than this costly and ultimately unsuccessful ground assault.[94] But that assault had been plenty nasty. At sunrise, it took Captain Black twenty minutes to get to the battalion command post, a walk of usually less than five, because of the damage and carnage all around him. "All along the way," Black said, "I saw Marines in tears for the hell they'd undergone and the buddies they lost."[95]

The NVA took most of their dead when they finally retreated before daybreak, leaving only fifteen bodies behind, nearly half of whom had been personally dispatched by Lieutenant Frank Ahearn. He and Ray Smith, classmates at OCS the year before, had just led synchronized charges into the teeth of a resolute enemy assault force, driving them from captured American trenchlines and bunkers. The courage and determination of them and their men saved this last, isolated battalion at Khe Sanh from being overwhelmed; denying

Hanoi a propaganda coup that would undoubtedly have had a significant impact on ceasefire negotiations then underway in Paris.

Fittingly, this closing fight at Khe Sanh was not decided by the sophisticated weaponry in America's vaunted arsenal, as envisioned by General Westmoreland when he helped orchestrate the siege six months before; but, by the audacity of officers and men in Marine rifle platoons, whose "tactical professionalism" he had questioned, meeting the enemy in the dark, face-to-face.

Before the battalion could leave the hill, they had to devise a scheme to recover the numerous dead still outside the wire. After two days of preparation, the final plan unfolded on the night of July 9. A "box of steel" would be created around the bodies with coordinated machine gun, mortar and close air support, while four-person "body snatcher" teams, well-camouflaged and faces smeared with black paint, carrying only pistols and a body bag, would, just before the rising of the moon, move into the box to recover a predesignated body. The mission was over in thirty minutes, when all but two of the dead were located and recovered. This time, no one was killed in the effort. The last Americans left Hill 689 three days later on the afternoon of July 12, 1968.

Despite Khe Sanh having dominated front-page world news just three months before, western media now barely mentioned the abandonment of the place. A brief account could be found buried in most U.S. newspapers. TIME magazine, which featured Khe Sanh as a cover story ten weeks before, now gave it a half-page blurb. Hanoi, on the other hand, devoted 70 percent of its radio broadcast time in several Asian languages over the ensuing five days to descriptions of the "American defeat" at Khe Sanh. Newspapers in Vietnamese, French and English language editions dedicated days of banner headlines and pages of detailed accounts about the final fighting. A variety of editorial cartoons were produced to gloat, one showing a caricature of a braying Marine, "USMC" printed on his uniform, with his buttocks on fire. Another showed a stunned Lyndon Johnson fainting backwards into the arms of a waiting physician upon hearing the news.[96]

One overwrought front-page piece in the *Vietnam Weekly*, while implying their own losses had been negligible, claimed that during the battle for Ta Con (Khe Sanh), "liberation forces" killed 14,000 Americans, took hundreds more captive and shot down nearly five hundred aircraft. Such hyperbole by the government-controlled media helped Party leaders in Hanoi provide their people with what they had been promising them all along about Khe Sanh—a duplication of the overwhelming 1954 victory at Dien Bien Phu.

In reality, viewing the battle of Khe Sanh as a fifteen-month-long engagement from the Hill Fights in April 1967 through the abandonment of Hill 689 in July 1968, 2,030 Americans had been killed and an estimated 8,000 wounded. North Vietnamese Army losses were staggering. Estimates fluctuate wildly, but it is generally accepted that, during this same period, NVA dead and wounded may have exceeded 50,000.[97]

A month before Hill 689 was abandoned, General Westmoreland departed South Vietnam and was succeeded by his deputy commander, General Creighton Abrams. Westmoreland still did not want to abandon Khe Sanh, but Abrams did. On June 19, after a grace period of just a week, the new commander initiated Operation Charlie for the final evacuation and destruction of the Khe Sanh Combat Base. It was the same scheme proffered by Generals Rosson and Cushman at Phu Bai the previous April 15, just as the siege was ending, but denied by Westmoreland because he did not want the base abandoned "on his watch."[98]

Oblivious to the unnecessary bloodshed and suffering his personal vanity was causing, Westmoreland even objected to the "cover statement" prepared for him by MACV to explain the abandonment of the combat base, proposing instead a version that included the phrase "we are taking military action to reinforce the successes won by General Westmoreland at Khe Sanh earlier this year." Abrams rejected Westmoreland's correction, explaining, "It is not quite true, since basically we are not reinforcing success."[99]

While on his return to Washington, D.C., Westmoreland stopped on Guam where he gave a speech to officers of the Third Air Division who had flown many of the B-52 bombing missions over Khe Sanh. The general told them that "the battle at Khe Sanh was won by you and exploited by the 1st Air Cavalry Division of the United States Army and the Marines."[100] Commenting on this years later, Marine Lieutenant General Victor Krulak derisively noted that, "While the order in which the General assigned his applause is open to serious question," Westmoreland seemed to have missed the point. [101]

Krulak, who in 1966 had tried to convince him not to defend Khe Sanh, went on to point out that Westmoreland had initially declared it to be of major importance, a critical blocking position, crucial anchor of our defense in the demilitarized zone, strategic jumping off place for an expedition to Laos. Then, "in a reversal that deserves Olympic honors for inconsistency," Khe Sanh was abandoned. Yet, the worst part, Krulak lamented, was "when it was over, nothing had changed—*nothing*." Other officers agreed. Army General Frederick Weyand, who later became the last MACV commander in South Vietnam, would say, "The Vietnam War was not unwinnable, it was just not winnable Westy's way."[102]

In the 1974 documentary film *Hearts and Minds*, Westmoreland attributed NVA/VC military successes not to his flawed scorched earth strategy, but to the Vietnamese being less-than-human: "The Oriental doesn't put the same high price on life as does a Westerner. We value life and human dignity. They don't care about life and human dignity."[103] The General could not imagine their willingness to take such enormous casualties for the sake of victories that usually provided only transitory political gains. Years later, Westmoreland still could only understand the concept in terms of what he valued most—career advancement: "A Western commander absorbing losses on the scale of Giap's would hardly have lasted in command more than a few weeks."[104]

If this three-month-long delay in abandoning Khe Sanh after the siege had been merely, as it appears, to spare General Westmoreland's feelings, it was a costly gesture. Several hundred Americans were now dead, including Tom Mahoney, and over a thousand wounded to accommodate this face-saving exercise. It also begs the question of from whom Westmoreland was trying to salvage his dignity. If it were the North Vietnamese, he was too late. General Giap had already formed an opinion of his aptitude as a military leader. Comparing Westmoreland to his replacement, Giap said, "General Abrams was different and had different fighting tactics. He based his leadership on research; he studied his own and others' experiences to see what he could apply to *the real situation here* [italics added by author]."[105]

🙰 🙰

On July 19, 1968, I received a letter from Tom Mahoney dated July 4—two days before he died. I was in Phu Bai when it arrived and had not yet learned of his fate. No longer the upbeat and optimistic guy he had been in his last few letters to me, Tom's tone was now grim. He had been watching the demolition of Khe Sanh Combat Base for the last few weeks and glumly commiserated with me about the waste it had been by so many who sacrificed so much to defend the place.

He was also frustrated by his battalion and regimental officers for allowing them to exist so dangerously exposed on the hill for days after destroying their own shelters. The men of Bravo were growing angry at the lack of proper planning that had left them in such a precarious situation and with still no reliable word on when they would be lifted out. There was no more talk from Tom about becoming an officer. More ominously, there was no mention of our planned New Year's Eve bash back home in Oakland (nor did he mention having received a letter from Linda). I was immediately concerned by this unanticipated level of despair from my usually optimistic friend and so quickly shot off a note full of inane, joking observations in hopes of providing a chuckle and lifting his spirits. I have no idea where that letter eventually ended up.

I learned of Tom's fate eight days after receiving his letter, while routinely reading U.S. casualty reports in the *Stars & Stripes*. His name was listed under the heading "Missing in Action." I had suspected something might be wrong because of a puzzling absence in mail from friends and family in the previous week, especially my mom who wrote almost daily. My unit was then located about seventy miles southeast of Khe Sanh and I had read about the desperate fighting Tom's battalion was engaged in there. On a hunch, I hitchhiked to a hospital several miles away to see if any casualities from Bravo Company might be there and could provide information about Tom's disappearance.

There, I found Bruce Bird still recovering from the near-fatal neck wound he had received during his attempt to reach Tom's body. Bruce said he had heard that Tom was acting "differently" because of a Dear John letter he'd received a few days before walking off the hill "and getting himself killed."

I was stunned. Until that moment I thought Tom was missing rather than dead. Bruce told me rest of the story in a detached, matter-of-fact monotone of one who had seen many men die. Still in shock, I turned to leave. Sensing my pain, he called out to me: "Hey, for what it's worth, if Mahoney hadn't done what he did, the whole platoon would have been lost, shot down with the chopper on the way out."

I suddenly recalled the vivid dream I had back in May 1967 of Tom being killed on Hill 881 South. At the time I dreamt this, Marines had just fought a well-publicized battle there, which he and I followed with great interest in the newspapers and on television. I did not mention the dream to Tom and now wondered if I should have. If I had, and he remembered it, would it have made any difference? Like most dreams, I didn't think it would come true; but now knew from firsthand experience that at pitiless Khe Sanh the unimaginable was a common occurrence—a lesson being painfully reinforced at that moment.

After leaving the hospital, I went back to my hut and intentionally picked a fight with the burliest enlisted man in my platoon, with whom I seldom spoke, and who was more than happy to accommodate, drilling me on the chin with a big right fist, knocking me back through the air onto the plywood floor dazed.

This incident was immediately understood by everyone present. In an environment where to weep was considered a sign of weakness by peers, a cause for doubt about one's toughness and trustworthiness under pressure, I had to do something quickly to extirpate the devastating sorrow I was experiencing. Physically punishing myself for having outlived my friend seemed like an acceptable course of action. Getting one's ass kicked was more dignified than crying.

That evening I wrote a letter to my parents:

Dear Mom & Dad,

I haven't been getting much mail lately. I guess I know why. I read about Tom, we get weekly casualty reports. I'm really going to miss him. He was about the best friend I ever had. I hope his mom will be able to take it.

As for me, I just don't know. I'm sick of it all, this lousy country and this war. A few more months and I'll be leaving and somebody else will take my place. One big waste. That's all it is. Well I'd better go. Take care. I'm O.K. And I'll write again soon.

Love,
Mike

PART II

To the living we owe respect,
but to the dead we owe only the truth.

~ VOLTAIRE ~

13
HOME

AFTER LEAVING OUR long-time quarters at Khe Sanh, the Twenty-sixth Marine Regiment changed locations about every month. I came under much less enemy fire than before, because the regimental air team's main duty now was coordinating close air support bombers, medevac and resupply choppers to Marine battalions out in "the bush," most often our First Battalion, who fought costly battles in May near Dong Ha and during the summer at An Hoa.

In an effort to keep troop spirits high, U.S. armed forces newspaper and radio attempted to soften news from home with carefully chosen stories and photos. However, we did have access to magazines like *Time* and *Newsweek* and our morale deteriorated with the endless stream of bad news arriving from the U.S. and around the world. Reverend Martin Luther King, Jr. had been assassinated even before we left Khe Sanh, spawning riots in over a hundred cities and student strikes closing campuses. In early June, Senator Robert F. Kennedy, front runner for the Democratic Party's nomination for president, was also murdered.

In Paris and Prague enormous demonstrations by students and workers were violently suppressed. The summer months were filled with more rioting and violence across the United States, peaking in August at the Democratic National Convention in Chicago, where days of indiscriminate clubbing by the police of demonstrators and bystanders alike, shocked the nation. In early October, five thousand students and workers demonstrated in Mexico City until troops and police dispersed them with gunfire, killing hundreds. In that same city, two weeks later, during an Olympic medal ceremony, African-American athletes Tommie Smith and John Carlos raised their black-gloved fists in protest against racial discrimination during the playing of America's national anthem.

Just before the presidential election in November, Lyndon Johnson, who had chosen not to run again, ordered an end to the bombing of all North Vietnam. Those of us engaged in endless interdiction of supplies coming into South Vietnam from the north were not pleased with that news. A few days later, Richard M. Nixon, promising to bring law and order to an internally battered nation, and "Peace with Honor" in Vietnam, was elected thirty-seventh President of the United States.

As 1968 came to a close, new people populated the ranks of our company. Often bored, and with little respect for just how dangerous an enemy we faced, many turned to chronic drug use and became serious threats to our safety. Steve Orr and I were anxious to get out of there,[106] and gratefully received our orders home, departing on December 17, 1968.

While standing on the Da Nang airfield waiting to board a commercial airliner out, I watched silently as troops disembarked from that plane and walked past. Some in our group sang out, "You'll be sor-e-e-e," the same serenade I'd received there a year before. Most, like me, just stared with surprising indifference at those passing by. Yet there was something else. Unlike past wars, most American troops in Vietnam did not perceive it as a shared sacrifice in the common cause of victory, but rather as a personal, finite exercise in self-preservation. While the war would still go on for years after I left—my war was now over.

Three days later, I sat down to dinner at home with my parents and younger siblings, Sue, Kevin and Brian. I had just arrived back in the United States that morning for thirty days of leave before reporting to my next duty station at Camp Pendleton. Mom was visibly relieved and could not stop grinning. I was happy for her because she was a relentless worrier and for two of the last three years had endured the anxiety of having sons at war.

The previous January, I had written them hurriedly to say I was being temporarily reassigned to a platoon in Khe Sanh village.

Ten days later they were stunned by a news headline in the San Francisco Chronicle blaring "MARINE BASE AT KHE SANH ATTACKED" and, even more painful for them, a column heading just below that stating "Village Overrun." I had written as soon as I returned to the base to tell them I'd survived, but because of the chaotic conditions, mail did not leave Khe Sanh for six days and it took another week for my letter to reach home.

During that excruciating interval, my parents waited each day for the sound of the doorbell and the telegram they were dreading, or a uniformed Marine waiting to extend official condolences. It was very difficult for my mom. Of all the things I did in my youth to make her worry, I most regret having put her through those two weeks. I also knew she was having a hard time dealing with Tom's loss and the pain his mother was enduring, wanting so much to help her, but also conscious of the awkwardness of the situation, especially now that I had arrived home safely.

I could sense my family felt uneasy about my presence there at first, not quite knowing what to expect. Later, thirteen-year-old Kevin told me that because the media had so often depicted the behavior of American troops in Vietnam as depraved and savage, he was expecting me at any minute to show them some human ears I'd removed as souvenirs from enemy dead. Dad probably believed that too, but mostly just repeated the phrase: "Geez it's good to have you back," and occasionally asked me carefully worded questions about the flight home and the weather in Vietnam. I answered in short replies, my conversation skills rusty and inhibited by a reluctance to let slip any salty expletives in the presence of mom and the kids.

Later that evening, some of my high school friends came to gawk. I did not have much to say to them, or they to me. We made small talk in the kitchen for about an hour. None of them had been to Vietnam and so discussion of the war was awkward and uncomfortable and, of Tom's death, even more so. Of them, only Jack Mooseau, who had been close to Tom, remained an unwavering friend.

The next day I visited Tom's family, stopping first at a florist to buy a poinsettia plant to take with me. Before my enlistment, I had driven a delivery truck for that shop and it was good seeing those I had worked with. However, the owner's eighteen-year-old son was visiting that day and, as I chatted with the father, the boy approached and interrupted us to rebuke me: "How can you justify what you've done? How can you live with yourself?" His questions were laced with such self-righteous conviction that I was momentarily at a loss for words. It was the first time, but not the last, I would be scolded for my participation in the war by those who had not been there. His father apologized to me for the rudeness. However, none of this affected me deeply because I was preoccupied with the unpleasant task ahead—and dreading it.

I then drove to the house on Fairmount Avenue and knocked on the door. Tom's grandmother Ruby answered and stared at me for a moment with a look that clearly said, "Why are you alive instead of my Tommy?" Then, without having said a word, she turned wearily and disappeared into the house leaving the door half-open. I waited on the porch for a while longer and then Tom's sister, Claudia, came to the door, gave me a hug and led me into the house.

I sat down in the living room and soon Tom's mother entered. I did not know what to expect after the grandmother's reception, and so was relieved by her warm greeting. On a piano, next to a beautifully decorated five-foot high Christmas tree, was a frame containing a photograph of Tom in his Marine dress blues uniform, the citation for his Purple Heart and the medal itself. His mom picked it up and handed it to me. We both started to cry.

She then left the room, soon returning with a small cardboard box containing several envelopes. These were letters that had been among Tom's personal belongings, she explained, shipped to her from Vietnam by his company commander. Two of the letters were those I had sent him in the months before his death and two others were of condolence from Captain Black dated July 12, 1968, six days after Tom was lost, and Ken Fernandes, dated July 24. Ken wrote that he was deeply sorry, not just in losing a close friend, but, as Tom's squad leader, he felt responsible for not keeping a better eye on him.

Another letter was from Tom's former girlfriend. As Mrs. Mahoney handed it to me, I asked her if she ever saw Linda. She said that the girl had come by once after the news of Tom's disappearance. Linda had gone into the living room and sat on the floor by the piano, not saying a word for about an hour, then departed. Tom's mother thought it was "all very odd" and had not heard from her since.

As I began to read, I realized it was the Dear John letter that Bruce Bird had mentioned to me in the hospital at Phu Bai. I guessed the letter would be harsh, but was stunned by the level of hostility and the wild epithets. "Babykiller" is one I vividly recall because, to that point, I had not heard the expression, and was immediately shocked by its horrifying insinuation and the grave injustice to my friend. However, it was the last sentence that must have hurt Tom the most, when Linda wrote that she could not believe she'd ever cared for him and never wanted to see him again. Given his despondency about the abandonment of Khe Sanh to the North Vietnamese at the time this letter arrived, her timing could not have been worse.

Speechless, I could not imagine that in Mrs. Mahoney's long months of grief, pain and pursuit of answers, she had missed the possible role this letter played in the loss of her son. However, she made no comment. I handed it back to her and she carefully placed it in the envelope and returned it to the little box. We sat for several minutes more, not knowing what to say next, our throats too constricted by grief to get words out even if we knew what they were.

The silence was finally broken by a question I hoped she would not ask, "Do you think Tommy is still alive?" I responded dishonestly, saying that "anything is possible." Although the Marine Corps had determined him to be dead, it was clear she could not fully accept that as the truth. And I could not bring myself to extinguish her last flicker of hope. I later wondered whether my lie helped her, or merely prolonged her pain. After several more minutes of silence, I stood up, gave her a hug and left.

Mrs. Mahoney's belief that her son could still be alive and might return home was not entirely the overwrought reaction of a grieving mother. Bureaucratic clumsiness had fed this suspicion. While

Captain Black and Ken Fernandes both wrote within days of Tom's death to express their condolences, she was simultaneously receiving a series of messages from the Twelfth Marine Corps District, Alameda, California informing her to the contrary:

13 JULY 1968 - I DEEPLY REGRET TO CONFIRM THAT YOUR SON LANCE CORPORAL THOMAS P. MAHONEY III HAS BEEN REPORTED MISSING IN ACTION SINCE APPROXIMATELY 2:00 PM JULY 6, 1968 IN QUANG TRI PROVINCE, REPUBLIC OF VIETNAM. YOUR SON BECAME MISSING IN ACTION WHILE ENGAGED IN A HOSTILE FORCES DURING AN OPERATION. EVERY POSSIBLE EFFORT IS BEING MADE TO DETERMINE HIS WHEREABOUTS. YOU'LL BE KEPT INFORMED OF ALL DEVELOPMENTS AS ADDITIONAL REPORTS ARE RECEIVED BY THIS HEADQUARTERS. ON BEHALF OF THE UNITED STATES MARINE CORPS, I EXTEND OUR SINCERE SYMPATHY DURING THIS PERIOD OF GREAT ANXIETY. L W WALT JR LTGEN USMC ACTING COMMANDANT OF THE MARINE CORPS. [107]

No representative from the Marine Corps ever came to explain, and she received a similar message each week throughout July and early August, saying that Tom's status was still "missing," and search operations were continuing "to determine his fate."

What she was unaware of at the time was that back in Vietnam, First Lieutenant Stuart A. Dorow, the personnel officer in Tom's battalion, was busily conducting an investigation to determine if he might still have been alive when the hill was abandoned. Dorow, from Beaumont, Texas, had turned down a scholarship from the Juilliard School of Music to join the Marine Corps and was regarded as a highly intelligent officer with a keen eye for detail.

His investigation began just a few days after Tom was lost and contained statements from Frank and Captain Black, as well as Richard Delucie, the first man attempting to reach Tom. Richard, who was bedridden recovering from his wound at Tripler Hospital near Honolulu, stated that, contrary to what he told Frank on the hill that day, he had never seen Tom's body. Dorow would explain away this discrepancy in his final report by saying, "it is understandable some of the facts would be blurred slightly by the mental and physical strain of combat conditions placed on those solicited to recall the action."[108]

In the time allotted him, Dorow was unable to locate and interview the other four men who volunteered for the recovery effort that afternoon. A grieving mother was waiting in Oakland to know if her son was dead or alive and Lieutenant Dorow did an exceptional job under chaotic circumstances. On July 27, Lieutenant Colonel Van Winkle officially concurred with Dorow's findings that Tom was killed in action, body not recovered, and forwarded the decision up the chain of command. For some reason, it took another twenty-three days to process.

On August 16—forty days after his death—Tom's tormented mother was finally visited by a representative of the Marine Corps, a captain, to advise her that Tom had been killed in action and provide her with this official message of condolence on behalf of the Commandant:

> I DEEPLY REGRET TO CONFIRM THAT THE STATUS OF YOUR SON LANCE CORPORAL THOMAS PATRICK MAHONEY III USMC HAS BEEN CHANGED. INFORMATION RECEIVED BY THIS HEADQUARTERS REVEALS HE DIED 6 JULY 1968 AS A RESULT OF GUNSHOT WOUNDS TO THE BODY FROM ENEMY RIFLE FIRE. WHILE YOUR SON'S PLATOON WAS PREPARING TO BE HELILIFTED FROM THE COMPANY'S POSITION ON HILL 881 TO HILL 689, THOMAS STEPPED OUT OF THE COMPANY PERIMETER AND, IN DOING SO, HE EXPOSED HIMSELF TO HOSTILE SNIPER FIRE. HIS MOVEMENTS AT THAT TIME WERE NOT DISCERNIBLE DUE TO VEGETATION. HIS REMAINS WERE LOCATED BUT COULD NOT BE REACHED BY RECOVERY FORCE DUE TO THE NEARNESS OF HOSTILE FORCES. RECOVERY ATTEMPTS WERE TERMINATED BECAUSE MEMBERS OF THE RECOVERY TEAM WERE WOUNDED BY ENEMY FORCES IN CONCEALED AMBUSH. ON BEHALF OF THE UNITED STATES MARINE CORPS I EXTEND OUR HEARTFELT CONDOLENCES IN YOUR BEREAVEMENT. LEONARD F. CHAPMAN, JR. GENERAL USMC COMMANDANT OF THE MARINE CORPS.

Tom's sister Claudia later recalled how wise it was that the captain thought to bring with him Monsignor Nicholas Connelly, pastor of Saint Leo's Church and an old friend of the family. As she walked toward the door responding to the bell, Claudia saw the crestfallen look on that cleric's familiar face through the leaded glass and knew immediately her brother was dead. The remainder of that mournful visit, the anguish of her grief-stricken mother and grandmother, and the words of comfort from the captain and monsignor, are mercifully blurred in Claudia's memory. "But at least," she later said, "the agony of not knowing was finally over."[109]

Three days later, a letter from the Personal Affairs Office at the Naval Air Station, Alameda, California, tried to explain the delay, but, because it was written in such impersonal "bureaucratese," could not have provided the family with any solace:

> The intensity of the action and subsequent medical evacuation of the wounded personnel made the quest for completing compilation of facts relating to the status of Thomas difficult to immediately ascertain. Every reasonable doubt had to be thoroughly investigated before a determination of his status could be made.

After the visit, Patricia Mahoney agreed to a memorial service for Tom to be held in late August at Saint Leo's Church, where he had attended grade school just six years earlier. Because I still had four months left to go on my tour of duty in Vietnam, I was unable to attend. Sue Thomas, our friend from the "Yellow Submarine" days, later told me that the gathering was large and heartrending. Sue had been a high school friend of Linda's and so they sat together during the service. Linda, who insisted on being in the last row of pews, kept nervously commenting to Sue that she felt everyone was staring at her and blaming her for Tom's death. She left as soon she could do so without drawing further attention to herself.

Before the year ended, Patricia had an epitaph for her son engraved on the reverse side of his father's gravestone. After my return from Vietnam, I went to the National Cemetery in San Francisco and found that marker beneath a wind-bent cypress tree on a hillside by the bay, just a few hundred yards from the Golden Gate Bridge. Two brief inscriptions etched into a single stone, two generations of Mahoney men lamented by the doleful moan of a nearby foghorn. It still breaks my heart to go there.

14
RICH MAN'S WAR, POOR MAN'S FIGHT

RICHARD M. NIXON was inaugurated as President on the afternoon of January 20, 1969. After participating in the ceremony, Lyndon Johnson departed Washington, D.C. for Texas in the early evening, which, in Vietnam, was the morning on January 21, precisely one year—almost to the hour—from when the attack on Khe Sanh began, signaling the start of the siege and the beginning of the end of his presidency. Johnson left office an emotionally broken man and, in some respects, became a physical casualty of the war. He resumed chain-smoking that day, his first cigarette since a massive heart attack in 1955. It proved to be the start of a self-destructive spiral from which he died of heart failure four years later.

I completed my home leave on the day after the inauguration and joined the Fifth Communications Company at Camp Pendleton. In September, I transferred to the Marine Corps Air Station, Kaneohe Bay on Oahu. The U.S. had begun downsizing its forces in anticipation of a negotiated ceasefire in the war and my occupational specialty soon qualified me for early separation from active duty. In February 1970, four months before my enlistment contract required, I was sent to the Treasure Island Naval Facility in San Francisco Bay for transfer to civilian life.

My friend Steve Orr had been discharged a few days earlier in Yuma, Arizona and was there to pick me up. During the siege, Steve and I kept a morning chow routine in my bunker as a way to ensure, at least once a day, that the other was still alive. We always started the morning with a little game of trying to be the first to utter the phrase, "Tonight's the night," a reference to the big attack we were expecting from the thousands of NVA troops massing just a few hundred meters away. The joke was in the absurdity that one of us was going to be correct eventually, but probably not live to gloat about it the following morning. Steve has remained a close friend. Such a life-long bond occurred rarely among returning Vietnam veterans, and I have long since stopped wondering why this happened. I just consider myself lucky.

I had witnessed antiwar demonstrations in Berkeley before Tom and I went to boot camp in the spring of 1967 and, since then, had read about the escalating violence occurring in American cities throughout 1968. Yet, I arrived home expecting, at the very worst, to be merely ignored by the civilian population for having served in the war and so was not prepared for the degree of hostility, on a personal level, I encountered upon my return to civilian life.

I was also surprised to learn that, what I believed to be a national peace movement, had morphed into vigorous allegiance to the communist government in Hanoi, and so returning to the Oakland-Berkeley area added an almost surreal aspect to my growing sense of alienation. Viet Cong flags were draped from the eaves of houses around campus and posters of Ho Chi Minh and other communist icons, like Giap, Mao and Che Guevara, could be seen hanging in windows block-after-block. The Berkeley City Council had changed Willard Park, where I played two-hand touch football as a kid, to Ho Chi Minh Park, although would-be revolutionaries around town claimed it had been "liberated," rather than merely renamed.

The place often had the feel of a battle zone. Several months earlier, in May 1969, I had come home from Camp Pendleton for a weekend, arriving just after six thousand rioters clashed with police over access to a vacant lot in Berkeley they called People's Park. Governor Ronald Reagan ordered 2,700 National Guardsmen to restore order in the city. Tanks were now rumbling along the streets of Berkeley and when I finally made it to my parent's home in the hills above town, they were sitting outside on lawn furniture because tear gas being used to disperse the rioters had wafted up the canyon and was now trapped inside the house.

While away in Vietnam, this was the place I'd longed to be more than any other, the land of my dreams and the endless topic of conversations with buddies. And, when I had only a few days left to scratch-off on my short-timer's calendar, I uttered the word "home" in sappy and sentimental murmurs that made my insides go light with excitement. However, it proved to be none of that, and I was soon overcome by the pitiful realization that all those treasured memories of home and friends, that I'd used to survive the worst times, had been mostly fantasy. I was hurt and slightly humiliated at my naiveté.

However, I was now no longer so naïve that I didn't understand how financiers and industrialists were not grudgingly, or accidentally, reaping huge profits from the war. While still in Vietnam, most of us had begun to understand that the endless rain of bombs and shells expended throughout the country around the clock, and all the materiel necessary to support that war, had to be good for someone's bottom line. General Westmoreland's last assignment before taking command of U.S. forces in South Vietnam was as superintendent of West Point, a distinctly political post, cozy with America's business and government elite; members of what former Army General and President Dwight D. Eisenhower warned the nation against in his 1961 farewell address as the "military-industrial complex."

"Westy," historian Stanley Karnow observed, "was a corporation executive in uniform."[110]

In Vietnam, the General saw to it that his forces were provided with a staggering excess of personal amenities—at least those who served in the rear areas—along with an equally astounding amount of materiel for his "big war" strategy. This required the construction of seven deep-water ports and other major infrastructure projects that poured billions of additional dollars into private industry; despite most of these ventures being deemed completely unnecessary by those in the military who best understood the war. The direct cost of it all would eventually reach $140 billion (equivalent to nearly a trillion in 2016 dollars).

The loss of Tom Mahoney was a perfect illustration of what I perceived to be wrong, especially in light of the abusive letter he received just before his death from the daughter of a wealthy international scrap metal dealer who profited handsomely from a decade of accelerated armament manufacturing. However, such profiteering was nothing new. In 1933, Major General Smedley Butler, one of the Marine Corps' most celebrated heroes, twice awarded the Congressional Medal of Honor, wrote about those who "profited in blood" during the First World War (in terms hauntingly reminiscent of daily life at Khe Sanh):

> How many of these war millionaires shouldered a rifle?
> How many of them dug a trench? How many of them
> knew what it meant to go hungry in a rat-infested dug-
> out? How many of them spent sleepless, frightened nights,
> ducking shells and shrapnel and machine gun bullets? How
> many of them were wounded or killed in battle?[111]

The following year, President Franklin D. Roosevelt, concerned that the arms industry exerted too powerful an influence on the country's foreign policy, convened a conference on how to sever that connection, saying "The time has come to take all profit out of war." A decade later, in the midst of the Second World War, distinguished American war correspondent Edward R. Murrow spoke prophetically from Britain that, "one hears, here and at home, the rising chorus of the brittle voiced businessmen who have done very well out of this whole thing, and who are at heart not in the least appalled at the prospect of a repetition in a few years' time."[112]

During my time in Vietnam I often heard my fellow enlisted men utter the bleak, sardonic maxim used by Confederate soldiers during the Civil War, "Rich man's war, poor man's fight." It was a shameful, but inescapable, truth.

While I was away, a number of radicalized political movements had gained national influence in the country, most notably the Students for a Democratic Society (SDS). The organization's membership had risen to over 25,000, with chapters springing up on scores of college campuses. The SDS viewed the fighting in Vietnam as not only misguided foreign policy, but the consequence of a social system based primarily on profiting the nation's ruling elite. With a growing militancy modeled after the recent "Black Power" radicalization of the civil rights movement, student activists across the country were now forcefully, often violently, protesting university participation in defense research and military recruitment.

The SDS's national convention in 1968 voiced a distinctly anarchist platform—destroy the current political system in America, but with nothing specifically to replace it. However, by the fall of 1969 at their convention in Chicago, a majority of delegates backed an ideology of replacing the current U.S. government with a socialist system modeled on variations of existing communist states. Chris Harman, British journalist and long-time member of the Socialist Workers Party, later wrote of that convention: "Everyone thought himself or herself a Marxist; most were Maoists; and while some found it hard to swallow, the bulk of the leadership openly identified with Stalin."[113]

Yet given mounting evidence at the time that the Soviet gulag state was responsible for the democide of over sixty million of its citizens, and that within the People's Republic of China thirty-five million were killed as Chairman Mao Zedong consolidated power, it was difficult for me to see how the practical application of existing communist systems was morally superior to U.S. imperialism. A timely example of this, called the Great Proletarian Cultural Revolution, was still occurring in China during my transition to civilian life. Mao, concerned about losing influence, had unleashed a campaign of domestic terror across the country in 1966. By the time the chaos subsided ten years later, an estimated thirty-six million had been persecuted and nearly a million killed. Mao's minions also destroyed countless temples and historical treasures, burned books and closed the universities.

I had experienced by then, to a greater degree than most Americans, what an imperfect world it was; yet saw as significant that those calling for the overthrow of the U.S. government were allowed to do that under the nation's constitutional right to free speech, press and assembly, though certainly under surveillance of, and infiltrated by, U.S. intelligence operatives and police. This kind of public criticism of the government was unmistakably absent in prevailing forms of communism I'd observed.

After the "blood profit" excesses of America's ruling class and the arrogance and deceitfulness of the Johnson, and later Nixon, administrations, I understood why so many Americans wanted change. Yet, for all its imperfections, I believed the nation still retained the legislative and judicial tools to improve, and saw such legal remedies to be absent in the party dictatorships of communist governments. Recent civil rights legislation, which had overcome powerful segregationist forces in Congress, and sweeping federal consumer product safety, environmental and occupational health regulations, surviving influential corporate lobbying, were evidence to me that the U.S. Constitution was still viable.

I had grown to despise the war, primarily due to the wasteful and counterproductive way it was conducted in alienating the population of Vietnam against us; but, at the same time, I was filled with resentment toward antiwar protestors. I felt they had not earned the privilege to be against it, and was offended that they saw their acts of civil disobedience as dangerous and sacrificial. Unlike the danger of real battle, they could return each night to the safety of their homes, often to get high and recreate with friends. Avoiding military service, and the dangers inherent in it, was, from my perspective then, just too convenient, too self-serving. Upon reflection, I think I most resented them for still being able to act their age and be so unabashedly idealistic; yet was grimly amused by the irony that the historical record of successful communist revolutions revealed intellectuals and visionaries were the first to be taken away for "reeducation," as the Party hierarchy consolidated power.

Their idealism led many young Americans to conclude that the National Liberation Front and the Provisional Revolutionary Government of South Vietnam were independent of the north and that the latter's participation was based on a common nationalism and would result in restrained retribution when the fighting was over. Those who escaped Vietnam in the years following the war told a different story. The new regime had summarily executed over 65,000 of those who associated with the South Vietnamese government and the Americans and sent over a half million southerners to suffer the horror of concentration camps, some for as long as ten years.[114] Over 165,000 perished in these camps and at least another 50,000 died performing slave labor in "New Economic Zones."[115] Those who were eventually released back into society would barely eke out a living due to their perpetual status as "non-people."[116]

Of the approximately 1.5 million people who eventually fled by boat, or other means, to escape their "liberators," more than 200,000 died from disease, starvation, drowning and pirate attacks.[117] This exodus by a people so tied to their land and ancestry, whose deepest spiritual beliefs told them that to leave Vietnam and die elsewhere was to condemn their souls to wander in misery forever, is probably the single most damning evidence of just how bad things were under the onerous North Vietnamese form of communism forced upon the south.

But this should not have been a surprise. Northern and southern Vietnam had begun a separate political existence over three centuries earlier when the Nguyen of the south constructed two enormous walls near the narrow center of the country to protect it from the Trinh armies of the north. This animosity persisted, and at the conclusion of the war in 1975, legions of modern-day carpetbaggers descended on the south to control things for the central government in Hanoi. They brought with them a centuries-old conviction in their cultural and ethnic superiority and an engrained mistrust of southerners, and their cruelty soon exceeded what western apologists on the political left argued was "a necessary evil" to avoid a reactionary return to imperialist domination.

The Communist party in Hanoi quickly disbanded the National Liberation Front, which was created to fight the Saigon regime and Americans, and merged these VC forces into the NVA in a way that destroyed its separate identity. Many Front members, who led the struggle and had suffered gravely in the process, were now considered a threat to the new order, and dealt with accordingly. Non-communists in the Provisional Revolutionary Government were quickly purged. Some endured persecution, others fled the country.

State security forces, like the Cong An, continued to intimidate and bully the citizenry in an effort to keep power concentrated in the hands of the old Party hierarchy. Pervasive government corruption, often cited as a reason to remove the South Vietnamese regime, remained endemic under the communists. In short, Vietnam did not become the beneficent worker's paradise envisioned by the American radical left who had uncompromisingly supported the communist cause, but rather an endless tragedy.

Because my hometown now bred within me so many bad feelings, I moved to Sacramento, California in the fall of 1970 and attended American River College and later California State University. I majored in history, largely because I felt more comfortable in the distant past than the present. I did well in my studies, voraciously consuming all the information I could, believing that in knowledge I might find some logic in what had happened to me and my friend. I enjoyed the college environment, despite being philosophically unacceptable to most of my classmates and professors by questioning the altruistic motives of the North Vietnamese Communists and our other Cold War adversaries. Soon frustrated, I quit discussing it, and my resentment grew.

I often tried to see things through Tom's eyes, wondering how he would have handled such disillusionment. If he had been able to overcome the dual emotional blows in July 1968 of his sense of betrayal by U.S. government and military leaders at what he witnessed in the chaotic, final days of Khe Sanh, and then the painful rejection by his girlfriend for having fought in the war, would he have been less disappointed or resentful about it all than me? The bitterness I felt was understandably magnified by the fact that he was not there—and in my knowledge of the despair he experienced just before dying.

It was not that I felt responsible for his death, for I had, long before, conceded that luck determined who walked away from the slaughter at Khe Sanh. Rather, it was a localized form of survivor's guilt that had me convinced the better person had not come home. Instead of the charming, confident, handsome and optimistic young man for whom doors would have opened the rest of his life—the world got me. Tom's trust in me to share with him what we naively thought would be a splendid adventure, had given me my first taste of truly believing in myself. Now, three years later, I returned home devoid of confidence, exhibiting self-destructive behaviors like heavy smoking and binge drinking, and seeking out the dirtiest and most arduous jobs I could find to help pay my way through college.

On sweltering summer days in the Sacramento Valley I would routinely offload fifteen tons of animal feed—one fifty- or seventy-five-pound sack at a time—from a steel-walled, railroad boxcar in which the oven-like interior afternoon temperature often exceeded 160 degrees. On other days, I would hoist nine tons of hay onto a flatbed truck, then drag each bale with hooks into dusty, airless, stifling barns or other storage outbuildings at ranches around the valley, the sharp alfalfa stems ripping deep scratches in my arms and face that stung all day from the salt in my sweat. It was the worst work I could find, but still not penance-enough for having been the wrong one to survive.

I hoped that by immersing myself in such grueling manual labor I would forget about the war, unaware that experts treating combat-related stress disorders had determined that such filthy, hot, painfully laborious and mindlessly repetitive activity was so close to the Vietnam experience, it was precisely what I should not have been doing.

As if this wasn't bad enough, at midmorning on a Friday in September 1975, I was driving a load of feed sacks away from a railroad spur in an old residential section of Sacramento when I stopped at an intersection. As I turned my head to the left to see if it was safe to continue on, I was suddenly overcome by a disorienting sensation of *déjà vu*. A rickety, wooden, two-story building, about three doors down, was completely surrounded by a dozen armed men, some with

M-16 rifles, all behind the cover of trees or parked cars and aiming up at the second floor ready to shoot. This unanticipated war zone so stunned me that I sat there, mouth agape, until a uniformed police officer rushed up barking commands for me to turn right (the wrong way on a one-way street) and get out of there.

I later learned that the upper floor of the house was rented to several "hippies," one of whom was Lynette "Squeaky" Fromme, a disciple of Charles Manson, who had just attempted to assassinate President Gerald Ford a mile away on the State Capitol grounds. Fromme had neglected to chamber a round in her military .45 caliber semi-automatic pistol before trying the first shot at point blank range and was wrestled to the ground by Secret Service guards before she had another chance to fire. The armed men I had seen around that old house were federal and local police waiting to move in on any accomplices living there. The shock of that combat imagery distracted me for weeks afterward.

❦ ❧

After my return to civilian life, I rarely paid attention to reports in newspapers or on television about the war in Vietnam—hoping it would all just go away. It finally did. On January 27, 1973, representatives of North and South Vietnam and the United States signed a promise to follow guidelines for peaceful national reconciliation, commonly referred to as the Paris Peace Accords. Within a few weeks, photographs taken by a South Vietnamese Ranger reconnaissance unit of the former Khe Sanh base revealed three Soviet antiaircraft missile (SAM-2) launching sites in clear violation of the agreement. The U.S. government warned that if the missiles were not removed they would be bombed. Subsequent reconnaissance confirmed they were gone.

In April, North Vietnamese soldiers killed thirteen members of the International Commission of Control and Supervision (ICCS) established by the Accords to monitor war materials entering South Vietnam through the Lao Bao-Khe Sanh corridor along Highway

9. The remaining ICCS staff, intimidated by these attacks, withdrew from the area, opening the door for North Vietnam's final invasion. The following month SAM-2 missiles were back at Khe Sanh along with antiaircraft guns and heavy field artillery pieces, a large fuel depot and numerous storage, supply, headquarters and communications buildings. Protests by South Vietnam and the United States about these violations of the ceasefire agreement went unheeded in Hanoi, largely because by then Richard Nixon had been rendered virtually powerless due to revelations of his abuses of presidential power by the Congressional Watergate Committee investigation.

In November of that year, over Nixon's veto, Congress passed the so-called War Powers Act, limiting presidential authority to deploy military forces into combat without congressional endorsement. Subsequent deep cuts by Congress in aid to South Vietnam caused economic chaos there and a sharp decline in civilian and military morale. After Nixon resigned the presidency in August 1974, Congress did not honor promises he made to the government of South Vietnam to intervene militarily if the country was invaded. Throughout the remainder of that year, the ARVN retreated before a mechanized NVA onslaught. In April 1975, Saigon fell and was renamed Ho Chi Minh City by the victors.

The refusal by the United States to intervene militarily in South Vietnam's final crisis sealed its fate. But George Herring suggests that nothing the Americans could have done at that point would have changed the outcome. "The Nation," Herring said, "simply collapsed."[118] Just after midnight on April 30, 1975, as northern tanks rumbled into the center of Saigon, CIA station chief Tom Polgar cabled Washington:

THIS WILL BE THE FINAL MESSAGE FROM SAIGON STATION. IT HAS BEEN A LONG FIGHT AND WE HAVE LOST... THOSE WHO FAIL TO LEARN FROM HISTORY ARE FORCED TO REPEAT IT. LET US HOPE THAT WE WILL NOT HAVE ANOTHER VIETNAM EXPERIENCE AND THAT WE HAVE LEARNED OUR LESSON. SAIGON SIGNING OFF.[119]

15
ALL THE THINGS I THOUGHT I KNEW

AFTER RECEIVING A BACHELOR'S DEGREE in history, I went to work for the Social Security Administration, first in Glendale, California, then transferring to Reno, Nevada in 1978. I was married at age twenty-four and divorced after sixteen years. Now, with my life in disarray and two young children whose affection I did not want to lose, I was forced to reexamine my beliefs. I had spent years reading philosophical works and so understood the concept of critical thought and the logical process and, as it began to dawn on me that I really knew very little about the Vietnam War, the words of Epictetus came to mind: "It is impossible for a man to learn what he thinks he already knows."

During the siege of Khe Sanh, as I slowly came to grips with the capricious selectivity of death from the relentless artillery bombardment, I realized much of what I'd learned at home, school and church—intended to nurture, motivate, and guide me—were no longer effective tools in my struggle to cope. I later supplanted that tattered belief system with a rationally unsupportable conviction that my experiences in Vietnam automatically made me wise beyond my years. The war may have taught me to endure terrible things, but it provided no information about what was going on outside my immediate area of observation, or why it was important for me, Tom and the others to have been there. I now recognized that most of what I knew about the war came from boot camp propaganda and rumors I had heard while in Vietnam.

One of the many things I did not know was the growing clinical evidence of what was being labeled Post Traumatic Stress Disorder (PTSD). Not to be confused with battlefield psychological injuries, often termed "shell shock" or "battle fatigue," PTSD can range from normal stress responses to a full-blown, incapacitating, life-long anxiety disorder. It can manifest well after a traumatic event occurs with a variety of symptoms, including clinical depression, rage, panic, chronic insomnia, substance abuse and self-destructive impulses.

For the decade after my return from Vietnam, little was understood about PTSD, or the unique psychological problems associated with the Vietnam War. Even if more information was available to veterans immediately following the end of the war, I, like many others, might have refused to accept help because it would have appeared to be an example of weakness, or in the parlance of the Corps, "not hacking it."

Returning to an ungrateful and often hostile American public was exacerbated by the way we were treated by veterans of prior wars. Many in our fathers' Second World War generation considered us unworthy of their respect. Returnees from Vietnam were frequently unwelcome at their local VFW and American Legion halls. They were blamed for the embarrassment of the nation's only military defeat, the not-so-subtle implication that this younger generation of American warriors had not been up to the task.

Movies produced about the Second World War depicted American soldiers, sailors and Marines as tough, heroic and rarely frightened by their combat experiences. While most veterans must have realized these Hollywood versions of combat were fabricated, far too many of them failed to mention it to their children. Accordingly, we kids spent hours at movie theaters and in front of black-and-white TV screens awestruck by such prodigious gallantry.

The subsequent rejection of us by so many of them, because we had not lived up to such unattainable standards, only deepened our later sense of alienation. In that regard, some experts believe PTSD has been over-diagnosed to include a form of non-traumatic stress described as a continuing cynicism on the part of many veterans about how the Vietnam War was conducted and their treatment by the American public upon returning.[120]

I have been lucky to avoid serious, long-term issues with stress disorders and often wondered why. I still had eighteen months left on my active duty obligation after leaving Vietnam. Though bemoaning that predicament constantly, wanting to get out of the military as soon as possible, I now see how helpful that extra time among my fellow Marines may have been, especially spending the last six months on balmy and beautiful Oahu.

There, I was with an airborne unit, the First Air and Naval Gunfire Liaison Company, and though not parachute jump-certified, I joined the others in their daily physical training, which included running several miles. I kept the habit of running regularly for exercise from that point on throughout my life. I believe this routine may have mitigated some symptoms. In addition, I had the good fortune to remain close friends with Steve Orr who shared almost exactly the same experiences I had in Vietnam, and so we were able to mutually support each other through dark moments. Steve has also avoided serious problems with PTSD.

While PTSD is not necessarily tied to the degree or length of exposure to combat, there was a correlation. Despite my scary experience when the NVA overran Khe Sanh village and the intense enemy artillery pounding of the combat base for the next seventy-six days, I always felt that I had it better than many others, especially those in Marine rifle platoons, like Tom, who patrolled almost daily in constant fear of being ambushed—a predicament in which they found themselves with shocking regularity and high casualties.

My self-deprecating sense of humor tended to snap me out of occasional bouts of melancholia and had been a big factor in surviving the war with my faculties reasonably intact. A few years after leaving the military, a friend from Khe Sanh sent me an audio tape he had been making for his parents on a small recorder while I happened to be standing near him with two other Marines. Incoming shells suddenly began exploding along the trench line, sending us diving down through the hatch of a nearby bunker, just as the last round burst exactly where we had been standing. It was a close call, but by no means an unusual occurrence.

In his haste, my buddy neglected to turn off his recorder and for the next few moments the only audible sounds are the rattling of rifle slings and the scraping of boots and helmets against the hard earth as we struggled to untangle from one another. We then spontaneously burst into fits of uproarious laughter, interspersed with mocking arguments about whom among us was too dumb or too slow to survive the next one. About three minutes later we could be heard filing out of the bunker and back into the trench line as if nothing had happened.

As our voices reached me across the years, I could not help but marvel at the composure and audacity of these young men, who, just seconds before, had escaped certain death. It reminded me that the only way to survive then, and now, was not to take things too seriously—if you could. No one spoke more eloquently to this point than Rudyard Kipling, who suffered throughout his adult life from chronic depression. In 1907, Kipling told the graduating class of McGill University that the best cure was to focus on an issue not personal to oneself, "in another man's trouble, or, preferably, another man's joy." Above all else, Kipling said, "take anything and everything seriously except yourselves."[121]

For about a year after my return to civilian life, I had a recurring dream of being called back to join our group from the Khe Sanh command bunker, Captain Steen, Captain Baig, and my fellow radio operators, at an unidentifiable dreamland location other than Khe Sanh, which was under siege and required our expertise. I can still feel the contentment I experienced upon rejoining them, as if it were the only natural place I belonged. I also experienced minor anxiety reactions. Auto backfires, thunder, slamming doors and other sudden, loud sounds sent me scrambling for cover; nor could I sit in places with people behind me. I do not recall how soundly I slept before Vietnam, but have not slept well since. For decades thereafter I awoke at the slightest sound, routinely prowling the house checking and rechecking doors and windows. Sleep disturbances such as nightmares or intrusive thoughts went away as time went on, though my insomnia remains chronic.

I came to realize that, while I had generally acquitted myself well and never neglected my duty, there were times I was dangerously agitated by panic, or locked in despair. This brought me to the final and most difficult transition I needed to make—to accept myself for who I was. I had always been ashamed of an incident that occurred about a week after the siege began. Several explosions had rocked our bunker and gas began seeping in. With my eyes stinging and nose running, I could taste the distinct, astringent tang of CS tear gas. I was familiar with it from my gas mask training at Camp Pendleton, and knew it was not lethal; but, persistent rumors had been circulating that the NVA were about to attack us with nerve agents and other highly poisonous gases. Everyone in the bunker immediately located their masks and put them on. I had left mine behind in the village a few days before. As I looked around at the faces of my buddies now housed behind hideous, bug-eyed, black rubber masks, my gag reflex triggered and I panicked. Grabbing my rifle I headed for the hatchway.

Steve Orr's muffled voice asked, "Where are you going?"

"I'm going to get a mask from the first person I see," I said, "even if I have to shoot him for it."

As I turned to leave, Steve's right fist crashed into my jaw. Other Marines pulled me down, threw a blanket over my head and began pouring water onto it. Whether this actually worked as a filter from the gas, it had the immediate effect of calming me down. As it turned out, there was no poison laced into the tear gas, but the NVA did follow up with a mortar barrage to catch those who fled in fear out into the open. Though I never again panicked in Vietnam, that event remained a source of secret humiliation. Decades later when I finally began to talk about it, I found that it did not matter to anyone else but me. So I decided, going forward, that I would not intentionally neglect the more humbling episodes from my war experiences. It proved to be one of the most liberating decisions of my life. I had done my best and that was enough.

About this time I began to recognize that countless others had it worse than me. Taking disability claims for the Social Security Administration put me in contact each day with people suffering from terrible, often, terminal illnesses, blindness, incapacitating psychological disorders, missing limbs, excruciating pain, both old and young—sometimes children—and the agony of their families. Yet, each day, the vast majority of them summoned up the strength and emotional resiliency to go on. I had inadvertently followed Kipling's admonition to lose myself in "another man's trouble." How could I feel unjustly victimized after seeing that never-ending parade of affliction and strength?

Only about one in three American men and women who served in Vietnam during the war saw some form of combat action, and for most of them that consisted of an occasional mortar or rocket attack on their installation. Data indicated that by the late 1980s "the majority of people, even those in high intensity combat, successfully adjusted to civilian life." [122] Indeed, of the dozens of former combat veterans I would later meet, most went on to become highly successful in the arts, business, entertainment, education, law enforcement and government work, with a high number of advanced college degrees, including several PhDs. Some PTSD experts suggest that many veterans choose to live with mild cases of the disorder rather than seek treatment because they haven't come to terms with losing friends in the war: "They hold on to the idea that if I let go of my PTSD I will be dishonoring my friend." [123] I may have been one of them.

Just before almost every Christmas for twenty years after the war, I would, without warning, suddenly burst into tears and weep for several minutes. The first time this happened I was worried that I would not be able to stop crying—EVER. But, as the years went on, I accepted it as part of my holiday season and often wondered if it was the result of my having had to confront Tom's family just two days before Christmas in 1968. I had always felt one of the saddest things about his loss was that there would be no little, Thomas

Patrick Mahoney IV, whose wondrous, beaming face on Christmas morning my friend would never have the good fortune to see.

For years after coming home, I struggled with a festering hatred of Tom's former girlfriend Linda for the scathing Dear John letter she'd written him, and often wondered how I would react if I suddenly found myself in her presence. I knew that nothing I would do, or say, could even the score; but also recognized that reasonableness would not be in play at that moment—only my pent up rage at the unfairness of it all. As it turned out, our paths never crossed again.

Decades later, I recognized that, as with my episodes of Christmas melancholia, the outrage I expected to carry for a lifetime had vanished somewhere along the way. It was not *forgiveness* that drove this transformation, but *indifference*—the place where all anger finally dies. While my awareness of that unspeakable injustice lingers, some internal mechanism within me had decided it was time to finally stop fighting what I would never be able to alter. "If you do not change direction, you may end up where you are heading," Taoist philosopher Laozi said, and I am convinced that such unremitting bitterness would have driven me to an early grave.

However, all my problems were slight compared to some veterans who could not put it all behind them, suffering to this day from complex PTSD, including debilitating depression and inability to love and care for others. Many, who as young men were put in impossible situations, like Army medics and Navy corpsmen, perpetually carry dark misgivings, second-guessing their actions in long-ago battles, unable to free themselves from the agonizing belief they were responsible for tragic endings far beyond their control.

There is no good data on how many Vietnam veterans took their own lives because they could not cope with such guilt, but no doubt many did. Psychiatrist and author Jonathan Shay suggests that twice as many died by their own hand than by the enemy's.[124] Even those of us who feel we have gotten well past all this, occasionally worry that a volatile unresolved issue may be lurking within some subliminal spider hole waiting to ambush us.

One of the most evocative descriptions of a post-traumatic episode I've ever read was penned four decades after the war in an email to Frank Ahearn from a former Bravo Company Marine who had recently struck a "cute little golden retriever" that bolted in front of his pickup truck without giving him time to stop:

> I got out and there it was lying in the grass along the side
> of the country road not making a sound except its hard
> and fast breathing. I called 911 and as I was waiting for the
> Sheriff to come, I just watched the dog lying there, breath-
> ing its last and then my mind went right back to Viet Nam
> and I saw the Marines dying all over again, breathing hard,
> laying in the grass looking so hopeless and sad. I cried for
> the little dog and those painful days in Viet Nam.[125]

16
THOSE WHO
NEVER FORGOT

I ATTEMPTED TO WRITE about my war experiences almost as soon as I returned to civilian life, but found myself unfocused and agitated just a few pages into each attempt. What I had hoped to describe—snippets of remembered terror, disillusionment and anguish—barely made sense even to me. In frustration, I quit trying.

In the mid-1990s my manager insisted I become the office computer automation person and I immediately saw the enormous potential of email and the fledgling Internet. This seemingly insignificant career-development step was critical to my later writing, especially once it occurred to me that I did not know the details of Tom's death. Moreover, in 1994 I married Becky, who helped stabilize my life to a point where I now felt confident and psychologically strong enough to reopen this painful wound and deal with it.

I was soon searching websites for former members of Bravo Company who might have information about Tom and in April 1999 found an electronic bulletin board entry posted by Al Zehner briefly mentioning his loss. I contacted Al and learned he had joined Bravo in 1967, knew Mahoney, but had been severely wounded in the Memorial Day battle and so was not on Hill 881 South when Tom was killed a few weeks later. He later learned about the incident while at Camp Lejuene, North Carolina "from a guy who was shot in the neck trying to get to him." I immediately recognized that as a description of Bruce Bird, who I had visited at the hospital in Phu Bai in July 1968.

Zehner did not know where Bruce was living, but put me in touch with Ernie Vaughn who had been on Hill 881 South the day Tom died. Ernie replied by email that he'd known Tom well, and remembered the day "he had gone outside the wire and was jumped by the NVA." He and other members of First Platoon had been told that a Marine recon team located Tom's body on the hill a few days after Bravo departed and it was returned to his family for burial. Ernie was shocked when I told him the remains never arrived home, and I was equally astounded to hear that his body had been recovered. I continued to search the Internet for information, but only a trickle of historical data from the war had made its way online. I seem to have reached a dead end. Nearly three years would pass before that changed.

In January 2002, Frank Ahearn received an email from Ernie who was seeking to reconnect with former Bravo Company mates. Frank called him and, when the topic of conversation turned to Tom Mahoney, Ernie told Frank that he had spoken to me a few years earlier (though he had forgotten my name) and that I'd told him the body never made it home. Frank was dumbfounded by the news and immediately contacted the Defense POW/Missing Personnel Office (DPMO) where he learned that, contrary to what he had been told in Vietnam, Tom's body was never recovered. He then called Captain Robert Black at his home in Tenafly, New Jersey to give him the news.

By that time I had also come in contact with Steve Busby, a member of Bravo's Second Platoon, who witnessed the attempts by Frank and his men to retrieve the body. After leaving active duty, Steve earned a pharmacy doctorate at the University of the Pacific in Stockton, California, and now lived in San Lorenzo, California, not far from where Tom and I grew up. Steve had recently reconnected with others from Bravo and begun searching government records to learn the status of Tom, and another Bravo Marine who had been missing since the Memorial Day battle.

With Steve's help I requested DPMO documents regarding Tom and was feeling optimistic because I'd recently learned that efforts to recover missing Americans at Khe Sanh began well before the war ended. In September 1971, Marine Corps legend Captain John Ripley, an advisor to South Vietnamese Marines, led perilous missions to the slopes of Hill 950 hoping to recover the remains of several American Marines killed there in a helicopter crash earlier in the year. The first two attempts resulted in Ripley's helicopters being badly shot up by enemy antiaircraft fire and forced to glide down into hard landings on the nearby abandoned Khe Sanh airstrip. Each time the men were able to escape capture. After recovering from wounds received during the second attempt, Ripley and his Vietnamese Marines made a third try, this time successful in locating the bodies.

On September 20, 1971, as the chopper lifted off carrying those remains, Captain Ripley looked out at the deserted airfield and crumbling bunkers where once the plight of thousands of besieged Americans had captured the world's attention.

Earlier that year, in February and March, the U.S. Army had reopened the base briefly as the springboard for a South Vietnamese Army invasion of NVA sanctuaries in nearby Laos to interrupt their supply chain. Despite some initial successes, and inflicting heavy losses on northern forces, the offensive soon stalled and turned into a disastrous rout, with South Vietnamese troops fleeing in a panic back into their own country, but not before over two thousand were killed or missing and another six thousand wounded. American forces, operating in support of the operation, suffered two hundred fifty killed and over twelve hundred wounded—another thirty-eight were reported missing. This appalling defeat was later determined to be largely the result of incompetence, corruption and, in some instances, treason within the ranks of the ARVN high command in Saigon.

But now, as Ripley watched that forsaken, shell-pocked, overgrown plateau fade behind him in the distance, he had no idea that he'd just commanded the final American military action at Khe Sanh.

About six weeks after requesting the documents on Tom, I received a large envelope from the Library of Congress—but could not bring myself to open it. I did not appear to be feeling any anxiety, nor was I burning with curiosity. I knew it was odd, but for some undefined reason I was not yet ready to open it. So that inch-thick manila envelope sat in plain view on my desk beside my computer each day as I wrote on for the next three weeks. Becky never questioned me about it, though I knew she was concerned. Then, one morning, after a bracing three-mile run in the crisp, high desert air; I poured a cup of coffee, sat down at my desk and decided it was finally time to discover exactly what had happened to my friend.

Wading through that half-ream of documents, I soon learned that, just two months after Captain Ripley departed Khe Sanh, American POW/MIA investigators considered the possibly of trying to recover Tom Mahoney's remains from Hill 881 South, just five miles west of Ripley's successful effort, but decided that "the continuing hostile threat in the area precluded any visits or ground inspections in his case."

The 1973 Paris Peace Accords would include provisions for locating those still unaccounted for at the conclusion of hostilities, creating a joint military team with all signatories represented. The U.S. component, called the Joint Casualty Resolution Center (JCRC), was responsible for field searches, excavations, recovery and repatriation activities negotiated through these accords, but was often hampered by ongoing fighting in the south. With the fall of Saigon in April 1975, Americans lost all access to the old battlefields.

For a decade afterward, most Americans sought to forget Vietnam in an effort to pull the nation together after a period of domestic unrest and violence that had bordered on civil war. While returned veterans were still considered pariahs by many, in the late-1980s President George H.W. Bush and Congress acted on growing public interest in locating missing Americans. This became the foundation for ending a nineteen-year trade embargo with Vietnam and establishing economic relations.

In 1994, American investigators returned to Vietnam, Cambodia and Laos, interviewing former NVA and VC soldiers, conducting field searches and excavations, and sifting through military archives in Hanoi. The mission of the JCRC was reassigned to the Joint Task Force-Full Accounting (JTF-FA) located in Honolulu and soon most U.S. government documents pertaining to MIAs in South East Asia were declassified and available through the Library of Congress.

From those records, I learned that on July 12, 1993, twenty-five years to the day after the battle of Khe Sanh ended with the departure of the last Marine unit from Hill 689, a four-person JTF-FA team traveled for the first time to Hill 881 South in search of Tom's remains. The investigators had no one to interview, because there were no local civilians in the region at the time of his death, and Hanoi's antiquated record-keeping system still prevented them from identifying the NVA unit involved in the incident. They performed a perfunctory surface survey of the area where Tom was last seen according to the Dorow report and "found no evidence of remains or burial."[126]

❧ ❧

In late July 2004, I received a call from Frank Ahearn who had tracked me down through information provided by the DPMO as a result of my earlier contacts with that office. I had never met Frank, but knew about him from reading the Dorow report and was awed by the sacrifice he'd been willing to make to recover my friend's body.

From already having spoken to some he had commanded, I also knew how quickly he'd become trusted and admired by those he led, an unusual circumstance for a green officer after such a short stint in the country. With no room for error, Frank's natural gifts of fairness and courage of conviction won him the immediate loyalty of his men. Mahoney and the others knew he would not let them down and considered themselves fortunate to have such a fine platoon leader.

In Vietnam, new officers were often stigmatized by their lack of experience and a common fear among enlisted men that their primary objective was to recklessly make a name for themselves in order to enhance their careers and earn medals at the expense of their subordinate's lives. As such, enlisted men were wary of them, in general, and often mistrustful of commands they gave. Even after a junior officer gained experience and expertise worthy of his troops' trust, their loyalty would not be forthcoming unless there was a fair distribution of risk. This not only required a willingness on the officer's part to share in the same deadly peril as his men, whether it was technically necessary to do so or not, but also display impartiality in the way he assigned risky duties, like night listening posts or walking point on patrol.

Jonathan Shay wrote that if such a social contract between a combat enlisted man and his platoon commander was broken, the moral injury became an essential part of any later combat trauma leading to a lifelong psychological injury: "[Vietnam] veterans can usually recover from horror, fear and grief once they return to civilian life, so long as 'what's right' had not been violated."[127]

During the terrible fighting in Hué, Frank had been approached one evening by a lance corporal who told him that the men of First Platoon, including Tom Mahoney, had decided he was "only worth two dollars." Frank did not understand what that meant, but soon learned it was popular to put a price on an officer's head reflecting how much someone would pay another Marine to "frag" him, or take some other kind of action that would eliminate him from the unit. "I took it to mean that no one in the platoon wanted me dead very badly," Frank said, "and was somewhat pleased, since I had only been in the country for two weeks at the time."[128]

During our initial phone conversation, Frank told me that after Bravo left Hill 689 on July 12, 1968, they were flown to the base near Quang Tri City and allowed to cleanup and relax for two days before returning to the field. A few weeks later, the company had another turn "in the barrel" at Con Thien.

Just after leaving Con Thien, Frank's six-month front line combat obligation was completed and he was reassigned as battalion intelligence officer. In addition to his Purple Heart (he could have claimed several) and the Vietnamese Cross of Gallantry for his efforts while fighting in Hué, Frank received the Bronze Star Medal. The latter, he added sardonically, "was for doing virtually nothing during Operation Meade River in November 1968."

It seemed odd to me that he received no official acknowledgement for his charge down the trenchline on Hill 689 the night of July 7, an extraordinarily daring action that likely helped save the entire battalion from annihilation. Lieutenant Ray Smith, the Alpha Company commander, engaging in the same counterattack that night, but from a different direction, had been awarded the Silver Star Medal. When I later asked Frank about it, he clearly chose not to express his opinion on the subject, replying simply that medals were not important to him.

Apparently Frank's achievement had been lost in the chaos of the situation. His immediate superior, Captain Black, left Hill 689 the following morning for R&R in Hawaii. Black would later explain that, between his return from R&R and the end of his tour of duty in Vietnam a month later, he did not have an opportunity to speak with Frank about his actions on Hill 689 and Frank never brought up the subject. It was decades later, Black said, before he would first learn from some of Frank's former enlisted men the specifics of his incredible feat.

Frank departed South Vietnam on January 1, 1969, and was stationed at Camp Pendleton. When his active duty obligation expired, he stayed in Southern California as a real estate broker for a land-acquisition firm. On a business trip north to San Francisco, he rented a car and drove to Oakland, parking across the street from the Mahoney house. At that time, he believed Tom's body had been recovered by a recon team and sent home for burial and so decided not to ring the doorbell in order to spare the family the pain of revisiting that grim episode just over a year before.

He later married, had two children and was divorced. Changes in his life and business took him to Wheatland, Wyoming where he was an engineer in the construction of the huge Laramie River Power Station, which began operation in 1980. Frank stayed in Wheatland, primarily because it was a good environment to raise his kids. There, he designed, built, and operated a state-of-the-art truck stop on Highway 87 and later worked with troubled youth at a juvenile facility near Riverton.

As I listened to Frank tell his story over the phone, it became clear to me that he was intelligent and articulate, honestly conveying the climate of the times, the misery and unpredictability of the combat he and his men endured, as well as almost every survivor's assessment that he could have done more. He also carried deep regret for not having been able to recover Tom's body. I told him it was obvious to me that he had done everything humanly possible, but that did not seem to change his feelings. I later learned of his father's admonition, "no excuses," and better understood Frank's high expectations of himself. He soon put me in touch with Captain Robert Black.

Immediately following the July battle on Hill 689, Black returned to the battalion's rear headquarters near Quang Tri City where he was asked by battalion First Sergeant Hugh Gatewood to sign a unit diary entry showing Tom Mahoney as MIA, rather than killed in action, body not recovered (KIA-BNR). Black refused to sign because a designation of MIA would have left doubt about whether Tom might still have been alive when Bravo abandoned the hill. Black ordered the first sergeant to have the status changed to KIA/BNR. Just before leaving for R&R, Captain Black composed a letter of condolence to Patricia Mahoney, heeding Gatewood's warning not to mention to her that the body had not been recovered. That function, the first sergeant explained to him, was the responsibility of a higher command, which Black assumed would be someone at the battalion level.

Upon returning to First Battalion headquarters on July 17, Black was furious to learn that Gatewood had been prevented by the battalion administrative officer, Lieutenant W.L. McIver, from annotating the unit diary as Black had directed him to do. McIver felt that such an action did not follow proper procedure; but Black remained suspicious that the overworked battalion administrative staff had been trying to coax him to quickly sign off on a finding of MIA in order to avoid the time-consuming investigation by Lieutenant Dorow that later determined Tom was, in fact, KIA/BNR. "I honestly believe,"

Black would say, "that had I not 'gone off' on the MIA issue, Tom would have remained in that status."[129]

This issue seemed to have resolved itself two weeks later when Dorow told Black that a Marine recon team had gone to Hill 881 South, found the body and "disposed of it." Captain Black passed the information on to Frank and the men of his platoon, who took some consolation in knowing Tom's family would now have something to bury.

Robert Black left active duty in 1969, earning a master's degree in political science and international relations at Columbia University, later lecturing regularly on college campuses, publishing academic papers and running an international management consultancy firm. After a return visit to Vietnam in 1999, he began writing articles about his war experiences. The visit, he said, "had gotten me out of my shell," but, as he began writing, Black found he "still had considerable rage."

❧ ❧

In October 2003, the functions of the JTF-FA mission shifted to the Joint POW/MIA Accounting Command (JPAC), now charged with the world-wide search, recovery and laboratory identification of more than 83,000 Americans still missing from past conflicts. Their researchers soon discovered an NVA military record in Hanoi titled *The History of the 246th Regiment,* which not only contained the incredibly graphic "eyes like a mean animal" description of Tom's death, but also the names of the five NVA soldiers involved.

Representatives of the Vietnamese government and a JPAC research and investigation team went back to Khe Sanh in August 2004 to locate these men. There, they spoke with members of the Huong Hoa District Veterans' Association and Veterans' Association of Quang Tri Province, but none recognized the names of the five soldiers. Back in Hanoi, researchers soon learned that the 246th Regiment had disbanded years before and the whereabouts of unit records was unknown.

The JPAC report of this field trip to locate Tom's remains concluded:

> This is a very difficult case. There are no direct witnesses. The people who fought in this battle were main force troops. When they were done fighting, they left, leaving responsibility for the area to the locality. Furthermore, the dead American was not buried, so there is no way to find the remains. Recommend cessation of investigation.[130]

Back in Hawaii, JPAC analysts concurred, saying there was no further information regarding the disposition of the remains and "no leads for further investigation."

Upon reading the report I was astounded that, given the significant historical and cultural divisions between the people of the north and south, and the family-centric nature of the society, JPAC researchers could somehow suppose that regular army forces from the north might have returned to settle in that neglected, poverty-ridden region so far from their roots. I was also curious how they could conclude with such certainty that the body "was not buried."

Because Captain Black had given Dorow exact map coordinates of where Tom's body was last seen, I was disappointed by JPAC's conclusion that "there is no way to find the remains," and baffled at the reluctance of the investigators while on the hill to probe beneath the surface of a location so precisely pinpointed for them in U.S. military records. It now seemed I had run out of options. Then, as if ordained, I received a call from my old friend, Robert "Doc" Topmiller, who I had not heard from in thirty-six years—and everything changed.

17

NO PLACE ANYMORE
FOR PEOPLE LIKE YOU

I THOUGHT OF CONTACTING DOC many times in the years after the war, but was prevented by what I later learned was a common, but largely unexplained, reluctance on the part of Vietnam veterans to reestablish such contacts. When my memoir, *A Patch of Ground: Khe Sanh Remembered*, was nearing publication in late 2004, I wanted Doc's input. An online search located him as being a professor of history at Eastern Kentucky University (EKU). Despite my hesitancy, wondering if he would even remember me after all those years, I sent a letter. Doc called immediately upon receiving it and was so excited about reuniting that he caught a flight west to see me.

I contacted Steve Orr to tell him the good news. After his discharge from active duty, Steve went to work for Holiday Inn and, by age twenty-four, had moved to Bakersfield, California, as one of that international corporation's youngest hotel/restaurant managers. Steve married his high school sweetheart and within a few years they moved to South Lake Tahoe, where he was hired to manage a large, upscale lakeside hotel and restaurant. He eventually went to work as a gaming dealer, later pit boss, at Harrah's Hotel Casino. But Steve's lifelong ambition was to become a cop and he joined Nevada's Douglas County Sheriff's Office as a reserve officer and later a full-time sworn patrol officer. His professionalism and work ethic eventually led him to the rank of captain and, after earning a master's degree at the University of Nevada, Steve moved on to become Chief of Police in Lewiston, Idaho.

Steve, Doc and I met in Reno and reminisced for two days with the woozy sensation that almost no time had elapsed; effortlessly finishing conversations we'd left interrupted four decades before in Vietnam. Doc told us that he was struggling with PTSD and had recently returned to his teaching position at EKU after taking medical leave to deal with it. My fear that our reunion would have an adverse effect on his emotional health was dispelled when he later sent me a copy of his book, *The Lotus Unleashed: The Buddhist Peace Movement in South Vietnam, 1964-1966,*[131] with the inscription, "To Mike, Thanks for reminding me who I was. Your buddy, Bob."

Also during his visit, I noticed how quickly the three of us relapsed into the cynical humor which allowed us to deal with issues in Vietnam that might otherwise have overwhelmed us emotionally. I now recognized that we had also used it to disguise the affection we felt for one another under those grim circumstances where one of us might be snatched away by death at any moment. Resilient people seem to recognize the value of humor—dark or light—in overcoming adversity and Bob Topmiller had prevailed over more than his share of hardship.

Born on October 18, 1948, in Cincinnati, Bob was the youngest of three sons whose parents divorced when he was six. Five years later his mother was diagnosed with a brain tumor and the kids spent most of their after-school hours caring for her. Upon learning of her illness, the boys' father moved the family into a new house and remarried the gravely ill woman. She died three years later.

Though Bob had great respect for the commitment his father made to her, the two never shared more than a distant emotional relationship, and he learned quickly to stand up for himself. As his brother Thomas later recalled, Bob's unwillingness to back down from bullies "became a prominent trait in him later as an adult."[132] At Archbishop Moeller High School, Bob was an excellent student and a competitive athlete, establishing the city's high school record in the one hundred-yard dash that would stand for over twenty years.

At his graduation party, Bob announced his intention of joining the Marine Corps. Worried aunts immediately implored his father not to allow him to go to Vietnam as a Marine. The father agreed, refusing to grant permission for his underage son to enlist in the Corps; but, believing it was safer, allowed him to go into the Navy instead. Bob began basic training in July 1966 at Great Lakes Naval Station near Chicago.

When asked to specify what occupational specialty field he desired, Bob chose hospital corpsman, later explaining that his mother's long illness had piqued his interest in health care. It was only later that Bob learned Navy corpsmen served with Marines in combat. Now envisioning himself rushing to the aid of wounded men under enemy fire, he was amused by the irony of his family's insistence that he join the Navy to stay unharmed.

After boot camp, he moved just across the road to Hospital Corps School and, except for a brief stint in field medical training with the Marines at Camp Lejuene, remained there while awaiting the inevitable journey to the war. During that period, he became "an ardent opponent of the conflict," yet, like many young men of his generation, wanted to go to Vietnam out of curiosity and a desire to prove himself in combat.[133] Now known by his occupational nickname "Doc," Topmiller received orders to South Vietnam in late 1967, with a stopover on Okinawa for additional combat training. There, instructors replicated harsh Marine Corps boot camp methods, with verbal abuse and vigorous physical conditioning intended to toughen up the corpsmen to increase their chances of survival in battle.

Doc arrived at Khe Sanh Combat Base in mid-January 1968 and soon realized he was part of a large troop buildup in preparation for an attack by thousands of NVA soldiers now massing in the nearby mountains. As such, he was appalled to find the Twenty-sixth Marines Regimental Aid Station (RAS), where he was assigned to work, nothing more than a cramped, cinderblock bunker, half above ground and covered by a flimsy, plywood roof that barely gave the occupants protection from the rain, let alone enemy artillery fire.

His concern about the structural integrity of the RAS was validated just nine days later when North Vietnamese incoming shells began hitting the combat base. As the little bunker filled with wounded men, the base ammunition dump, just a hundred meters away, suddenly went off with a thundering explosion, shock waves collapsing the flimsy roof. After regaining his senses, Doc dug out from under the dirt and shattered lumber, stunned by the "bedlam" around him as doctors and staff struggled to move the many wounded from the now-crumbling structure to another bunker nearby. As enemy shells exploded around them and tear gas from the still-erupting ammo dump seeped down into the new location, it quickly became "a gruesome chamber of horrors filled with moaning wounded men, packed like sardines."[134]

That evening, in the glow of the burning ammunition, Doc worked his way around the area looking for more wounded, filling a single body bag with parts of several Marines who'd been literally blown to pieces. During the effort, he was wounded by shrapnel from the exploding ammunition but was able to continue.

As time went on, the constant enemy artillery fire created unique problems for the medical personnel at Khe Sanh. Corpsmen had been trained primarily to treat in-and-out bullet wounds, but most of the injuries at Khe Sanh were the result of embedded shards of jagged shrapnel that almost always became grossly infected. Concussion injuries to the brain from the force of exploding shells were frequent, as were psychological casualties from the stress of the constant artillery pounding. Exotic diseases, including rat-borne rabies, were prevalent and almost everyone became ill upon arriving at the base, most developing diarrhea and vomiting because of the high bacterial level. Inadequate supplies of clean water contributed to dehydration, which increased susceptibility to these and other health problems.

Doc and I eventually became close friends at Khe Sanh, but our first encounter did not go well. I had gone to the RAS for some Kaopectate because of chronic intestinal problems. As he handed me the bottle, I cynically joked, "Does this qualify me for a Purple Heart?" Doc, laboring daily among maimed and manic victims, was not in the mood for my depraved humor and squinted at me loathingly. However, we soon discovered that our backgrounds and education were similar and that we enjoyed reading history and good literature.

We also shared a dislike for the minutia of day-to-day military life, a hankering to question authority and a comparable sense of sarcasm. Despite Doc's grisly business, he maintained a quick, self-deprecating wit.

In less dangerous situations, the traditional antagonism between Marines and sailors goes on as it has for centuries; but in war, no one is held in higher regard by a Marine than his Navy corpsman. Doc quickly gained a reputation for courage and competency and was widely admired by those in his area of responsibility at the combat base, although self-consciously deflecting praise by Marines with curmudgeonly insults, calling us "morons," and the like. At these times, he especially relished mentioning a sign he had read at the hand grenade range during his combat training on Okinawa:

Pull Pin.
Prepare to Throw.
Throw.

"After dealing with you halfwits for months," Doc quipped with mock disdain, "I can now see why they felt it necessary to add that final word of instruction."

In the summer of 1968, Doc completed his tour of duty in Vietnam and returned to the Great Lakes Naval Hospital where he lived in a barracks for a year with other combat-experienced corpsmen, most of whom were angry, alienated, drank heavily and often became violent or suicidal. While at Great Lakes, Doc met fellow corpsman Theresa "Terri" Nicks, a petite, outgoing young woman from Wesier, Idaho. Though not having gone to Vietnam, Terri was not spared the horror of war, caring for some of the most severely maimed, burned, grossly infected and mentally unhinged survivors of combat who were shipped to Great Lakes for advanced treatment. Once discharged, Doc returned with Terri to her hometown in Idaho, where they were married in 1969.

The Topmillers stayed in Idaho and Doc, at age twenty-four, became manager of a large retail department store. They would have three sons and a daughter and, because his own father had been so emotionally distant, Doc made a point of being affectionate to his children, never missing an opportunity to tell them how much he loved them.

As his responsibilities with the company became more stressful, the intensity of nightmares he'd been regularly experiencing since Khe Sanh grew worse. "Symptoms of post-traumatic stress disorder," Terri later recalled, "but we didn't know about it at that time." After fifteen years with the company, Doc left to open his own clothing store, but a local economic downturn soon drove him out of business. He returned to retail management and was soon promoted to corporate headquarters near Seattle, where the game of office politics further aggravated his PTSD symptoms. The sights, sounds and smells of the mangled and burned young men he treated at Khe Sanh now occupied his thoughts daily.

A psychiatrist at the VA hospital encouraged Doc to return to school and, in the autumn of 1991, he and the family moved to Ellensburg, Washington where, at age forty-two, he enrolled as a freshman at Central Washington University. Terri recalled their time in Ellensburg as happy and Doc thrived, graduating in four years with *both* a bachelor's and a master's degree in history. His thesis was on the Vietnam War.

Pursuing that academic focus, he entered a doctoral program at the University of Kentucky, studying under George Herring, the foremost Vietnam War scholar in the country. In 1996, as part of his research, Doc made his first return to Vietnam. He promised Terri he would not visit Khe Sanh, but once in the country, felt compelled to "settle the unfinished business of war." He'd heard of other veterans who had returned to the scenes of former battles and escaped their demons. Doc wondered if a visit to Khe Sanh would end his nightmares, or make them more terrifying. "Worst yet," he thought, "what if nothing changed."

The former combat base was now an extensive coffee plantation, but as Doc roamed the fog-shrouded plateau he was still able to locate several identifiable landmarks, including the site of his old Regimental Aid Station where he'd spent so many horrific hours piecing together lacerated, young bodies. Standing at that spot, he realized he would not find redemption in merely reacquainting himself with a piece of geography, because Khe Sanh—the place—was not the problem.

Doc had by now seen too many shattered lives and ruined minds from the war, both in the U.S. and Vietnam, and was seeking answers to deeper, more personal questions. After abandoning Catholicism during his time at Khe Sanh, he sought religious education for his children and became active in the Presbyterian Church. He later came to admire the Buddhist nuns and monks he visited during the course of his travels throughout Vietnam, some of whom were elderly religious-rights activists under house arrest by the government. He embraced their teachings and soon considered himself a Buddhist.

Doc now understood that, as much as American veterans and their families had suffered from that war, the South Vietnamese had suffered more, forfeiting their freedom and living under a political party "that hated them for fighting alongside the Americans, and punished them repeatedly for it."[135] He had wasted years of rage, hatred and resentment on people who did not hate him in return and, as he met more and more citizens and soldiers of the former nation of South Vietnam, found that most appreciated what Americans tried to do during the war. "Even if our attempt seemed misguided and caused an unacceptable level of destruction to the cultural fabric of South Vietnam," Doc said, "they realize that had we won, they would have avoided years of communist terror and not have borne the brunt of communist reprisals."[136]

He received his doctorate in 1998 and accepted a position teaching history at EKU. His academic colleagues soon came to know him as strong and outspoken in his opinions, but also possessing a fine sense of humor and great dedication to his profession. He quickly earned a reputation among his students as an enthusiastic and inspiring teacher, fearless in the pursuit of truth.

During the university's winter holiday break in 2002, Doc returned to Vietnam and experienced a life-changing epiphany. While in Hué, he, by chance, visited a treatment center called Thuy By, or the

School of the Beloved, run by the Buddhist nun, Minh Tan. Thuy By is a privately funded facility caring for over fifty children suffering the lingering effects of Agent Orange, most with appallingly severe neurological disorders. Millions of gallons of that toxic herbicide had been sprayed throughout the country by American forces during the war and was later recognized by the U.S. government as a contributing factor in numerous health problems among American Vietnam War veterans and their offspring.

Doc set about learning all he could about the appalling effects Agent Orange had on the health of the Vietnamese people, even generations later. Seeing this calamitous problem being largely ignored by those in the United States, he was determined to change that. He embarked on a crusade to help these young victims and dedicated his next book, *Red Clay on My Boots,* to "the sick children of Vietnam." In it, he wrote that the level of human suffering left over from the war was inconceivable to most Americans, many of whom still wanted to punish the people of Vietnam even decades after. "For what continuing purpose?" Doc asked. The U.S. was now Vietnam's primary trading partner, Citibank owned one of the largest buildings in downtown Ho Chi Minh City and members of the Vietnamese military regularly trained with U.S. forces.[137]

The long process leading to these trade and diplomatic relationships had included a visit to Hanoi in November 1995 by a delegation from the Council on Foreign Relations that included former Secretary of Defense Robert McNamara. There, he was received by his old nemesis, eighty-three-year-old General Vo Nguyen Giap.

A few months earlier, McNamara had released his book, *In Retrospect: The Tragedy and Lessons of Vietnam,* in which he admitted not having been "sufficiently truthful" with the American public about the causes and conduct of the war. There were many occasions, he said, on which the Johnson Administration should have considered withdrawing from South Vietnam, but did not. The CIA, he wrote, believed "the North Vietnamese had much greater staying power than the Administration and Westy [General Westmoreland] believed. It turned out the CIA was correct." He and the Administration "were wrong, terribly wrong."[138]

Many American military leaders had worn themselves out during the war trying to convince McNamara that his "timid pursuit of gradual, military pressure in hopes of nudging the North Vietnamese toward negotiations caused needless casualties."[139] But the Defense Secretary, like President Johnson, had seemed to agree with the French diplomat Clemenceau who, during the First World War, proclaimed that war was too important to be left to the military.

The book unleashed a firestorm of scorn from around the world. One of the most stinging reviews came from Harold Ford, the former CIA Staff Chief for the Office of National Estimates in the mid-1960s, who had drafted countless intelligence estimates about communist troop strength in South Vietnam. Ford called McNamara's accounting of history ambiguous, debatable and skewed. Nor, he went on, did his confession satisfy anyone, including war veterans, the families of war casualties, those who opposed the war, or even those who still believed it could have been won.[140]

In Retrospect, with its obvious insincerity and selective memory, infuriated Doc, and it only grew worse. In December 2003, *The Fog of War* was released, a documentary film exploring McNamara's decisions during the war. In it, the former Secretary of Defense admitted for the first time that an alleged attack on a U.S. vessel off the coast of North Vietnam on August 4, 1964, which gave rise to the Gulf of Tonkin Resolution by Congress to send U.S. combat forces into South Vietnam, "didn't happen."

I joined Doc and countless other veterans in revulsion at McNamara's admissions and his barely concealed resentment at being questioned about this after decades of silence. Many others in government and the military during that period in the war had summoned up the courage to remain faithful to their sworn duty to the nation, despite career-ending implications. McNamara had the same opportunity to do what he knew to be right, but, as former CIA Vietnam Chief-of-Station, Peer DeSilva later explained, did not because he was "arrogant, prideful, and dumb."[141]

At the conclusion of the film, McNamara gazes forlornly into the camera, appropriately through the rear view mirror of his car, but received no pity from me. He would die peacefully in his sleep at the age of ninety-three on July 6, 2009—exactly forty-one years to the day that Tom Mahoney fell on Hill 881 South.[142]

In Retrospect and *The Fog of War* were crushing for Doc because he had come to know, to a far greater degree than most Americans, the horrible consequences of the war. He became obsessed with it never happening again. In the spring of 2003, when President George W. Bush ordered the invasion of Iraq, Doc and another professor organized an event on the EKU campus as part of the Historians Against the War National Teach-in.

Doc presented pro-peace information focusing primarily on the welfare of U.S. troops and their families and the serious psychological consequences of combat they would experience for years afterward. It was not just a few "liberal" college students and professors who echoed Doc's concern about the invasion. Many intelligence community and foreign policy experts agreed. Subsequent findings from independent panels, including the Iraq Survey Group and the bipartisan Iraq Studies Group, appointed by Congress in early 2006, concluded that the American people were misled by the Administration as to why the invasion was necessary, that Iraq posed no threat to the United States, and that the war was poorly planned and poorly led by Secretary of Defense Donald Rumsfeld.

Rumsfeld, like Robert McNamara, had no confidence in the advice of the nation's military leaders and decided to run things himself. Eventually, a "Generals Revolt" of retired high-ranking American military officers publicly criticized the Administration, and the Secretary of Defense in particular, for the extraordinarily inept way in which the occupation of Iraq had been carried out. Rumsfeld resigned, but as Doc observed, this "Revolt" had been about assigning blame for starting the war, rather than ending it. "Everyone in Washington knows we cannot win in Iraq," Doc said, "but no one has the courage to bring our troops home." George Herring later said of Doc: "In a nation traumatized by the 9-11 attack and cowed by a Bush administration that sought to exploit the national fear to its own ends, he stood as a voice of courage and sanity."[143]

Although Doc's warning about the dire consequences of the Iraq invasion proved accurate, his views were not widely accepted at the time. At EKU, a staff member sent him an email saying: "There's no place in this country for people like you anymore." Her calculus of patriotism appalled Doc, who later wrote that in Vietnam he had pushed the intestines back inside of a horribly wounded man, tried to comfort men burned so badly their skin peeled off like a pair of gloves and abandoned wounded men to die so he could treat those more likely to survive. "And no place remains for me in America?" He asked. "I guess there really never was any spot for me after Khe Sanh."[144]

If any single event could be said to have crystallized Doc's resolve, it was that remark questioning his worthiness to live in United States. Such an intolerable attack on his senses of reason and fairness, combined with the personal pain from both old and new Vietnam experiences, whipped him into a level of indignation and zeal that was puzzling even to those of us who knew him well. As his PTSD symptoms grew worse, his visits to the VA Hospital in Lexington for counseling and medication became more frequent. Doc was soon granted a medical leave of absence from teaching, returning to EKU two years later in 2004.

He traveled again to Vietnam and Cambodia in 2006 and, upon his return, spent what he termed "an incredible five days" with the Marine Corps at Quantico while attending a USMC-sponsored educator's workshop. Accompanying him that week were a group of young officers, most having seen combat in Iraq, a few wearing Purple Heart medals. Doc later told me the experience demonstrated his "totally incomprehensible ability to remain dedicated to nonviolence, while still retaining the utmost loyalty to the Marine Corps."

In April 2006, Doc invited me to speak about Khe Sanh at EKU and took the opportunity to tease me by fabricating a darkly humorous hypothesis. The gist of it was that my platoon, having abandoned Khe Sanh village after the attack in January 1968, allowed the NVA to occupy the Huong Hoa District Headquarters there, the first seat of government in South Vietnam to be captured by communist forces. This boost to their morale "created by PFC Archer's surrender," transformed the NVA into a juggernaut and so was directly responsible for the fall of Saigon seven years later. Accordingly, he introduced me to each class as, "the person who single-handedly lost the Vietnam War." While most of his students knew it was a joke and laughed, there were always a few faces contorted in revulsion.

In March 2007, Doc and I spoke about Khe Sanh to a large audience at Bentley University in Waltham, Massachusetts. Earlier that day we had taken a drive to Concord and the Old North Bridge where the Revolutionary War began. The pastoral setting on that mild day prompted us to stay for about an hour discussing a variety of topics. Just a hundred yards away was The Old Manse, built in 1770 as the home of Unitarian minister William Emerson.

Doc pointed out that while the Revolutionary War began at this bridge, another revolution, in American philosophy, started in the old house when William's son, Ralph Waldo Emerson, began meeting there sixty-five years after the famous battle with leaders of the Transcendentalist movement, like Henry David Thoreau and Nathaniel Hawthorne. Transcendentalism, he explained to me, was influenced by Asian religions, especially the ancient Indian Vedas and the Buddhism Doc practiced had its origins in the Vedic culture as well. He spoke of the concept of the soul and how Buddhism differed in that regard from Hinduism, Transcendentalism and other religious doctrines.

Several decades after the Transcendental Movement had faded, Doc said, others, like Brigadier General Joshua Lawrence Chamberlain, Medal of Honor recipient for gallantry at Gettysburg and later Governor of the State of Maine, just about fifty miles north of us, still held this Buddhist-like notion of the soul. "In great deeds," Chamberlain said, "something abides. On great fields, something stays. Forms change and pass; bodies disappear; but spirits linger, to consecrate ground for the vision-place of souls."[145]

I was only half interested in what Doc was saying, rather wanting to discuss with him how far the Redcoats might have advanced on the Minutemen there in April 1775. As such, I could not have imagined that what he was trying to explain to me at that moment on this little, wooden bridge outside of Concord was the key to the next phase in the search for Tom Mahoney's remains—sending us on an unimaginable journey to Vietnam and Hill 881 South.

18
WANDERING SOULS

UPON MY RETURN from Massachusetts, I sent Doc copies of the JPAC reports on Tom's case, including the February 2005 determination that "there is no way to find the remains." I had not wanted to bother him about it because he didn't seem to have any time left for other projects. When not teaching, Doc was traveling regularly to Vietnam, had just published his war memoir, *Red Clay on My Boots*, and was writing two other books, including a history of veterans' health care in America. In addition, he was publishing academic articles and remained active in the Peace History Society.

Doc wrote back to say how disappointed he was with JPAC's methodology, particularly "their absurd effort" in August 2004 to locate veterans of the NVA's 246th Regiment who might be "still hanging around remote Khe Sanh village 36 years after the battle!" During his frequent travels throughout Vietnam, Doc had come to believe the Vietnamese government was "stringing the JPAC along" because the Americans spent a lot of money when they showed up. It was not unusual, he said, for locals to "salt" sites with a bone at a time, to keep that money coming in.

He was soon absorbed in the effort to recover Tom's remains, and traveled to Hill 881 South in May 2007 to learn more. In the area where the Dorow report showed Tom was last seen, Doc found several old NVA spider holes. Thrilled by this discovery, he wrote me that "days like today are the reason I became an historian," but added that "nothing ever works the first time in Vietnam," and before he returned to the hill, he would need more information.

Later that week he flew to Hanoi to meet with Phan Thanh Hao, a renowned poet and editor who had translated several important

Vietnamese books about the war into English. Hao was an admirer of Doc's scholarly work on the war, especially his 2006 article, "*Struggling for Peace: South Vietnamese Buddhist Women and Resistance to the Vietnam War,*" published in the Journal of Women's History, and for which he received the prestigious 2007 Charles DeBenedetti Prize in Peace History.

She provided Doc with information about a website where he could post the names of the five men who ambushed Tom. Phan also told him about a TV show and newspapers catering to the needs of former soldiers and carrying announcements by those seeking to reunite with comrades from that war. Doc left the meeting with a high degree of confidence. "She has major juice," he wrote me. "There is a photo on the wall of Hao and her grandchildren with General Giap."

Doc then visited Dr. Dinh Van Toan, professor and head of the Geophysical Department at the Institute of Geological Sciences at the Vietnamese Academy of Science and Technology. Toan's brother, Dinh Thay Duc, had been Doc's Vietnamese language instructor when he briefly studied at the University of Wisconsin-Madison. In addition to Toan's other duties at the Institute, he volunteered his time working with psychics to locate missing remains from the war, and so was eager to help us. "For the Vietnamese," Doc told me, "to die away from their home and not have their remains recovered is a source of immeasurable pain. They understand how Tom's friends and family feel and want to help us."

I replied in an email that I did not understand what Doc meant by "psychics." Knowing I was skeptical of such things, he promptly telephoned me and delicately suggested that since the JPAC had failed to find Tom's remains, and appeared to have given up the search, "we should now try doing things the Vietnamese way and see what happens."

For a westerner, Doc had an unusually profound understanding of the subtle nuances in Vietnamese culture and religion, and went on to explain that, "the Vietnamese way" is one of unwavering ancestor worship and worked essentially like this: The soul of a deceased person whose remains are not returned to his or her family is always sad and wandering. If the wandering soul can be contacted, often through the services of a psychic, there is a good chance that whatever physical remains still exist can be located with the assistance of that soul.

Doc paused for several seconds and, when I didn't say anything, added, "I know you don't believe in things like this, but I've just got to believe the Lord Buddha is involved here." I still didn't know what to say. Doc, sensing my uneasiness, implored me to "keep an open mind."

The following day he tried to lighten the mood by emailing me that communists authorities were questioning him about the identity of those he had treated at Khe Sanh for "combat incontinence," a joking reference to how we first met at the aid station during the siege. He continued the absurdity, stating, "If I have to name names, then I must offset the shame of your 'combat incontinence' by also naming you as the one who delivered victory to the NVA at Khe Sanh village."

His next message, a day later, was more serious. He had met with Toan and the psychics. "They've had amazing success in contacting wandering souls," Doc wrote, "and are actually quite eager to help us." Toan had outlined a number of methods they might employ, ranging from staying awake for several nights meditating to reach Tom's soul; to holding a séance with us on Hill 881 South.

The psychics, he said, rely heavily on dreams to help locate these souls and wanted to know if I could remember any I'd had involving Tom since his death. While I had not dreamt about Tom for decades, at least that I recalled, surprisingly I had done so just two weeks before. He and I were sitting at a table in the afternoon at an outdoor cafe in Paris having a leisurely conversation over wine and bread about things of no great importance, with no hint we had ever been to war, or even that an inordinate amount of time had elapsed since our last meeting. I do not recall whether we were young men, or old, because I really did not see his face. I just intuitively knew it was him.

Doc passed this along to Toan and the nun, Minh Tan, who replied a few days later that she was thrilled to hear this and deemed it an indication that "communication" was established between me and Tom's soul. It occurred to me how strange it was that the only other dream I could recall ever having about Tom, as described earlier, was one in which I saw him dead on Hill 881 South. Having dreamt a year before his death that he would fall on that exact hill was strange enough, but, when combined with the information I was continuing to receive from his Bravo Company comrades, who were convinced his inexplicable behavior that day saved all their lives, things were now taking on a distinctly supernatural feel.

Earlier that month, Robert Black spoke at a ceremony dedicating a monument to Vietnam veterans and told his audience, "We remember Tom Mahoney, who made a fatal mistake on Hill 881 South and in so doing, unwittingly saved Bravo from being annihilated by enemy machine guns and mortars when helilifting to Hill 689."[146] I mentioned to Frank how all this was giving me an uncomfortable "other worldly" feeling. He replied, "Mahoney was a smart Marine, an experienced Marine, and he certainly didn't want to die. But he probably would have been willing to make the sacrifice. He was that kind of person."

The diverse collection of lives changed by Tom's baffling stroll that July afternoon in 1968 was growing. After mentioning the circumstances of his loss in *A Patch of Ground*, I was soon busy responding to an outpouring of interest from around the world. This resulted in numerous, often implausible, always poignant, ongoing interpersonal connections with both his civilian and former military friends, as well as total strangers, all deeply moved by Tom's tragic end and the unresolved issue of his remains. I had rekindled in some, created in others, a sorrow about his loss that I now felt responsible for putting to rest.

Doc recognized this and urged me to consider joining him in Vietnam, writing, "I have come to realize how many people (including me now) need some closure over Tom's death. But, we can't do that unless you are here." Knowing I did not want to return, Doc continued pitching the plan: His contacts there would make all the arrangements for hotels, guides, translators, drivers, the psychic and necessities for the Buddhist religious service. All I had to do, he urged, was show up and "again, keep an open mind."

I truly had no desire to return to Vietnam. It held nothing of sentimental value for me, nor was I curious to see how it had changed. I'd spent most of my time there learning to mistrust the local population as a survival mechanism, and did not care much about their welfare then, or now. This was all about to change. As much as I did not want to admit it, I knew Doc was correct and that I must go back. If I didn't, I would be abandoning Tom there again. This seemed the only chance we now had of finding his remains. After consulting with Becky, I decided to go. I then contacted two people who I felt strongly should join us. The first was Steve Orr who, like me, never had a desire to return to Vietnam, but now unhesitatingly wanted to join us. Three old friends returning together after forty years in search of the "wandering soul" of a fellow Marine was just too intriguing for him to miss.

The other person was Claudia Harris, Tom's sister, who I had reconnected with in 2005. The Buddhists assisting us in Vietnam, Doc told me, expected a blood relative to make the journey. Connecting with Tom's wandering soul would be far more difficult without the presence of a family member. In lieu of that, something from Tom's past which held strong sentimental value might help.

Claudia graciously declined the offer. She and her mother had suffered a great deal in the years after his loss and I respected her decision and appreciated her encouragement with regard to our efforts. She did, however, provide me with Tom's old baseball glove to take to the séance. It was a sad, sweat-stained relic of his boyhood with a proprietary machine-stamped Ted Williams "autograph" on the front, but a more authentically inscribed "Mahoney" on the back strap, created by its young owner with a patient redundancy of strokes from a blue ballpoint-pen.

As the trip approached, I grew increasingly uncomfortable with the whole idea of ghosts. I did not believe in such things and not just because reason and the absence of scientific evidence suggested they did not exist. I also had a philosophical concern that if I departed from the logical process, then *anything* was acceptable. If I brought the possibility of ghosts into the realm of problem solving, it rendered the process worthless. Because how would I then know if something occurred from natural phenomenon or from spirits? Did the wind blow the door open or did a ghost push on it? Most importantly, who would decide that?

Yet, at the same time, I admired many people who held such beliefs, Doc high among them. Before we left for Vietnam, I asked him how an intellectual as he was could believe in wandering souls. Doc explained that, to him, "spiritualism" was not the same as religion. Spiritual people, he said, do not want to *believe*, they want to *know*. He constantly strove for insight, called "enlightenment," saying that, while no system of thought contained "absolute truth," all were useful guides in seeking it. Though I was still unable to understand how wandering souls fit into all this, I knew I would have no problem respecting the millenniums-old practices of the culture I was about to visit. And, having exhausted all other practical means of locating Tom's final resting place—what had I to lose?

As our departure drew near, I was having difficulty sleeping. On the surface, I felt confident and calm about going, but clearly my subconscious was working overtime on these issues. Frank Ahearn understood this and offered sage advice that put things into perspective for me, "You are being lead on an amazing journey. Just keep an open mind, and everything will happen as it should."

❧ ❧

On the morning of December 9, 2007, I found myself squeezed into an economy-class seat between Doc and Steve aboard a United Airlines 747 winging westward on a journey both chillingly familiar and incomprehensible. As I clamped my eyes tightly shut in an unsuccessful effort to sleep, I could not conjure up even the vaguest imagery of the events to come.

We arrived in Ho Chi Minh City, formerly Saigon, about midnight and caught a cab to our hotel. The next day, Doc located his usual scooter driver, a former ARVN enlisted man who had spent six years in a "reeducation" camp after the war. In addition to losing his right eye in combat, he was also without the first phalange of his right trigger finger. Doc had noticed this unusual amputation among several former ARVN soldiers who'd spent time in the camps. He believed that to help secure an early release, they were allowed to cut off that particular fingertip as a gesture assuring their captors they would never take up arms against that government again. While the driver never spoke about the injury, years of reeducation had not diminished his resentment at losing the war, and he was utterly convinced that the American military was going to return any day and force the communists out of the South. No matter how often Doc would tell him that was never going to happen, the driver remained unconvinced.

My scooter driver was a former VC soldier who wore an apologetically sad face even when he tried to smile. He told us how, in 1974, he decided that he wanted no more to do with the war, handed his rifle to his superior officer and went home. His timing was poor, because a few months later his side won. The new communist government located him and, while not sent to a camp as a deserter, he was deprived of any opportunity to be successful in life. Like his former ARVN foes, he and his family were social pariahs in their own country and so he was relegated to driving a scooter for the equivalent of a dollar a day. I was fast learning that, despite the passage of so many decades, the war's impact was still widely and very personally felt.

Two days later we flew to Hanoi and prepared to meet Doc's friend, Dr. Dinh Van Toan. Steve and I were uneasy about this because Toan had been an NVA soldier badly wounded outside the Khe Sanh Combat Base in March 1968, literally just a few hundred meters from where the three of us were then dug in. Our concern about the awkwardness of that introduction was fueled largely by the fact that we knew almost nothing about the people we fought against, believing they were all soulless, automatons of totalitarianism.

The North Vietnamese Army remained an enigma even for American military tacticians and intelligence analysts until the early 1970s when "think tanks," like the Rand Corporation, began crunching data from various sources, including deserters, to better understand how they operated. This information would have no practical value for Marine combatants, however, because all their infantry battalions had departed Vietnam by mid-1971.

A typical North Vietnamese soldier was given basic training for about eight weeks before going south. Contrary to the popularly held American belief that they were natural jungle fighters, most recruits came from the metropolitan Hanoi/Haiphong area, or from the rice farms along the Red River and South China Sea. The average Vietnamese had no reason to enter the jungle.

The basic organizational unit, or "cell," consisted of three people. Three cells comprised a squad, three squads a platoon, three platoons a company, and so on up the line, with continuous indoctrination from political cadre at every level. Such concentrated control, and the regular use of group criticism and self-criticism sessions, usually maintained correct behavior, though beginning in 1968 the NVA began to suffer from high rates of desertion. An acquaintance of mine, Hoang Tran Dung, who had fought against the Americans late in the war, said that after his first taste of the horrors of combat, his patriotic fervor quickly diminished and, like many others, what kept him going for the rest of the war was not dedication to his country or the army. "I never turned back," Hoang said, "because it would have been an embarrassment and dishonor to my family."[147]

Once in the south, soldiers were granted occasional respites from combat at R&R centers in South Vietnam, Laos or Cambodia, but rarely returned to the North unless too severely wounded to continue. Despite such rigid management, NVA soldiers acted much the same as troops everywhere. Bao Ninh, author of *The Sorrow of War*, spent six years with the Glorious Twenty-seventh Youth Brigade, one of only ten members to survive the war of the five hundred with whom he went south in 1969. During a 1999 interview, Bao said the average age of his comrades was about nineteen. Like soldiers everywhere, they missed their wives or girlfriends, mothers and families and exhibited occasional emotionally crippling episodes of sadness and nostalgia; but coped the rest of the time by employing the sardonic humor and toughness common to all warriors, exchanging gags and exaggerated yarns and making ample use of profanity.

The subjects of their conversations, Bao said, were almost always about sex or food. Soldiers from the poorer, rural agricultural areas did not usually understand the more urbane banter from the city dwellers and were often the butt of practical jokes. To keep morale from slipping, they usually avoided talking about past or recent battles, but cried and grieved over the loss of friends. "We were not robots," Bao said, his voice cracking with emotion. "We were human beings." [148]

Doc's friend in Hanoi, Phan Thanh Hao, who had translated *The Sorrow of War* into English, and was now actively trying to reach Vietnamese war veterans for information to help us in our search for Tom's remains, would later reinforce Bao's passionate observation in a *New York Times* op-ed piece. In it, Hao spoke of meeting an old friend returning from the war just after it ended in 1975. The man was indifferent to the national celebration of victory, instead only wanting to talk about the day he had killed an American soldier with a bayonet:

> My friend turned him over on the ground and saw his
> young and handsome face. 'Mama,' the man said before
> dying—the same word so many of our own soldiers uttered
> before they died. My friend's heart tightened and, from
> then on, he said, he could never forget the American's cry. [149]

Her friend died sometime later, Hao said, because he "felt guilty about living."

The NVA's cadre system provided training and leadership at all levels within the organization. Cadres were selected for promotion by dint of their talent, virtue and bravery and were essential to unit effectiveness. But, because they led by example, the best cadre were frequently lost as the intensity of combat with the Americans increased. This created a need to regularly redevelop expertise. But because new cadres did not receive the specialized training their predecessors had earlier in the war, successful techniques on how to best fight the Americans were often lost with each succession of replacement troops.[150]

American troops had a similar vulnerability as the result of DEROS (Date Eligible for Return from Overseas), which promised the combatant a way out of the war after about a year.[151] While well-intentioned, the system created problems. As one's DEROS approached, an individual typically became fixated on his personal safety. These "short timers" were often excused from dangerous duty by their superiors, despite them often being in the best position to train new arrivals.

The NVA understood DEROS and how it fostered the unlearning of lessons and were confident American military units would adapt slowly and act in a predictable pattern in battle. This was often correct and American causalities stayed consistently high because effective lessons learned by the survivors of ambushed patrols were continually being redeveloped through trial-and-error by new personnel. Nguyen Tien Thanh, who fought against the Americans around Khe Sanh in the spring and summer of 1968, would later say that while he found the average U.S. soldier and Marine to be a capable fighter, "not all American soldiers fought with the same level of intensity or motivation or with the same spirit." The Americans' conventional style of ground warfare, Thanh said, "Was easily tricked, ambushed, or circumvented because they generally made a lot of noise as they approached."[152]

One lesson not lost on the NVA was that U.S. Marines prided themselves on being the best assault troops in the world and pushed onward in an attack with characteristic boldness instilled by the Corps. Therefore, by planning carefully, fortifying and supplying in advance, and designing a battleground that would entice the

Americans forward, the North Vietnamese could accomplish what was most important to them—creating maximum casualties.

So it was with some unease that Steve and I met Toan in front of our hotel in Hanoi that morning so he could escort us to our meeting with the psychic at the Center for the Investigation of Human Capabilities (CIHC) at the Vietnamese Academy of Science and Technology.

On the cab ride there, Toan, who is fluent in English, told us a little about his life, how he had joined the NVA at the age of sixteen and was assigned to the 304th Division as an antitank gunner. He was part of the attack force that overran the Lang Vei Special Forces camp in February 1968 and, a few weeks later, sustained multiple and serious wounds during a B-52 bombing near the combat base. In addition to life-threatening internal injuries, the bomb blasts left him deaf. Toan began to regain his hearing about a year after his medical discharge from the army. He was soon recognized for his scientific brilliance and sent to the University of Moscow where he earned a doctorate in Geological Sciences.

Toan then went silent for a moment, finally turning to us from the front seat of the taxi with an expression of unconcealed sorrow and haltingly uttered, "We are all very lucky to be alive." This simple observation, recognizing that we had simultaneously shared the terrible ordeal of the Khe Sanh battlefield, perfectly articulated what we were all feeling at that moment, and was followed by a long hush while we struggled to clear our throats now constricting with emotion.

We soon arrived at the CIHC office located on the same floor as the Department of Physics, an indication of the Center's status among the so-called "hard sciences" within the university system. Nguyen Thi Tuyet Mai, a professionally dressed female journalist and Deputy Director of the CIHC, led us into a meeting room and invited us, in near-perfect English, to sit at a long table with her, Dr. Toan and three others, including the psychic, Nguyen Buu Thuan.

Thuan, a handsome, thirty-three-year-old father of two young daughters was wearing a thin, powder blue sports jacket. Like most

Vietnamese psychics, he had developed his unusual abilities after surviving a life-threatening event, in his case, a serious and prolonged illness five years earlier. It took Thuan a while to fully comprehend the significance of his "gift," but he now dedicated almost all his time to locating deceased civilians and soldiers, claiming to have identified over three thousand wandering souls and the location of over one thousand graves, earning him a level of respect bordering on national celebrity status.

Belief in the afterlife and the care of deceased souls are deeply rooted in the Vietnamese culture and, for a grieving family, retrieving the mortal remains of a missing relative is of the highest importance. This is not only to ensure the soul's safe transition to the "other-world," but until their physical remains were found and "honored," often by reburial in an ancestral cemetery, unhappy ghosts of the uncared-for dead were a problem for the living—responsible, many believed, for almost every misfortune that befell a family.

For centuries, mediums and "soul callers" (who invite souls to temporarily possess their own or another person's body) have been used to communicate the wishes of the dead to the living. However, during the high point of state socialism in Vietnam in the 1960s and 1970s, these practices were stigmatized as superstition and officially discouraged.

After the war, pressure mounted on the government from families and veterans groups who wanted to know the status of missing soldiers. By the mid-1990s, Hanoi admitted having lost over a million military men and women during the war, 300,000 of whom, they said, were still unaccounted for. These numbers were immediately challenged by some who pointed out that the vast majority of that million were left on distant battlefields in South Vietnam, Laos and Cambodia, meaning it was more likely that as many as 700,000 bodies still were not recovered or otherwise unaccounted for.

Later identification of these remains became nearly impossible, especially those killed after the beginning of the 1968 Tet Offensive, when record keeping by units in the field became virtually nonexistent. In addition, North Vietnamese soldiers were discouraged from carrying personal identification when they went south in order to maintain the ruse that only local southern popular forces were fighting the war. For most who did not return, the only record of their military service was located at a local conscription office in the north, merely showing they had signed an enlistment contract.

During the war, NVA and VC soldiers did all they could to recover their wounded and dead after battle, often sending specially trained transportation porters and reconnaissance soldiers back under cover of darkness, even with American or South Vietnamese forces still close by. But, during periods of extended contact with the enemy, as around Khe Sanh, most were not recovered. Some were later buried in unmarked mass graves by American and South Vietnamese soldiers, while others moldered where they fell due to the elements of nature or were disintegrated by bombs, napalm or artillery shells. Even those who were killed later in the war within communist-controlled areas of the south, seldom had their name recorded on a grave marker.

Eventually death certificates were granted to some families of the missing who petitioned for them. Most of these documents were based on affidavits of those who had witnessed the death and survived the war to tell about it. Some relatives even became eligible for a small monthly stipend from the government, though barely enough to cover the cost of the incense they burned to entice their loved one's soul home. In 1985, when veterans groups demanded better accountability and honor for their fallen, the Hanoi government built several monuments to "The Martyred," hoping to appease those questioning their official estimates.

However, as the general population of Vietnam came to grasp the vast numbers of NVA and VC who died during the war, the Party had a more difficult time selling them on the glory of having sacrificed for the cause. Impetus for change arrived in 1991 when Bao Ninh published his novel *The Sorrow of War*, which was immediately banned by the Party as subversive, but flourished on the black market. His countrymen seemed to be waking up from a long dream and saw the truth, Bao said, and the war veterans "also woke up and wanted change."[153]

The opening pages of his book churn with the macabre imagery of "The Jungle of Screaming Souls" in the Central Highlands where the protagonist, Kien (also the name of the mythological figure responsible for the concept of wandering souls) leads a squad of soldiers to find, and rebury with honor, the remains of hundreds killed there in battle with the Americans years before. They experience no joy at having won the war, only grim fatigue—and dread: "The sobbing whispers were heard deep in the jungle at night, the howls carried on the wind. Perhaps these really were the voices of the wandering souls of dead soldiers."[154] Kien and his comrades take no chances. Despite such practices being banned by the government, the men build an altar and pray before it in secret to the restless souls and "sparkling incense sticks glowed night and day at the altar from that day forward."

The mounting public demand to locate wandering souls of their war dead forced the Party to act. The role of soul callers and spirit mediums was soon officially tweaked to "specialists in extrasensory perception," called telepaths or psychics; better conforming to Marxist socio-scientific precepts. Before long, news accounts of lost remains being routinely located by psychics launched a huge demand for their services.

This prompted the establishment of the CIHC, funded through the Vietnam Union of Science and Technology Association, a national, nongovernmental organization of Vietnamese intellectuals who specialize in various fields of science and technology. The stated mission of the CIHC is to locate those with extrasensory abilities, test and verify their "merit and genuineness" and establish hypotheses to explain it. In reality, it provides a government-sanctioned method of publicly practicing ancient beliefs in the supernatural.

᳝ ᳝

As Doc, Steve and I sat down at the table with the CIHC staff and the psychic in Hanoi that morning, I was far out of my comfort zone. We made our introductions and engaged in small talk while tea was served. Two videographers were present to record the meeting. Hanoi was soon to host an international convention of psychics and video footage of our meeting, Mai advised us, would be used in television advertising to promote the event. She and the other CIHC members were unusually excited about our visit because Thuan had never before attempted to communicate with the wandering soul of an American. Knowing I was skeptical, added more incentive to that challenge.

During this preliminary conversation, Thuan sat silently staring at an atlas lying open on the table to a page displaying a map of central Vietnam. At one point, he looked up and stared in my direction as if focusing on something just behind my head. Mai sensed my discomfort and explained that Thuan was in the process of communicating with the spirit world and so was not really observing much around him in the room. After several minutes, Thuan, through an interpreter, asked me some questions about Tom, including whether he had "a long face." Before I could answer, Doc reminded Mai that a folder in front of her contained a copy of Tom's high school yearbook photo that he had provided them. Mai, who appeared to have forgotten the photo was there, immediately produced it for Thuan. After carefully studying it, he seemed satisfied that this was the same face as that of the soul with whom he was now communicating.

Thuan then seemed confused about Tom's exact age. When Doc had sent them information earlier, he had assumed Tom and I were born in the same year of 1948. I then advised Thuan that Tom was born in 1947, dying in 1968 just three months before his twenty-first birthday. This information seemed to clear up whatever inconsistencies were bothering him. Thuan would later explain to us that his images of wandering souls were often vague because they were sometimes reluctant to be found, making it difficult to be sure he was dealing with the spirit he was seeking.

He then closed the atlas and began writing notes on a piece of typing paper and, upon finishing, took another sheet and began sketching. This process lasted about ten minutes and Mai explained that it was okay for us to talk among ourselves quietly because he was so focused on information he was obtaining from Tom's soul he could not hear us. We used this opportunity to ask questions, which the group was eager to answer.

Despite it being the end of the school year, and Dr. Toan had an enormous amount of work to do back at his office, he decided to stay and translate for us. I was relieved he did, because the young man the CIHC provided for that purpose spoke English in such an unusual dialect that I could scarcely understand him. Doc agreed, and jokingly speculated later that the man sounded like he learned his English from a German who learned his English from a Cajun.

After Thuan finished the drawing, he asked Toan to translate it. The three of us immediately recognized it was a rough diagram of Khe Sanh Combat Base, with the fairly accurate locations for the main ammo dump, airstrip, helicopter revetments, and even Doc's small regimental aid station. The drawing also showed two howitzer batteries and some tanks parked on the southwest side of the combat base near the U.S. Army Special Forces Forward Operating Base compound.

I recalled that during the siege, Colonel Lownds distrusted the indigenous troops living there and so placed tanks between them and his Marines as a precaution. At first I wondered how Tom's "wandering soul" might have acquired this information, since he was not stationed at the combat base. I then recalled that his first days at Khe Sanh were a top lofty Hill 950 and had to admit, for argument's sake, that the layout in Thuan's diagram would have been what Tom saw from that hill.

Doc, Steve and I were asked how precise we thought the diagram was and all agreed it was probably 90 to 95 percent accurate for the relative locations of what it attempted to show. The attendees were visibly elated by that news. Thuan even smiled. I was asked to sign and date the original drawing and note on it that I believed it was, as described to me, about 95 percent accurate.

Mr. Thuan then drew a rough map of the Hill 881 South area. Since Doc had been to the hill earlier that year, I asked him to check it. Doc replied that, as he understood the translation by Toan of the points of reference on the drawing, it was 90 percent accurate. I subsequently signed and dated it.

This drawing showed that Tom's remains were located near the home of a "Mr. Nguyen" outside a small village at the base of Hill 881 South. The location was several hundred meters down slope from the spot Tom was last seen, and, although it seemed highly improbable to me, I didn't express my concern because I wanted to see where this was going.

Mr. Thuan then wrote a list of reference points and the items we would find at the site of the remains. All that was left of Tom, he said, were three small teeth, demonstrating the size by covering up all but the tip of the little finger of his right hand with his left. He added that we would also find a canvass ammo pouch containing a deteriorated metal M-16 magazine and the remnants of some bullets. He then pointed to the left side of his abdomen to show where Tom had been carrying the pouch. These items, he said, will be found 1.6 meters (slightly more than five feet) below the surface. He then repeated, for emphasis, that the teeth were unusually small.

The significance Thuan placed on the size of the teeth underscored what I had been told by others familiar with the search for remains at Khe Sanh. In the climate and soil there, especially over the span of forty years, most remains now consist of only teeth, small fragments of what had once been larger bones, and pieces of durable clothing, like boots. Thuan would later tell me, with obvious pride, that he had been able to locate remains that were completely decomposed into a thin layer of "black earth."

He then asked me to close my eyes and think of Tom for five minutes. As I did, mental images raced in an unusually rapid manner, like the riffling pages of a book; but I felt no unusual sensations, such as that of "a presence" or revelation. After opening my eyes, Thuan said that Tom had "visited me" and my skin should feel abnormally warm now and would be so again when I was near the location of his remains. I did not feel the sensation of warmth he was describing and told him so.

Thuan showed no sign of disappointment at my reply. After a brief conversation with the CIHC members, Mai advised us that Thuan was scheduled to escort two families in search of remains in Laos. The trip would take them past Khe Sanh and Mr. Thuan had offered to stop there and lead us to the spot on Hill 881 South where Tom's remains were located. Thuan then looked at me with a kindly, confident smile and said, "I will bring your friend to visit you." We gratefully accepted his offer.

As we got up to leave, Steve and I felt an enormous sense of relief. Because we were not as familiar with the Vietnamese people as Doc, we had been apprehensive about how we, as former American combatants, would be received, particularly by the older ones who endured the war. At the time of our visit, the city of Hanoi was not only celebrating its millennial birthday, but also marking the thirty-fifth anniversary of a massive U.S. bombing campaign, which street banners and newspapers were referring to as "The Dien Bien Phu of the Sky."

Following the breakdown of peace talks with North Vietnam in December 1972, President Nixon ordered an aerial pounding of the north called Operation Linebacker II. By the time the bombing ceased after North Vietnamese negotiators returned to the table two weeks later, American aircraft had dropped over twenty thousand tons of bombs, primarily on Hanoi and Haiphong; but not before losing fifteen B-52s and eleven other aircraft to surface-to-air missiles, antiaircraft guns and MIG fighter attacks. North Vietnam claimed over sixteen hundred civilians were killed in the bombings. The Paris Peace Accords were signed a few weeks later.

After such enormous destruction of their city, we would not have been surprised by lingering animosity toward Americans. However, when our meeting ended that morning and we shook hands with everyone and said our goodbyes, the genuine goodwill and compassion shown us by those in the room dismissed any apprehension Steve and I had. Outside, on our way to catch a cab, we asked Toan to join us for lunch. Knowing that lunch among men in Vietnam customarily involved drinking several beers, Toan graciously declined our offer, citing the need to keep his head clear while grading his students' finals exams.

Despite his unassuming nature, Dr. Toan was a world-renowned geologist, frequently engaged in seismic wave experiments with colleagues at the University of Texas, El Paso. Doc reminded us that if American war veterans and their families could glimpse the human side of people like Toan, who many continued to demonize decades after the guns had gone silent, their real healing would finally begin. I had to admit it was difficult to equate this generous and intelligent man as being the inhuman wretch I believed him to be when I cheered the rain of bombs that eventually maimed him. As I watched Dr. Toan hurry off toward his office across campus, I shook my head in disbelief that the last thing I ever could have imagined in all my years of bitterness after the war, was to finally meet a former NVA soldier from the Khe Sanh battlefield—and offer to buy him a beer.

In the taxi back to our hotel we spoke about the psychic's accuracy and knowledge of things known to us, but not widely published, and struggled to understand what had just happened. It left us with a vague sensation that we were being "summoned" to the hills of Khe Sanh by something beyond our comprehension.

We flew from Hanoi to Hué the next morning and waited excitedly for that journey, staying at the excellent Saigon-Morin Hotel where the Trang Tien Bridge on National Highway 1 crosses the Perfume River. In early February 1968, The Morin was the main building of Hué University and held by NVA soldiers. It took the Marines two-days of intense fighting to capture the building, during which an enemy RPG knocked out a Marine tank as it was about to crash through the area of what is now the hotel's elegant lobby.[155] Tom Mahoney and his platoon had moved from that intersection northeast along the river to secure the critical Navy boat ramp.

The day after we returned from Hanoi, our travel agent, Nguyen Thi Dieu Van, received an email from Toan with our itinerary. We were to meet the psychic in the city of Dong Ha the following day. Dieu Van would also make arrangements for a Buddhist religious ceremony to be held at the site of Tom's remains located by Thuan. This required her to shop for an assortment of flowers, fruits, prepared foods and beverages to be set out as offerings in the hope of enticing his wandering soul from the old battlefield.

Toan also wanted to be sure we understood there was to be no digging at the site. We had already discussed this and come to the same conclusion. Steve, a former police detective, pointed out that such activity by nonprofessionals might inadvertently destroy important evidence. Doc, savvy in the ways of the culture, echoed Toan's concern that both the Vietnamese and U.S. governments would frown upon Americans digging up part of Vietnam without permission and that our driver would; for legal, cultural and religious reasons, almost assuredly refuse to carry the remains of a dead body, regardless of how minuscule, in his car back to Hué. I added the practical consideration that we did not have the archeological expertise or proper tools, such as sifting screens, to locate the tiny fragments described by Thuan. Moreover, the thought of banging a shovel blade into one of the countless unexploded land mines, shells or grenades on that hill was most unappealing.

19
YOUR FRIEND IS HERE

IT WAS RAINING STEADILY as we drove north along Highway 1 through the area made famous by historian Bernard Fall as the "Street Without Joy." With the exception of some houses and shops clustered at intervals along the way, that section of the highway appeared to pass through one, long military cemetery.

I vividly recalled my last trip along that stretch of Highway 1. Coming from R&R in early May 1968, I hitchhiked a ride at Dong Ha on an ARVN truck heading south. I had arrived back from Singapore that morning and was still in my summer service khaki uniform, shiny leather dress shoes and a garrison cover, called a "piss cutter" by Marines, pulled down tight over my head to avoid it blowing away. Perched ten feet above the road, on a load of grimy, drums of diesel fuel, I was a target even the most myopic NVA/VC sniper could not miss. Evidently, none tried and I safely reached my unit near Quang Tri.

After arriving in Dong Ha, we quickly located Thuan and the others he was leading up to the mountains that day. He asked to ride with us, then climbed into the backseat of our small van between me and Steve. Along the way, with our interpreter Mr. Tam translating, Thuan answered my many questions in a friendly and open manner.

I asked Thuan why he was doing this for us. He explained that Vietnam had a "national problem" because there were still too many American souls roaming the land. The U.S. government, he said, spends millions of dollars each year trying to locate remains and was seldom successful anymore. He and other psychics would be happy to locate them all—at no cost.

Doc then asked Thuan if we could at least help defray his expenses for food and lodging. He politely refused, explaining that, if psychics took anything for their efforts, the Lord Buddha would remove their "gift." Thuan added that he hoped his success in finding Tom's remains would lead "to more unhappy souls of your war dead returning to happiness back among their families in the United States."

As we traveled west on Highway 9, Thuan offered detailed historical information about the countryside through which we were passing. This impressed us because, like over 70 percent of the population of Vietnam, he had not even been born until after the war ended. Near a large military cemetery at Cam Lo, close to the former American base of Camp Carroll, he told of how he was once there looking for a lost NVA soldier and unexpectedly came across three other wandering souls: two were Vietnamese and the other was an American artilleryman. Before he could learn more about the American, the spirits fled. I wanted to ask Thuan if the two Vietnamese souls were South Vietnamese soldiers and whether he was permitted by the government to search for deceased ARVNs. Doc had told me that the communists obliterated all ARVN military cemeteries with bulldozers after the war ended, and so I decided not to ask the question and spare Thuan from a potentially awkward situation.

Unlike the deeply rutted, single lane dirt road I had first traveled in 1968, Highway 9 is now a high quality, well-maintained asphalt thoroughfare. As such, we were able to cruise along through the less congested areas at about forty-five miles an hour. The rain stopped after leaving Cam Lo and, as our van ascended into the mountains, we passed the long-abandoned American position of LZ Stud/Camp Vandergrift. Looking through the windshield at the sinister peaks looming ahead, I experienced an immediate sense of foreboding. During my time at Khe Sanh, this represented the westernmost point along Highway 9 past which no American dared to venture due to the certainty of ambush by the NVA. As we sped onward, the words of Dante came to mind: "Abandon all hope, ye who enter here."

Montagnard hamlets soon appeared along the way. These "Minority People," as the Vietnamese now call them, had been killed in the thousands by bombs and artillery during the fighting at Khe Sanh and I was pleased to see they had returned in such numbers. Most resided in traditional houses built on stilts with woven reed walls and no windows. The Montagnards were still largely animists and the architecture of their dwellings was designed to keep evil spirits, who they believe live in the tall grass and forest, from entering at night and making mischief. Absurdly, nearly every one of these primitive dwellings had a TV satellite dish attached to its thatched, slat or corrugated metal roof.

As we drove into Khe Sanh town I was astounded by the size and economic vitality of the place, a virtual metropolis compared to the primitive village it had been when I briefly resided there in January 1968. Near the center of town, Thuan ordered our driver to turn right on to a nondescript road of pounded, red earth. About two miles further, he asked that we stop at a small family compound where Thuan questioned a farmer for several minutes. We then proceeded another half mile to a crossroads, similar to one he had sketched during our meeting in Hanoi. Thuan appeared to be lost.

There Thuan walked about a fifty meters up one road and then back, apologizing for the confusion, saying he often became temporarily disoriented when he arrived at a place that he'd only envisioned. The house of "Mr. Nguyen," shown on the diagram, was, he told us, not as close to the location of Tom's remains as he had believed. He then asked me where the "airfield" was located. When I told him it was more than a mile to the northeast of us, in the opposite direction from Hill 881 South, Thuan politely disagreed (this exchange will be explained shortly). We then drove northwest into a narrow, fertile valley.

Despite never having been at this particular location before, I was suddenly engulfed by an overpowering sorrow and began to sob. I immediately recognized this as a recurrence of my Christmas episodes, which had now been absent for years. Steve and Doc uncomfortably pretended not to notice in an effort to spare me embarrassment; but Thuan gazed at me, his expression a mixture of curiosity and mild surprise. I regained my composure after a few minutes, just as we arrived in the Montagnard hamlet of Lang Ta Tuc, at the foot of Hill 881 South.

While Thuan and Tam were making arrangements for us to leave our vehicles there, Steve, Doc and I noticed a man from the other van who was about our age. He was wearing a green, gabardine uniform of the People's Army of Vietnam, with a necktie and polished, formal leather dress shoes, but no medals, insignia of rank or unit designation. We introduced ourselves through the interpreter and learned he was traveling with family members to locate the remains of his brother, an NVA soldier who'd been killed during the war near the A Shau Valley, about twenty miles to the south. Doc asked him if he, too, had fought in the war. The man replied that he had, against the Americans at Tay Ninh, located between Saigon and the Cambodian border. Despite the potential for another uncomfortable moment, the man was quite friendly and sympathetic with our mission, asking to join us to pay his respects to our fallen friend. We agreed.

It was now clear that Thuan believed Tom's remains were much further up the hill than he had previously thought. As we prepared to hike there, our group now consisted of us three Americans, the former NVA soldier, our driver Phouc, Tam the translator, Thuan and two fellow psychics. One, a woman, had attended our meeting in Hanoi on the previous Friday. The other was a man who I had not seen before. Also with us for the climb were two teenage Montagnard guides we hired in Lang Ta Tuc, one armed with a machete and the other a long-handled hoe.

After leaving the hamlet, and still on relatively level ground, we passed along the rim of several rice paddies and then into a small grove of coffee bushes. After crossing a shallow twenty-foot-wide stream, we began ascending a steep, jungle trail for about a mile, then on to an equally precipitous dirt road through open grassland for another mile. It had not rained at Khe Sanh that day and so our hike up the hill was mud-free, a great relief because during the last

December I had been there in 1967, the entire region was a gelatinous mire.

As we approached the summit, Doc, breathing heavily as we all were from the exertion, told us of the fight to seize the hill in the spring 1967 when Marines, heavily laden with gear, attacked up the even more vertical northern slope, opposite our climb, covering the last tortuous few meters in the face of withering enemy gunfire. Hill 881 South had been central to the survival of Khe Sanh from the first days of American occupation until that last, grim, July afternoon in 1968 when the Marines finally abandoned it, leaving Tom's body behind. Although Doc, Steve and I had a difficult and dangerous life at the base during the siege, conditions on 881 South were far worse.

The sense of isolation by those defending the hill was not just the result of it being the most distant outpost from the combat base in the midst of thousands of enemy soldiers. The NVA were also monitoring radio transmissions, so the Americans had no secure means of communicating with the outside world. This meant they could not report the often-dire shortages of food, water and other supplies, as well as their exact troop strength, so as not to tip off their weaknesses to those who closely encircled them. The hill's commander, Captain William Dabney, later said "It was as though we had been sent to detached duty on another planet."[156]

In-person or written communication with the outside was hampered by the infrequency with which choppers were able to land on the hill due to fog, rain and antiaircraft fire. When conditions allowed a rare helicopter landing, the LZ would erupt in deadly mortar explosions. Because it took time to off-load replacement troops and carry badly wounded men from cover to the helicopter, the process almost always created additional causalities. By the end of the seventy-seven day siege, three hundred sixty-seven dead, or severely wounded, Americans had been flown off the hill.

The isolation was made worse by the lack of regular mail from home. Going weeks at a time without being able to communicate with worried loved ones took its toll on unit morale. Because of the constant incoming, normal military formations, even informal gatherings of more than two people outdoors were prohibited. This absence of social interaction amplified the sense of loneliness.

What little building material they received was dedicated to reinforcing the ammo bunkers that held over eight thousand rounds of artillery, recoilless rifle and mortar ammunition, as well as sundry grenades, machine gun and small arms ammo, stockpiled there in quieter times. Given the narrow confines of the fortification, the Marines were virtually living on top of their ammo dump. "They [the NVA] tried, but never hit one of our main ammo bunkers," Dabney said. "Had they done so, they'd have blown us all off the hill!"[157]

This psychological burden was intensified by the knowledge that if the North Vietnamese attacked, there was no possibility of reinforcement or withdrawal. Since such an assault would inevitably happen at night, bombers and helicopter gunship support would be negated. Except for supporting artillery fire from other American positions, they were on their own. Marines there knew that if wounded, they would not be evacuated to a medical facility for days, or even weeks, and that the only medical attention available to keep them alive was from a Navy corpsman who could provide little except words of encouragement and morphine. Despite all this, few broke from the strain.

Doc finished his account of the rigors endured there just as we were reaching the summit. He had made this climb seven months earlier and, using information from the Dorow investigation of Tom's loss, found what he believed to be the location of where the body was last seen. As we now approached that spot, Doc made sure not to cue Thuan in any way, and so intentionally walked past the site. It was not that he was suspicious of the psychic, he just wanted to avoid inadvertently tainting the process, should we later need to scrutinize some inexplicable occurrence.

Thuan soon arrived and, as he passed the point that had once been the location of the Marines' westernmost defenses on the hill, stopped and squatted alongside the road. He peered intently down the northwest edge of the narrow ridgeline, then walked to the opposite side and looked down the hillside for a full minute. It was in that direction, according to Dorow's sketch, that Tom's body was last seen. While Steve was photographing all this, Doc and I remained poker-faced and whispered to each other out of the corners of our mouths like two inept ventriloquists: "Holy crap!"

Then, as if confused, Thuan began walking farther along the ridge-line, past us, and part of the way down into the saddle. He was clearly looking for something specific. After about five minutes, he returned and, as he had done an hour earlier when stopping our van at the crossroad, asked me, "Where is the airfield?" I pointed in the direction of the former combat base and replied, "Eight kilometers that way." Thuan, slightly frustrated now, then asked to see the sketch he had drawn three days before in Hanoi. I took it out of my backpack and spread it on the ground, holding it down with both hands against a steady breeze that was starting to blow in from the southeast.

Thuan repeated his question. I gave him the same reply, and was now becoming disillusioned because he seemed to be confusing the combat base with this hill. He then slightly rephrased his question to Tam, who asked me, "Where did the aircraft land here?"

"Do you mean the LZ?" I replied.

Thuan understood that expression and nodded vigorously in renewed excitement as I explained that, according to the official July 1968 report of Tom's loss, we were now standing about thirty feet east of what had once been the LZ Captain Black intended to use that day. Thuan leapt up and his gaze traversed the horizon before coming to an abrupt stop facing southwest. He walked rapidly in that direction to the edge and, without hesitation, started down the slope. Doc, Steve and I watched as he made short switchbacks in the two-foot-high elephant grass, finally stopping fifty feet down beside a lone, leafless sapling. Thuan then looked up the hill at me, his eyes revealing no emotion other than earnestness, and said quietly, "Your friend is here."

He then dropped to the ground and began retching for the next several minutes. The woman standing near me explained that such episodes of emotional exhaustion occurred after every successful effort by Thuan in locating remains. He rose after a few minutes and was in a noticeably more cheerful mood than I had seen him since we met three days before.

Because the sketch he had drawn in Hanoi showed the location of Tom's remains to be much further down the hill, I immediately asked him if the three small teeth and ammo pouch were beneath where he now stood. Yes, he said, at a depth of 1.6 meters. Thuan then described how a "rocket or a bomb" had struck Tom, moving his arm over the top of his head in an arc to indicate the direction from which the plane had come.

I was astounded. Few people knew the location of the 1968 incident, or that U.S. fighter-bombers had briefly helped in the effort to retrieve the body; or that the Dorow report contained a statement by a Marine helicopter pilot who'd been flying above the hill that evening and believed the body had been damaged by the bombing. Several American witnesses later told me the planes attacked in a west-south-west direction—close to the line just indicated by Thuan.

If all this were not remarkable enough, while waiting for the others to bring offerings down the slope for a religious service, Steve noticed an unusually tall clump of elephant grass about ten feet from where Thuan said the remains were located. After a Montagnard guide hacked away the vegetation, we found ourselves staring down into an old NVA spider hole, about two feet wide and three to four feet deep. Three of the perfectly cut, interior walls still showed striations left there from a shovel blade, but the downhill side had been eroded away by running water long ago. The proximity of this hole to Thuan's site seemed to corroborate both Marine and NVA eyewitnesses who said Tom's body was dragged a short distance to a spot in front of their spider holes as bait for the ambush.

Once everyone finally joined Thuan at the site, a guide chopped away some of the grass and dirt with his hoe. Doc, Steve and I then observed a few moments of silence for Tom. Once we were finished, the Vietnamese began a Buddhist service, igniting clusters of smoldering incense sticks and covering the spot with an assortment of flowers, fruit, candy and even a bottle of Vietnamese vodka, all to lure his soul from the perpetual misery of the battlefield. One man began burning bundles of fake, votive paper currency.

Once this makeshift shrine was completed, Thuan asked me to stand before it and think of Tom in order to help bring his soul to that place. While I was doing that, several of the Buddhists, sidled up and began praying. Doc stood nearby in prayer, rolling the stem of a single burning incense stick between the palms of his hands.

At the end of the service, some in the group began picking up the offerings to take back with them, as was customary. One of the Montagnard guides began to dig and had gone down about twelve inches before we stopped him. From my backpack I took a black, lacquered, wooden plaque that I'd brought to bury on the hill, the gold engraved lettering reading:

In memory of
Thomas Patrick Mahoney III
Lance Corporal
United States Marine Corps
Age 20

Killed in action at this spot on July 6, 1968

They shall not grow old, as we that are left grow old; age shall not weary them, nor the years condemn. At the going down of the sun and in the morning we will remember them.

Dedicated this 20th Day of December 2007
by your family, friends and the loyal men of
Company B, First Battalion, First Marine Regiment
who so valiantly struggled to bring you home.

Semper Fidelis

As I placed the plaque in the little hole, Tam put the vodka bottle beside it, for what I guess he thought might make an interesting photo. But, when he went to remove the bottle, the old NVA shouted sternly in Vietnamese, "Leave it for the soldier!" A startled Tam set the bottle back down. The soldier's simple and spontaneous outburst of respect, tinged with what I distinctly felt at that moment to be his frustration with a younger generation's lack of appreciation for the sacrifices made here years before, was profoundly moving to us three Khe Sanh veterans.

That image of us standing alongside a uniformed former enemy from a nearly forgotten war, amid waving elephant grass and swirling smoke, in the midst of an Asian jungle, drawn there by a twenty-year-old kid's apparent mistake decades before, will always seem to me like some preposterous dream.

Just as the Montagnard boy was about to cover the plaque and bottle with dirt, Doc's cap, with a Marine Corps globe-and-anchor insignia on the peak, blew off his head in a gust of wind and landed upright in the middle of the little hole. As he reflexively leaned down to pick it up, several of the Vietnamese cried out for him to leave it there. Thuan then told us it was common for wandering souls to be "playful." Mahoney, he continued, was happy we had come for him and knocked the hat off Doc's head as a sort of a prank (an act definitely in keeping with Tom's impish nature). So, the cap stayed and was buried along with the plaque and vodka. While the young Montagnard began pushing soil over the items with his hoe, the old NVA soldier leaned down and scooped several clods of dirt into the little hole with cupped hands.

Before leaving the site, Thuan lit several more incense sticks, instructing me to carry them off the hill so Tom's soul would follow the fragrant smoke. After the sticks burnt about halfway down, Thuan caught up with me along the trail and snuffed them out. He advised me to keep them "safe" and I would receive further instructions after returning to Hué.

As we continued on, the ominous mass of nearby Hill 689 took up most of the southwestern horizon, the memory of its bloody past giving me the shivers. In June 1967, Marines had first tried to occupy its crest, but were unsuccessful after losing twenty-four dead and forty wounded. They would not attempt it again for another ten months, when, in April 1968, as the siege was ending, forty Marines and corpsmen were killed in a single day of fighting. The hill was finally captured the following month, then held by the Americans for seven weeks, and only barely, after the First Battalion, First Marines saved themselves from being annihilated there on July 7, 1968, the day after Tom's death.

Near the crest of that hill were the remains of two Marines who had suffered the same fate as Tom, even in the same week, being used as bait for ambushing rescue efforts. I hoped to ask Thuan if he sensed anything up there; however, he was in a "zone" all the way down the trail, squatting periodically to stare off in the distance, deep in concentration. At one point, sweeping his hand across 90 degrees of the small valley between us and Hill 861 to the northeast, Thuan said to me, "There are many ghosts down there." In the end, I did not find a propitious moment to ask him about those two Marines left up on Hill 689.

After a mile, we reached a narrow brook. The opposite side was elevated and slick. I climbed the slippery, four-foot-high embankment, anchored myself to a tree with my right arm, and started giving the others a hand up to keep them from sliding back. Somewhere along the trail, the old NVA soldier had taken out a small pocketknife with a slightly curved, four-inch blade, perhaps to clean his fingernails after helping bury the plaque, cap and vodka. As I grasped his left hand, he leapt upward, and, to maintain his equilibrium, his right arm, with blade pointing out, swung quickly up towards me—stopping about twelve inches from my neck. Our eyes met and seeing the mounting alarm in mine, he quickly snapped the knife down to his side. In that instant, we simultaneously recognized that four decades earlier he would not have given a moment of thought to continuing the upward arc of that blade into my throat.

He seemed mortified by the gaffe, but all I was feeling at the moment was the familiar, crushing sense of dread that I'd borne every day at Khe Sanh. Minutes later, Doc slipped off a small dike and landed on his back in rice paddy muck, but not before dragging ten feet of bramble fence line along with him in a futile effort to right himself. We all chuckled the rest of the way to the hamlet, a timely distraction from that unnerving moment with the knife. Once there, we said our goodbyes to Thuan and his group as they headed south to find the remains of other soldiers, and we returned to Hué.

Doc had often said that while the Vietnamese people highly valued etiquette, they could be maddeningly indirect in communicating. Thus, things in Vietnam "were complicated and never entirely what they appeared to be." Those who assisted us that day were no less paradoxical: tough, yet compassionate; philosophical, yet pragmatic; forthright, yet oddly secretive. The "nameless" NVA soldier seemed the most mysterious. Over dinner that evening we speculated whether there was more to his story about why he was with us that day. For seven months prior to our visit, Doc had been casting a wide net among his contacts in Vietnam to locate the five men known to have ambushed Tom. Given such broad family networks and the rapidity with which information traveled among social and veterans groups in that country, it seemed a strong possibility that at least one surviving member of that team would have gotten the word.

Could the man in the uniform been one of them? Both Steve and Doc pointed out that while the NVA soldier acted extremely tentative at first, once he arrived on the hill he became noticeably "involved." I distinctly recalled him wanting to show me, in an urgent way via hand gestures, several overgrown spider holes and an old, eroding bomb crater on the southwest slope. When he later shouted at Tam about the vodka bottle, the others were startled into respectful silence. Something about it all, we agreed, just did not add up.

I then wondered aloud if the two Montagnards might return to dig at the site. Doc, whose Vietnamese language skills were good enough to understand most conversations, believed these boys had figured out we were there to honor the place of Tom's death. As animists and afraid of spirits, they would not likely venture back there just for the plaque. However, as adolescents, the cap and vodka might be too much of a temptation, though they would surely not disturb the site any deeper than that.

All the astonishing things I'd witnessed that day were the result of Doc's expertise, connections and tireless efforts. Yet I could not pass up the opportunity later that evening over beers in the courtyard of the Morin to drolly mention his pratfall into the paddy. Doc seemed ready for my gibe, and was waiting with a quick, though implausible, reply: As with the loss of his cap, Tom's mischievous soul was responsible for bumping him into the mud.

We drove from Hué to Khe Sanh again the next morning with just our driver and translator. Our first stop was a visit to the site of the combat base, where most of the plateau was still a privately owned coffee plantation. A low concrete wall and locked wrought iron gate barred our entry into what had once been the center of the base. Undeterred, we climbed the wall and began our search for specific landmarks, such as our living holes and the regimental command bunker. It was nearly impossible to get our bearings due to the density of the bushy, six-foot-high coffee plants and also because familiar reference points, like Hills 950 and 1015, towering over the place to the north, were completely shrouded in clouds that day. Doc had been there in 1996, before the trees had grown so thickly, and so was able to locate the site of his old regimental aid station and the COC bunker. The latter was still a significant depression in the landscape after being blown up by Marines in July 1968.

An old, disheveled Vietnamese man suddenly appeared from the coffee plants, like the ghost of a fallen soldier, startling us. He carried a shallow wooden tray filled with American military insignias of rank, tarnished Zippo lighters and other trinkets supposedly left behind. There were about twenty-five corroded dog tags in the tray, a number that seemed to me impossible to be authentic. I had read about a thriving cottage industry in manufacturing, and then intentionally "aging," such items for sale to returning veterans and tourists. The thought of that irritated me and so I nodded for him to go away. It was only after I left Khe Sanh that afternoon that I cursed myself for my cynicism in not at least looking at each of the tags on the chance that one of them might have belonged to Tom, killed just five miles away.

Our wandering was soon interrupted by another Vietnamese man, this time well dressed in clean stylish clothes, including a thin, black, cotton sport jacket, and clearly too young to have been in the war. He introduced himself in excellent English as Nguyen Viet Minh, curator of the nearby Khe Sanh interpretive center, and politely advised us that we were not allowed in the area where we now stood. His suggestion triggered our immediate resentment, reviving a territoriality we'd developed while dodging death there each day as nineteen-year-old boys. Rather than saying what was on our minds, we simply ignored him and continued to search among the bushes. Minh didn't persist and, lighting a cigarette, quietly followed us at a distance for a few minutes and then disappeared.

We later visited the interpretive center, where Minh graciously reintroduced himself and was eager to show us around. As we expected, the various exhibits demonstrated examples of military superiority by "liberation forces" over the Americans and the South Vietnamese "puppet army." One display contained a picture of Marines racing to board the back of a C-130 transport plane on the Khe Sanh airstrip. The caption, in English, described it as American troops "fleeing" the base in July 1968; but the photo was clearly taken early in the siege, before the airstrip was closed to such aircraft. A small sign in the display asked the rhetorical question: "What must President Johnson have been thinking?" We found the quaint use of that verb form amusing and for weeks thereafter, Doc and I jabbed each other for laughs with it, such as when discussing his falling into the rice paddy, I would say, "What must Doctor Topmiller have been thinking?"

When we told Minh that the three of us were veterans of the siege, he seemed genuinely fascinated and his subsequent questions had the tone of honest, scholarly interest. Another glass display case contained a crude flag of pale blue and crimson, with a large yellow star, hand-sewn slightly off center. The caption claimed the flag was flown over Hill 689 on the night of July 12, 1968, just after the last Marines departed. It was the national liberation flag of the southern Viet Cong and so was misleading because only North Vietnamese troops had participated in that battle. Doc courteously told the curator, "I'm an historian and would be happy to help you fix the historical inaccuracies in some of these displays." Minh smiled and politely declined.

Upon leaving the interpretive center we drove down toward Khe Sanh Town about two miles away. The road was paved and smooth, a far cry from my agonizingly bumpy jeep trip from the base to the village in January 1968. Near where the plantation house had once stood, the van struck a rooster standing defiantly in the road. Our driver accelerated away, looking pensively in the rear view mirror until we reached the intersection at Highway 9, where he quickly turned west.

In a poverty-stricken area like this, Doc later explained, if the driver stopped to find the bird's owner it could have resulted in the entire neighborhood turning out to watch the drama of blame and negotiations for suitable compensation, which could get thorny and take up the remainder of our morning. This was further complicated by the Buddhist belief in levels of rebirth appropriate to one's karmic accumulations, which might make a case for the rooster being someone's relative.

In the decades after the fighting there, the Khe Sanh area languished in obscurity, remaining virtually uninhabited by civilians until the mid-1970s when surviving Bru Montagnards returned and some Vietnamese began to trickle in. No other province in all of Vietnam contained more unexploded ordnance than Quang Tri, and no district within Quang Tri Province contained more than Huong Hoa, with about 85 percent of the total land area affected by the litter of battle.

As late as the 1990s, the average wage of a Vietnamese farm laborer was equivalent to only about nine cents a day. To eke out a living, many became willing potential victims of these explosives by digging them up to sell as scrap metal. The situation did not improve until later in that decade when international groups with expertise in locating and neutralizing unexploded ordnance arrived. By then, over seven thousand people had been killed and tens of thousands more injured by this terrible detritus of the war. Despite these problems and its remote location, Khe Sanh Town was now remarkably urbanized. This prosperity was largely due to the success of the Highway 9 East-West Corridor construction project completed a few years before, allowing unfettered commerce from the Mekong River, at the Lao-Thai border, west to harbors on the South China Sea.

Because of this unanticipated growth in the population, I had difficulty locating points of reference. In 1968, the old French fort hill was some distance east of the village, but was now surrounded by the new town. I eventually found where the District Headquarters compound had been by first locating a stream that once passed under the highway just to the east of the 1968 village and, from there, using the van's odometer and an old military map I'd brought for that purpose.

The site is now occupied by a modern, bright, cobalt colored inn and adjacent apparel shop. Although nothing there was recognizable to me, I shuddered for a moment with anxiety as I stood on the opposite side of the road, facing the spot where I once believed I'd be drawing my last breath as hundreds of North Vietnamese assault troops slammed into our paltry defenses.

For years after the fighting I had remained incredulous that they were unable to capture the compound. Our above-ground communications bunker was in plain view and less than fifty meters from the attackers' Soviet-made, state-of-the art, rocket-propelled grenade launchers. A well-placed rocket into that bunker early in the fighting would have likely prevented my call for the prearranged defensive artillery fire until it was too late to stop them from overrunning us. I eventually located a Vietnamese military history and learned why the attack had failed.

At noon on January 20, 1968, about eight hundred soldiers of the NVA's Seventh Battalion, Sixty-sixth Regiment broke camp several miles south of us and began to move into position to attack. These infantrymen were heavily reinforced with a recoilless gun company, a mortar company, a transportation platoon, and a sapper/ engineer squad.[158] About three miles from our compound, a massive Arc Light bombing erupted just ahead of them, pulverizing their planned route of march and leaving it strewn with toppled trees and enormous bomb craters. Without predesignated landmarks to guide them, and trees to disguise their daylight advance from American air observation, the soldiers moved forward slowly and a number of them became lost. This forced them to delay the assault on us until shortly before sunrise the following day, breaking with their usual practice of attacking American positions in the dead of night.

Still greatly outnumbering us, the NVA rushed into the attack and were decimated by the artillery mission waiting for them. Their battalion commander was killed and his entire staff was so badly wounded that a company-level political officer, himself bleeding, and with a broken arm, directed the remainder of the attack. To make matters worse for them, due to the accelerated schedule for launching the attack, which had been decided upon just five days before, they had only half the ammunition and rations they needed.[159]

By the NVA's own reckoning, the two days of fighting at Khe Sanh village resulted in six hundred forty casualties, of whom one hundred fifty four were killed. It would be their costliest, single engagement at Khe Sanh during the siege.[160] No Americans were lost during the fight, except the four soldiers killed in the ambush at the old French fort during the ill-fated, helicopter-borne relief effort.

Now, standing with Doc and Steve across Highway 9 from where the compound had been, I vividly recalled the morning I left there, peering out through the barbed wire at the western edge of our defensive perimeter, trying to count the bodies of our attackers. I could clearly recall the poses into which some had fallen, but could not, afterward, visualize a single face. I attributed that lapse in memory to my exhaustion after spending so many hours on the radio, but secretly worried that returning to this place someday would bring those faces back—or even worse memories I might have buried.

Over the ensuing years, I'd forgotten just how mentally and emotionally depleted I was after surviving that battle until I received a letter in 2013 from Khe Sanh historian Ray W. Stubbe. In it, Ray included a copy of a Marine Corps Oral History he had transcribed years before and had, by chance, just come across again, recognizing my name.

In March 1968, Staff Sergeant William J. Enochs questioned Sergeant Harry Stroud at Marine Corps Base Twenty-Nine Palms, California. Harry had just arrived there from Khe Sanh, which was still in the midst of the siege, and, like most of my buddies at the combat base, had been listening worriedly on the radio as the drama unfolded during that ordeal in the village just six weeks before this interview:

> ENOCHS: What was the longest watch that you personally know of that was stood there on a radio?
>
> STROUD: It was 37 hours solid nonstop. This ville was getting overrun and when this man got off the radio after calling artillery missions and talking back and forth to our regiment using call signs, he didn't even know his name—you asked him his name and he used our call sign. That man took two days to recuperate. I personally feel the man should have gotten some kind of recommendation or some kind of commendation because without him I can assure you we would have lost at least thirty Marines and about a company of ARVN.
>
> ENOCHS: Do you remember the man's name?
>
> STROUD: Yes I do. His name was PFC Archer. [161]

Now, in 2007, as I stood beside the roadway fretfully remembering back forty years, envisioning the insufficient, rusting coils of barbed wire and the low, cramped, sandbagged bunkers occupied by our under-equipped Montagnard militia near the front gate of the compound, something extraordinary happened. Several clusters of young school children came walking past the site, boys with boys, girls with girls, some holding hands, all in sandals and immaculate white shirts with little, crimson scarves. The kid's paraded by, busily chatting and giggling, oblivious to the three, graying Americans across the road from them or the terrible things that happened there decades before. If any dead NVA faces, or other dark memories, were about to emerge from my subconscious at that moment, they were driven off by the sound of the children's laughter. This place couldn't harm me anymore.

The next day, after returning to Hué from Khe Sanh, we visited the Duc Son Pagoda, adjacent to the School of the Beloved to thank the nun, Minh Tanh, for having urged us to make this trip to Vietnam. She had just received a telephone call from the psychic, Thuan, who provided her with instructions on what to do next. After removing our shoes and entering the temple, we saw an altar dedicated to Tom Mahoney immediately off to the right on which his black-framed high school graduation photo was surrounded by food offerings similar to those brought to the hill. Incense sticks burned in a small, maroon-colored clay holder, replaced hourly, Minh Tan said, by young novitiate nuns. She then asked me for the half-burned incense sticks I'd carried from the hill, which she reignited one at a time and had me place in the holder. Tom's soul, she said, will now follow them to this place and reside among his "Vietnamese friends" until such time as his mortal remains are recovered. If they are not, she said, his soul will remain perpetually in the temple.

Minh Tan then invited us to sit on cushions at a low, lacquered table in the main hall of the temple, beside wide-open double doors. On the table was a variety of foods, including two round, western-style layer cakes, all designed to lure Tom's wandering soul inside. A novitiate appeared and began burning a great deal of incense in a brazier on the front step of the temple and soon a haze of sweet smoke filled the open doorway. Eight other novitiates soon appeared from behind the main altar and for the next thirty minutes chanted an ancient hymn for the safe arrival of Tom's soul. Lost in the soothing cadence of the chant, I finally experienced something that had been missing for the last forty years—a sense of peace about Tom Mahoney.

A few months later, I would receive an email from Dianne Williamson who was in Vietnam to memorialize a close childhood friend, Kyle Coles, a young Marine who died along with nearly two dozen others on a helicopter inbound to Khe Sanh that was shot down on February 28, 1968. In her message, Dianne said she had visited Minh Tan in Hué and stayed to observe the festival of Lu Van (Wandering Souls). Lu Van is celebrated with a variety of moving ceremonies, like the floating of paper lanterns down rivers at night to illuminate the way home for lost souls. Thousands of family altars across Vietnam are stocked with food to nourish hungry souls on their journeys.

During the ceremony, Dianne positioned herself near Tom's altar to watch. The courtyard outside the temple was full of large tower-like altars, with parading monks under giant parasols. An orchestra played as participants chanted to summon wandering souls to be fed. It was, Dianne wrote, "one of the most moving spiritual experiences of my life and your friend Tom Mahoney was nurtured, fed, and lovingly cared for by hundreds of devoted people."[162]

❦ ❦

In late December 2007, shortly after I returned from Vietnam, I received a telephone call from Captain Black. He advised me that the sketch of Hill 881 South drawn by Lieutenant Dorow for his report of Tom's death was inexact. Black, and other eyewitnesses, had been unavailable to check that diagram for accuracy during the rushed investigation in July 1968. Now, having examined it closely for the first time, Black saw that the entrance to the gate shown on the sketch was facing west, when it actually had faced in a more northerly direction. Mahoney, he said, had definitely walked down the northwest side of ridgeline, rather than the southwest as indicated. As such, the place where Tom's body was last seen was fifty meters west of the location determined by Dorow [163] and about one hundred twenty meters northwest of where Thuan believed Tom's remains were located. Despite this, Black refused to dismiss Thuan's site as being a possibility, theorizing the body may have been moved at some point just over the top of the narrow ridgeline to the other side for hygiene reasons if the NVA believed they were staying there for any length of time. Or perhaps, he said, later bombing struck the body and the blast sent his teeth over the crest in the direction where Thuan claimed them to be.

I still did not know what to make of Thuan's psychic abilities, and soon learned that wiser people than me were also grappling with these issues. One was Wayne Karlin, with whom I had been conversing regularly since 2005. Wayne is an award-winning author and editor (including an anthology of Vietnamese literature), as well as a professor of literature and languages at the College of Southern Maryland. He was also a Marine helicopter door gunner in South Vietnam in 1966-1967.

Wayne's extraordinary book, *Wandering Souls: Journeys With the Dead and the Living in Viet Nam,* tells the true story of U.S. Army First Lieutenant Homer Steedly, Jr. who, in March 1969, shot and killed NVA medic Hoang Ngoc Dam when they suddenly met on a trail near Pleiku. Steedly took a notebook and documents from the body and, rather than turning them over to his unit's intelligence officer, sent them to his mother for safekeeping. Homer survived the war and, after his return home, suffered painful memories, particularly of having killed Dam. Eventually, he retrieved the items from an attic and began looking for a way to return them to Dam's family. He came in contact with Wayne, who was involved with Vietnamese writers and journalists helping in reconciliation projects in that country, such as building schools and providing education about unexploded ordnance.

In 2004, Wayne located the Hoang family in a small village outside of Hanoi and returned Dam's belongings the following year. He learned that after Dam was shot, Steedly's men tossed the body down a hillside (as Captain Black had suggested Tom Mahoney's body may have been by the NVA on Hill 881 South). Local Montagnards later found Dam and two other NVA bodies and buried them. The three were disinterred in 1975 by an army recovery team and re-buried in a small military cemetery, each grave marked only as *"Ly Siet"* (War Martyr).

Members of the Hoang family later traveled to that cemetery, but were unable to locate Dam's remains and subsequently fired their psychic, believing her to be a fraud. However, in May 2008, five months after our search for Tom on Hill 881 South, the family returned, while Homer and Wayne stayed in nearby Pleiku. Though officially denied permission to dig, the family went ahead and retained the services of another psychic who stayed in Hanoi communicating with Dam's spirit. The psychic guided the family members to the gravesite by cell phone and told them it would contain a red poncho, in which Dam's remains were wrapped. They soon located this and immediately returned to Pleiku, where they showed Homer and Wayne the bones and a Polaroid photograph of the grave. Wayne later observed that the Hoangs "were utterly certain the remains belonged to Dam," and any suspicion about the possibility of deception, or even wishful self-deception, must be tempered by their deeply held conviction that, had they disinterred a different soldier, that soldier's ghost would have invoked a disastrous curse on the family. Hundreds later attended Dam's funeral in his home village.[164]

Wayne's experiences helped me sort out the conflicting feelings I was now faced with after my recent visit to Vietnam: sorrow, relief and the unexpected warmth and concern by former NVA soldiers, like Dr. Dinh Toan. But, like Wayne, I also harbored reservations about the validity of psychic powers. "I feel the same way as you do," he later wrote to me. "I'm a skeptic who wants to believe."

As much as I would have liked to disagree with Wayne's observation that I wanted to believe, there appears to have been some truth in that. Back on January 21, 1968, while sitting on the floor of the communications bunker at Khe Sanh village in despair that I would probably not live through the night after learning our reinforcements had just been ambushed, I looked down and saw a Kennedy half dollar pressed into the mud floor. I survived the night and, though I did not really believe the coin had been responsible for that, was now afraid to part with it.

As an eighth grader in March 1962, I had gone to hear President John F. Kennedy speak at Memorial Stadium on the campus of the University of California in Berkeley. Because of its long reputation as a breeding ground for "communists," the Secret Service considered the city unsafe and so, despite being a clear and warm day, the President arrived with a transparent bullet-proof, bubble top on his limousine. Later, as he stepped to the podium in the center of the football field, I was surprised to discover he was a redhead (we did not yet own a color TV at home).

After his speech, Kennedy departed through a nearby gate. I joined some other kids running up to the rim of the stadium to look down on his car. He tilted his head back and waved to us through the plastic. After meeting Tom Mahoney a few months later, I learned that he was also in the audience, and might have been among us kids jostling for a peek at the President in his limo.

I was awed by seeing the President and so his assassination the following year left me cynical and depressed. This, in turn, led to a series of reckless life choices and eventually Khe Sanh. So when I saw Kennedy's silvery visage gleaming out of the damp earth floor that very bad night in the village, it had the feel of a mystical experience. On the day I left Vietnam, I checked the buttoned pocket that I had used to keep the coin safe each day for the last year and discovered it had somehow vanished since I had checked on it the day before.

During my return in 2007 to the site where that battle for the district headquarters had taken place, I could not shake the totally irrational feeling that, despite last seeing the coin thirty-eight years earlier, and a hundred miles south of there, I was about to look down and suddenly find it again. This sensation persisted until we were back in the van and driving away, but left me momentarily in a dizzying, disorienting panic that my personal reality had nearly come undone.

I was too embarrassed to tell Doc or Steve about this, but my Vietnamese friends would not have been surprised by such a scenario, confident that Tom's mischievous wandering soul was not only responsible for the disappearance of the coin nearly four decades before, but was, by distracting me with this bizarre expectancy, now communicating approval of my quest to bring him home.

While I remain unconvinced of the effectiveness of paranormal involvement, I also know that until the day Tom's remains are discovered, we cannot rule out with absolute certainty the location identified by the psychic Nguyen Buu Thuan. I am grateful to him, Thich Nu Minh Tan, Nguyen Thi Dieu Van, Dr. Dinh Van Toan and the others at the CIHC, and profoundly touched by their sincerity, quiet dignity and compassion in helping ease the pain of Tom's family and friends by trying to reach this single soul among countless who they believe still wander their land. I began to wonder if, in that journey back to the place where I lost my youth, innocence and best friend, I may have inadvertently found a little part of myself that died there. In that context, perhaps *two* wandering souls were working their way home.

Doc Topmiller (left) and regimental air team radio operator
Denny Smith all cleaned up after leaving Khe Sanh, April 1968.
(Courtesy of Joe Haggard)

(L-R) Author, Steve Orr and Doc Topmiller in
Hanoi, December 2007. *(Courtesy of Steve Orr)*

Psychic Nguyen Buu Thuan at CIHC in Hanoi drawing a
diagram of Hill 881 South while in communication with Tom's
wandering soul, December 2007. *(Courtesy of Steve Orr)*

Dr. Dinh Van Toan, (center with finger on Thuan's drawing)
translates the document into English for us.
(Courtesy of Steve Orr)

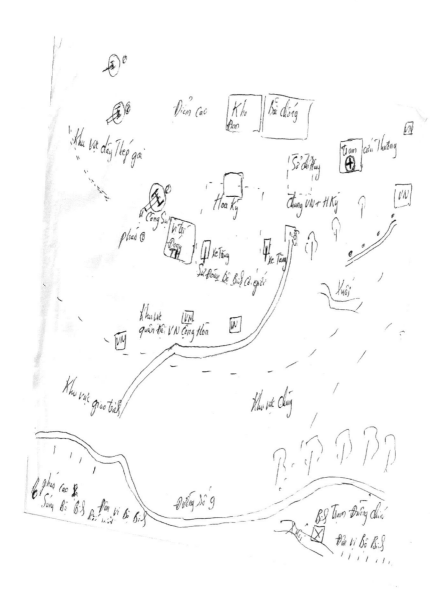

Thuan's drawing of the 1968 Khe Sanh Combat Base.
(Courtesy of Steve Orr)

Thuan's drawing of the current Hill 881 South area showing
where he believed Tom's remains were located.
(Courtesy of Steve Orr)

Author in village of Lang Ta Tuc preparing to ascend Hill 881 South, December 2007. The two young men directly beyond his arched back are the Montagnards guides who would lead them. *(Courtesy of Steve Orr)*

Steve Orr and Doc Topmiller in the final ascent to the top of Hill 881 South, December 2007. *(Courtesy of Steve Orr)*

Thuan checking the map he drew three days earlier in Hanoi.
Author kneeling beside him, Doc Topmiller, in tan baseball cap,
standing at right, December 2007. *(Courtesy of Steve Orr)*

Buddhist prayer service for Tom at the site Thuan located on Hill 881 South. *(Courtesy of Steve Orr)*

Offerings to entice Tom's wandering soul to this site, including bottle of vodka. *(Courtesy of Steve Orr)*

Former NVA soldier helping bury the plaque and offerings.
(*Courtesy of Steve Orr*)

Infamous Hill 689 as seen in the distance from Hill 881 South,
December 2007. (*Courtesy of Steve of Orr*)

Comparison of two photos of the western sector of Hill 881
South. In the top photo, taken from the main position on the hill
in April 1968, the white arrow in the upper right shows the area
in which Tom Mahoney's body was last seen. The white arrow
to the left, midway down the hill, shows the relative position
of where our group was standing in the bottom photo, taken in
December 2007. The white arrow in the bottom photo, upper
right, shows the area where Tom's body was last seen.

Buddhist nun Minh Tan beside Tom's altar at the Duc Son
Pagoda in Hué. (*Courtesy of Steve Orr*)

Site of destroyed Khe Sanh village in April 1968. (*Courtesy of Jim Singer*)

District Headquarters compound beside Highway 9 in Khe Sanh
village before the attack in January 1968.

Site of the destroyed District Headquarters along Highway 9 in
new Khe Sanh Town, December 2007. *(Courtesy of Steve Orr)*

Nguyen Tien Thanh (last surviving member of the NVA scout team that ambushed Tom Mahoney) and his bride before going off to war in 1967. (*Courtesy of Gary Foster*)

Bác Hồ Và Đoàn Đại Biểu Anh Hùng Dũng Sỹ Diệt Mỹ
Tháng 5-1969

Thanh receiving his "Courageous One" award from Ho Chi Minh and General Giap in Hanoi, April 1969. Thanh is in back row, center, directly behind Ho. (*Courtesy of Gary Foster*)

Thanh serving refreshments in his home to American guests
Gary Foster and Mike Najim, January 2013.
(*Courtesy of Gary Foster*)

A special evening with Tom's sister Claudia Harris in Lake
Forest, California. (L-R) The author, Claudia (her husband Bill
behind her), Al Maumausolo and Alan Williams.
(*Courtesy of Carrie Williams*)

A comparison of the 1968 photo (top) taken of the western sector on Hill 881 South from the hill's main position, with the mural (bottom) in the Vietnam War gallery at the National Museum of the Marine Corps, where the location of Tom's remains has been "hiding in plain sight" just down the road from the Pentagon.

Tom Mahoney's epitaph inscribed on the reverse side of his
father's grave marker at the National Cemetery in San Francisco's
Presidio. (*Courtesy of Walter Stone*)

20
BABYKILLER

BY AN ODD SET of circumstances, Bravo Company, First Marine Regiment would have a disproportionate number of former members figure prominently in the national debate regarding war crimes committed by U.S. forces in Vietnam.

Ken Campbell, a friend of Tom Mahoney's, who was on Hill 881 South the day he was lost, survived the terrible fighting on Hill 689 the following night, and then saw continued action, first at Con Thien, then further south in the equally dangerous "Arizona Territory" near An Hoa. The VC still maintained a strong presence there and, unlike the NVA, relied heavily on booby traps and hit-and-run ambushes to fight the Americans. These tactics proved so effective that Bravo took 50 percent causalities in just the first two weeks, including the loss of a company commander, a platoon commander and two platoon sergeants. Ken was also wounded, but not severely enough to be medevaced.

While there, Ken was ordered to call in an artillery strike on a village near where the company had just suffered grievously from booby traps and small arms fire. Despite seeing several children in the target area through his binoculars, Ken obeyed. Because Khe Sanh and Con Thien were virtually free of civilians, this was the first time he had faced such a moral dilemma.

By the time of his discharge from active duty, Ken was opposed to the war; but, like many returning veterans, could not tolerate the idea of being associated with "snotty, college kids running around university campuses waiving Viet Cong flags."[165] However, with the 1970 U.S. invasion of Cambodia and the killing of war protestors by the Ohio National Guard at Kent State University, Ken could no longer remain uninvolved. He joined the Vietnam Veterans Against the War (VVAW) and helped organize the Winter Soldier Investigation in January 1971, a three-day media event sponsored by actor/ activists Jane Fonda and Donald Sutherland challenging the morality of U.S. policy in Vietnam by exposing a pattern of war crimes.

The most powerful testimony came on the first day from former Marine Sergeant Scott Camil, who had also been with Bravo Company, although leaving Vietnam before Ken, Tom Mahoney, Captain Black and Lieutenant Ahearn had arrived in the unit. Camil's countenance was described by some as "angelic," as he calmly recounted in horrifying detail how he and his fellow Marines routinely tortured, raped and mutilated Vietnamese civilians, luridly dwelling on the most perverse details of sexual degradation. Other witnesses followed in the same vein, describing the ghastly torment American troops inflicted upon innocent civilians, often women, young children and the elderly. Ken Campbell's testimony that day was unique in its absence of salacious detail, telling only of how he participated in the killing of civilians by the indiscriminate use of artillery fire and that he had witnessed the mutilation of dead bodies.

Because it appeared most testifiers on that first day were trying to out-do each other in telling the most outrageous story, organizers sought to back away from such graphic tales on subsequent days. Some observers noticed that details of the most inhumane treatment of Vietnamese women, as told by Scott Camil and others, closely resembled stories in the recently published book *Conversations with Americans* by Mark Lane. [166]

Lane already had a reputation for sloppy investigative work and self-aggrandizement as a result of his best-selling book, *Rush to Judgment*, an attack on the Warren Commission Report into the assassination of President Kennedy which accused the CIA and FBI of a broad and high-level conspiracy. As part of the Fonda entourage, Lane had been an early organizer of the Winter Soldier Investigation, even suggesting the name. However, because of his penchant for exaggeration and shock tactics, many VVAW members, including

Ken Campbell, found his participation in the event a distraction and he was soon ousted.

The speed with which Lane put together *Conversations* indicated his desire to coattail on publicity being generated by the trial of Lieutenant William Calley for mass murder at My Lai in March 1968. The victims included children, the elderly and women, some of whom were raped and mutilated. These atrocities had been covered up by the U.S. Army until helicopter door gunner Ron Ridenhour, disturbed by rumors of the slaughter, had the unwavering moral courage to track down eyewitnesses and, despite the threat of physical harm and disciplinary retaliation, inundated the Pentagon and Congress with letters until an investigation was begun. In addition to Calley, twenty-six other soldiers were charged with criminal offenses related to My Lai. Lane hoped the book would give widespread attention to his theory that such monstrous behavior by American soldiers was not an aberration, but frequent and deliberate.

Conversations was quickly discredited by serious journalists. Neil Sheehan, who would soon help leak the Pentagon Papers, and so was no apologist for American policy in Vietnam, was disgusted by Lane's "hysterical propaganda" and asked if it was morally justifiable for those opposing the war to practice such deceit, just as they accused those in power of doing.[167]

One of the deserters Lane interviewed, Terry Whitmore, had also been with Bravo Company and was badly wounded during the fighting near Con Thien on December 15, 1967, in what had been Tom Mahoney's baptism of fire. After recovering from his wounds at a hospital in Japan, Whitmore defected. He first went to Moscow, briefly becoming a media darling for propaganda purposes, then took up residency in Sweden among a growing enclave of U.S. military deserters who were welcomed there.

Whitmore told Lane that, as a member of Bravo, he participated in a massacre of civilians in Quang Tri Province in 1967 during which he helped burn down "13 hamlets in one night" and kill nearly four hundred villagers, including children. In one strange digression, Whitmore describes how, in the midst of this night of alleged mayhem and murder, he established a warm relationship with some children there and planned to adopt one of them. "They were so groovy to me." Whitmore said. "I really dug those kids."[168] Sheehan followed up on the Whitmore story and determined that he was referring to the killings at Thon Nai Cuu in October 1967; Tom Mahoney being among those who replaced the men involved.

South Vietnamese government officials had determined the village of Thon Nai Cuu, and adjoining hamlets, to be "chronically VC controlled" and so relocated most of the population. Some villagers chose to remain and others, who initially moved, later returned from the relocation camp several miles away to retrieve personal belongings.

On the night of October 21, Marines observed enemy mortar fire coming from the village, which had been the scene of several recent, bloody encounters between American and VC units. The following morning, as Marines entered the area to investigate, First Platoon's well-liked radio operator tripped a booby trap and was killed. The newly promoted company commander, Captain Robert Maynard, a former enlisted man and trusted by his troops because he had previously been their Third Platoon leader, ordered the village and its inhabitants destroyed as payback. The killing of children, Maynard told his men, would be "left to your consciences." [169]

Second Lieutenant John Bailey led First Platoon into the village. Raised in North Carolina where his father was a dean at Davidson College, Bailey had arrived in Vietnam just a few months earlier. As the men progressed through the darkened village they fired at anything that moved and tossed grenades into underground shelters, often without checking first to see if they were inhabited by civilians.

Sergeant Don Allen, however, was checking. Allen, on his second tour of duty in Vietnam, had already earned the Silver Star Medal for ambushing an NVA company in 1966, later badly wounded by shrapnel to the face and skull. In the village that night, he soon found a man, woman and several small children hiding in a bunker and ordered them out. A member of Allen's' squad, Lance Corporal Rudolph Diener, a nineteen-year-old from New Jersey, argued that the order had been given to kill everyone, but the sergeant insisted the children not be harmed. According to witnesses, Diener then shot the woman. The Vietnamese man fled into the darkness and Marines fired on him, later claiming a body was never found. The children were taken to a relocation center and the Marines burned the remaining structures in the village before returning to their camp.

One member of the patrol, twenty-one-year old Lance Corporal Olaf Skibsrud, the son of a Lutheran minister in South Dakota, was troubled by what he witnessed and went to a chaplain. The chaplain reported the story to his superiors and, far from being covered up by higher ranking officers as the Army would do after My Lai, an investigation was begun immediately and the accused were either relieved of command, or sequestered until it was completed.

During the Article 32 hearing, the military equivalent of a civilian grand jury proceeding, some witnesses, both officers and enlisted men, closed ranks to protect themselves and their fellow Marines, making it difficult to determine what occurred in the village that night. This was further complicated when the lead investigator, Major Arthur Bergman, and several defense counsels, went to the crime scene to obtain evidence and were driven off by automatic weapons fire from "uniformed VC or NVA," but not before two Marines in the group were wounded.

However, other First Platoon members cooperated with the investigators. Sergeant Allen testified that he was present when Captain Maynard ordered that no one be left alive and all structures burned to the ground.[170] Another witness largely corroborated Skibsrud's account. Bergman was unable to bring perjury charges against those he knew were lying, and all were later returned to duty, dispersed throughout units other than Bravo Company. His report recommended that charges against Second Lieutenant Bailey should be dropped for the killing of several civilians, including children, by allowing his men to toss grenades into bunkers, because such acts were not premeditated, but "rather the result of actions that would be automatic from military training and experience in a combat environment."

But, Bergman found that there was no excuse for Diener's action, concluding: "He does not possess the same set of values in regard to human life as that required under all circumstances by the rules of engagement." Diener was tried by court martial on one count of *attempted* murder, because the woman's body was never found. He was acquitted by a unanimous verdict on the basis that the company commander who issued the order was responsible, and a lance corporal should not bear the brunt of that responsibility. Captain Maynard was later tried by court martial on murder charges and, while all records of that court proceeding are, oddly, missing, it is clear he was acquitted. Maynard did, however, receive an official reprimand for failure to report the deaths of civilians, as required for battalion record-keeping purposes, and soon left the military.

Later evidence indicated more than a dozen civilians may have been killed that morning at Thon Nai Cuu, either murdered or legitimately misidentified as VC,[171] but far from the four hundred Terry Whitmore had alleged. Neil Sheehan was astounded: "Is Whitmore transmogrifying this incident into a massacre of several hundred? The conflicting accounts certainly raise the question."[172] Steve Busby, who knew Whitmore in Bravo Company, recalled him being a "slacker" always trying to evade difficult and dangerous duties and "a coward who made up a fictitious life to justify his desertion and collaboration with the enemy."[173]

Whitmore's memoir, *Memphis–Nam–Sweden: The Story of a Black Deserter,* was published the following year. Written entirely by antiwar activist Richard Weber, it told a far more subdued version of the event than Whitmore had allegedly described to Lane, in which he did not mention the "groovy" children and admitted that he had not actually killed any people, just some cows.[174]

The killings by Bravo Company at Thon Nai Cuu were also mentioned in the film, *Winter Soldier,* a documentary record of the Winter Soldier Investigation released in 1972. In it, Ken Campbell is overheard meeting Scott Camil outside the hearing room just prior to Camil's testimony and asking him about a rumor circulating in

Bravo at the time Ken arrived in Vietnam regarding a massacre in Quang Tri Province the previous autumn.

Camil, who claimed to have forgotten about it until Ken's question, now recalled that they had slaughtered exactly two hundred ninety-one civilians that day while on "Operation Stone," as he and others sat on a railroad trestle nonchalantly shooting villagers for sport. Operation Stone, however, was not in Quang Tri Province, but over a one hundred miles south near Da Nang, and conducted eight months before the Thon Nai Cuu killings. And, while there is no record of the atrocity Camil refers to, the official after-action report showed that precisely two hundred ninety-one VC soldiers were killed over the course of the eleven-day operation.

When testifying that morning before the cameras, Camil curiously failed to mention what he had just described to Ken Campbell; an event that, if true, would have been one of the most horrendous massacres of civilians in the entire war.

By Camil's and Whitmore's accounts, the Marines of Bravo Company murdered nearly seven hundred men, women and children during the twelve-month period ending in October 1967—far exceeding My Lai in savagery. For whatever reason these men concocted such exaggerations, they were, as Gary Kulik points out in his book *War Stories*, the first from any war to lie that they had committed war crimes, literally reversing the practice of those who customarily denied crimes they had committed. [175]

Still, American troops did kill civilians in Vietnam with shocking regularity and at times, committed rape, torture and the mutilation of the dead. About the same time Camil and Whitmore were publicly spinning their atrocity stories about Bravo Company, I was equally abhorred that so many Americans considered Lieutenant Calley a "victim" after his conviction and life sentence by court martial for the premeditated murder of twenty-two Vietnamese civilians at My Lai, mostly old people, women and children, including infants, shot to death as they stood defenselessly in a group under guard. Calley had originally been charged with the murder of one hundred four of the approximately five hundred civilians slaughtered that day. All of the other twenty-six soldiers and officers charged with crimes were eventually acquitted for their roles in the mayhem. President Nixon, responding to widespread public pressure, later bestowed a limited pardon on Calley, commuting his prison sentence and subsequent parole obligations.

It sickened me that so many wanted to excuse him, and by implication, all veterans of the war, for such acts; that butchery, sex crimes and the deliberate shooting to death of toddlers and infants was somehow defensible. I did not want to be included in their group absolution because it made me feel guilty of something I had not done. While I never witnessed such atrocities against civilians in Vietnam, wild rumors and sadistic tales abounded during my time there and I had no doubt such things were occurring.

Many of these crimes, on both sides, were committed as a matter of strategic policy utilizing special units to terrorize the civilian population of South Vietnam. Viet Cong terror squads, in the years 1967 to 1972, abducted and murdered over 100,000 South Vietnamese civilians, including over 3,000 during the fighting in Hué city.[176] The U.S. had its own version of this, the CIA-operated Phoenix Program, designed to "neutralize" civilian VC sympathizers by assassination and kidnapping. While U.S. government records indicate over 80,000 suspected VC operatives, informants and supporters were kidnapped, imprisoned or killed, the actual number is generally believed to be far higher.[177]

In addition to these specialized terror units, the Pentagon's Vietnam War Crimes Working Group, set up in the wake of the My Lai discovery, recorded several additional massacres by regular infantry units between 1967 and 1971, and other acts of physical abuses against individual civilians. The investigation's final report is of questionable value because it found a total of only two hundred U.S. soldiers who had been accused of harming Vietnamese civilians or prisoners, meaning countless more went unreported. Of them, fifty-seven were tried by court martial and just twenty-three convicted. Sentencing was light and often overturned, or reduced on appeal. The Working Group concluded that it was not "rogue units" who were responsible for most of these atrocities, but rather "a widespread, violent minority within U.S. Army units" who benefited from extensive cover-ups at various levels of their command structure.

Like the Americans, most NVA and VC soldiers believed they were fighting to help protect the people of the south from oppression. Yet many engaged in unnecessary and unauthorized violence against civilians, including murder (often of entire families), rape, torture and mutilation. While some of this can be attributed, as with Americans soldiers, to their inability to cope with the psychological stress of war, other factors were at play. Many came south with a mindset of ethnic superiority, spawned by age-old prejudices against southerners as lacking character and reliability, creating resentment among northern troops in the belief they were forced to suffer and die because southerners were too lazy to do it for themselves.

This was further aggravated by the Marxist dialectic that labeled as "cruel tyrants and reactionary elements" any villagers and townspeople in the south who refused to cooperate when they came to confiscate rice and other taxes, or forcibly conscript older boys and men—and so were deserving of violent retribution. In addition to these depredations against civilians, both sides frequently engaged in the torture and murder of military captives.

Because of the closed nature of communist society, and the absence of almost any kind of military records from their units in the south, widespread atrocities were never admitted or publicized; nor do we know how, or if, anyone was held accountable for such war crimes. The United States, however, was not a closed society and so, by the end of the Calley trial in 1971, millions of Americans were willing to accept the characterization of a typical U.S. soldier in Vietnam as a brutish, young man pillaging the countryside, abusing and murdering Vietnamese civilians out of revenge or boredom. That impression, reinforced in films, TV dramas and sundry publications for years thereafter, was far from accurate.

While prolonged contact with the enemy destroys a soldier's confidence in his own mental functions "as surely as would torture in a political prison,"[178] the majority of U.S. combat troops held it together and were later disgusted that their courage, character and self-control, and that of their fallen comrades, were disregarded by those wanting to paint them all with the same brush as their contemporaries who had failed to do so, gone berserk and crossed that line. In his critique of Mark Lane's *Conversations*, Neil Sheehan derided those who "failed to draw distinctions between the grim but understandable brutalities of war committed by both sides in the 'passion of battle,'" and more severe atrocities "like the direct, personal murder of unarmed civilians who posed no immediate threat."[179]

Author, screenwriter and former Marine Lieutenant William Broyles wrote that, in war, the line between killing and murder was not always easy to define, but every soldier knew the difference. "Murder is different from killing," Broyles said. "I saw many people killed, but I saw one man murdered and I will never forget it. My Lai was like that, not killing, not warfare, but murder."[180]

To generalize that American troops acted with consistent dishonor in Vietnam is to ignore countless acts of conscience, like that of Bravo's Sergeant Don Allen, who prevented children from being killed at Thon Nai Cuu. And, though it will not satisfy those seeking justice for the deaths of so many innocent civilians, or make sense to those who's moral compasses had not weathered the madness of war, the awful truth is that while most American soldiers and Marines were able to maintain their principles throughout the physical and psychological agony of life in a rifle company, others were not.

Which was Tom Mahoney? Controlled and principled, or a "babykiller" as his former girlfriend charged in the last letter he would receive? To a man, his platoon mates, many of whom were with him every step of the way, declared that assertion to be completely untrue and outrageous. As one of his closest friends in Vietnam later said: "To say something like that about Tommy, of all people, couldn't be more ridiculous."[181]

After the Winter Soldier Investigation, Ken Campbell attended Temple University, earning a PhD in 1989 and accepting a professorship teaching political science and international relations at the University of Delaware. In 2006, Ken read *A Patch of Ground* and invited me to speak to his "Lessons of the Vietnam War" honors class. On the commuter train from Philadelphia to Newark, Delaware that morning we spoke about the war, Khe Sanh and Tom Mahoney. Ken's throat constricted with emotion several times as he tried to speak, and tears welled in his eyes. It was a reaction I had seen repeated many times before in my conversations with veterans of prolonged combat. Such discussions, especially when dealing with specific people and places, briefly peeled away the security of the present and exposed a young man whose days in Vietnam were a constant struggle against death and madness.

He had survived the worst of the war and remained proud of being a Marine. Yet, in the summer of 1971, as part of a delegation of American veterans attending a conference on U.S. war crimes in Norway, Ken went to Moscow and met with representatives of the North Vietnamese government and the Provisional Revolutionary Government of South Vietnam. This visit was given international media attention and Ken, along with several others, was profiled in a feature article in *Esquire* magazine.

Because U.S. troops were still fighting in Vietnam at the time, his contact with these Vietnamese Communist officials generated widespread disapproval, some considered it treasonous. As such, he was ostracized by many with whom he had once shared that most elemental relationship in war—the last face you might ever see, the last voice you might ever hear.

Ken told me that he had hoped to make the primary message of the Winter Soldier Investigation about the "banality of the atrocities" resulting from the contempt most American soldiers had for the Vietnamese, and how they "felt free to do terrible things to them with no good military purpose." He was disappointed that this message had been lost, "overshadowed by testimony of the most psychotic, shocking atrocities," exaggerations for which he "reluctantly felt shame."

"That may not make sense," Ken added, "but Vietnam, if nothing else, was a great contradiction."[182]

I had to agree. When I arrived there in 1967, the established mission of the Marines was clear: Protect the civilian population. On my ride from the base to Khe Sanh village I traveled with a "MedCap" group, including an American physician and dentist, going there to treat civilians. Eight days later, as we prepared to repel the imminent attack by what we knew was going to be an overwhelming NVA assault force, we decided not to aim our command-detonated claymore mines (each of which fired hundreds of steel balls horizontally towards an advancing enemy) in the direction of the huts of villagers nearby, so as not to harm the kids living in them. It was a decision that could have cost us our lives when hundreds of NVA soldiers crashed into our barbed wire perimeter a few hours later.

But such "feel good" moments did not last long in Vietnam as the war grew rapidly in scope and ferocity. Just five weeks later, with the enemy massing their troops and tanks among civilian human shields in Khe Sanh village for one last attempt to capture the combat base, Captain Harry Baig ordered an Arc Light on the little town. The bombing likely wiped out a battalion of NVA assault forces and much of their supporting arms, ending any immediate plans by them to seize the base, but it also killed nearly a thousand civilians.

Surprisingly to me, our regimental commander, Colonel David Lownds, seemed to have been left out of that decision process. Just two weeks earlier, Lownds had told a *New York Times* correspondent that he'd experienced some misgivings about sending so many civilians back to the village after they had come to the combat base for refuge, concluding "This thing can come back to haunt me—all of us."[183] I was sitting near my radio in the underground COC bunker when Lownds stormed in that evening. I had never seen him so angry. "Harry," he shouted, "I understand that you bombed the ville?" Captain Baig courteously replied, "Yes, Sir." Lownds reminded him that he had forbidden it. Baig calmly explained the necessity of having to do it: enemy tanks, thousands of assault troops and anti-aircraft guns and then stood stoically silent.

I will never forget the look on the colonel's face. It was part anger at the insubordination, and part resignation to the fact that it was done, and there was nothing he could now do about it. He stared silently at Baig for several moments and then said, quite seriously, "Harry, I wouldn't want to be you when the war crimes trials start." The colonel turned and left the room. The whole episode again made me suspect that Baig was accountable to a superior higher up the chain of command, probably in the CIA, than Colonel Lownds—and I think Lownds knew it too.[184] After the bombing of the village, some enlisted men dubbed the captain "Butcher Baig." While this moniker spread quickly, I do not recall it ever being used in his presence.

Among those killed in that bombing were many of the same children we had tried to save on January 20 by not aiming our claymore mines in the direction of their huts. And, though there was nothing I could have done to prevent the bombing, I felt an immediate twinge of guilt because I was alive largely due to the courage of those local forces who had helped defend the district headquarters. I can still visualize the faces of some of them, their wives and their kids.

Nevertheless, by the time I left the combat base in mid-April, exhausted by another six weeks of relentless incoming artillery fire and hundreds more American casualties randomly cut down around me, I wrote contemptuously in a letter to my parents that "if every person in this lousy country has to die in order for me to get home alive and in one piece, I'm fine with that."

The Vietnam War was, indeed, "a great contradiction."

21
THEMSELVES THEY COULD NOT SAVE

DOC TOPMILLER INVITED ME back to EKU in April 2008 to address several history classes. As usual, he introduced me as the person who single-handedly lost the Vietnam War. The students did not always know what to make of our absurdities; however, the lectures soon turned unmistakably serious as the story of Khe Sanh with its carnage and long-term effects unfolded, leaving most somber and reflective as they filed out of class. Much to the regret of his students, Doc announced his retirement the following month. One of them, Jared Kelley, reflecting the feelings of many wrote: "Dr. Topmiller made a significant contribution to the quality of my life and, more so, to my core beliefs and growth as a human being."[185]

In June, Doc traveled up the Mekong River far into northern Thailand and the Golden Triangle area, where bandits and drug lords held sway; a place where native Thais seldom ventured. It was never clear to me what Doc was looking for and I could not help expressing my concerns in an email to him.

Doc deflected this with self-deprecating humor, replying that while out in an open boat on the Mekong, a monsoon shower had washed from his canvass shoulder bag the last of the mud from the year before when he fell into the rice paddy while we were returning from Hill 881 South. I fell for this diversion, quickly responding with mock indignation: "While a squall may have cleansed the remaining water buffalo feculence from your bag, nothing will remove the indelible stain your misstep into that paddy in front of a former adversary placed upon the honor of the United States Naval Service."

Sadly, these comical exchanges were becoming less frequent. As Doc contemplated his return from this trip, he dreaded facing the issues that weighed so heavily upon him when in the United States: the military quagmires in Afghanistan and Iraq, the shoddy treatment of American veterans and the seeming indifference of the American people to both. But, in July 2008, he arrived home from this, his fourteenth visit to Vietnam. It would be his last.

Two weeks later, Doc and Terri attended the annual Khe Sanh Veterans Association reunion in Reno. The first night there, Doc ran into Rick Noyes, an acquaintance from his high school days in Cincinnati. Coincidently, Rick had been the first wounded man Doc treated after arriving at Khe Sanh in January 1968. A reconnaissance Marine, Noyes had been injured by shrapnel while on a patrol seeking information on the NVA build up around the base.[186] Doc later treated him for a second injury, after Rick's bunker took a direct hit from an enemy rocket. Noyes suffered multiple shrapnel wounds and a ruptured eardrum, but four others in the bunker were killed. Doc patched Rick up and sent him back on duty; but, because of the dreadful sanitary conditions at the combat base, his wounds soon became infected and he returned to the aid station for additional treatment.

A few days later, Noyes was standing nearby when some Marines, frustrated by the number of rats in their trenchline, decided to burn them out with kerosene. After pouring the fuel into the trench and igniting it, a Marine slipped into the flames and was burned over nearly his entire body. Rick helped carry the man to the aid station. Doc knew immediately that the injured man would not survive and later learned he died the next day on medevac flight to the Philippines. Before Rick could leave the aid station, Doc noticed that he was now delirious from a serious, life-threatening infection and helped carry his friend to a helicopter. Rick was reluctant to leave his comrades behind at Khe Sanh, but later credited Doc's professionalism with saving his life.

This chance meeting with Rick in Reno awakened painful memories within Doc. I later learned from Terri that he had gone back to his hotel room and sobbed for nearly an hour. However, the next day he seemed revived and, during an interview with a local TV reporter covering the reunion, spoke of how helpful and healthy it was to renew acquaintances and share jokes with those who weathered the siege alongside him.

The following day Doc and my Khe Sanh air team buddy, Raul "Oz" Orozco visited my home. During the siege I had worked each night on radio watch with Oz, a friendly and helpful guy with a fine sense of humor, who hailed from San Antonio, Texas, and had been at Khe Sanh since the Hill Fights the previous spring. Doc and Oz were soon discussing various physical and emotional symptoms for which they were being treated by the VA. After about a half hour, I interrupted them, asking if we could change the subject to something else and asked Doc how he had earned his second Purple Heart.

Doc, mildly annoyed at my interruption of what he clearly considered an important conversation with Oz, nonetheless obliged, saying that one day late in the siege, incoming artillery fire had caught a group of Marines in the open. He was notified, grabbed his medical kit, and quickly went to the site. The first man he came across was missing both legs. As Doc looked around, he saw numerous others sprawled on the ground with a variety of serious wounds. "I realized that I had to abandon the man with his legs gone," Doc said, "in order to go to the guys who had a better chance of surviving." The man soon died. Doc, who was subsequently hit by shrapnel while tending to the others, ended his account of that terrible day by saying: "The look on that legless Marine's face, when he realized I was about to leave him, has haunted me ever since."

I now recognized this account as one he had briefly mentioned in his memoir *Red Clay on My Boots*, published the year before. However, it was not until I watched Doc retell that tragic story that I fully understood how no flesh wound could have matched the emotional destruction inflicted upon him that day when he saw the look of desolation—and betrayal—on that dying, young man's face. I was now speechless at the terrible nature of Doc's burden and no gallows humor materialized from either of us to drive off that haunting vision. In the awkward silence that followed, I wondered how Doc had, over the ensuing years, been able to bear such vivid recollections of the sights, sounds and smells of all that carnage, and was furious with myself for having just interrupted my two friends in their efforts to heal.

❧ ❧

Doc often said that part of the guilt he felt from his Vietnam experiences was because he had not been vocal enough in his opposition to the war after returning home. He was now remedying that with a vengeance. He became obsessed with educating the public on what the wars in Iraq and Afghanistan would mean in human suffering and national treasure—for generations.

While Doc had been pleased with the services he received at the Veterans Administration hospital in Seattle during his days as an undergraduate student, he was disappointed by the lack of similar care after he moved to Lexington, Kentucky. On his first visit there to obtain prescriptions for relief of his depression and anxiety, as well as a narcotic to take the edge off his recurring nightmares, he had to wait seven hours and was subjected to derisive comments by the intake staff, at one point hearing Vietnam War veterans referred to as "red, white and blue trash."

Doc was now ready to turn his sense of injustice and considerable research and writing talents toward the VA medical system and secured a contract from Paradigm Publishers in September 2007 to write a history of medical care for U.S. veterans. "It will be critical, but not spiteful," he said. "I want the VA to be the best it can be."

But, by early August, Doc told Terri the book was bringing up too many difficult emotions and he doubted his ability to finish it. His former mentor, George Herring, later recalled that during the defense of his doctoral dissertation in 1998, Doc had maintained "scholarly objectivity against moral engagement." However, this deepening reengagement with Vietnam "eventually took its toll."[187] Navy veteran and clinical psychologist, Kerby Neill, who had met

Doc and become friends in their common cause of world peace, agreed with Herring: "Bob's anger was palpable in some of what he had written and his objective-historian self must have been in conflict with his angry, anti-war self, adding considerable stress to his efforts to write."[188]

Doc also struggled on a personal level with the dichotomy that, despite abhorring war and advocating nonviolence, he remained proud of his own military service and that of his three sons, who had served in the armed forces in dangerous places like Somalia, Kuwait and Iraq.

By late August he seemed content once again, accepting a position at the University of Kentucky to teach a course on U.S. diplomacy and foreign relations and was preparing another class on the Vietnam War. On August 19, 2008, he called me to discuss a joint book signing we had scheduled in Reno for the coming Veterans Day. Doc had just purchased round-trip plane fare and spoke about how much he was looking forward to it. He told me how thrilled he was by his new position at Kentucky, calling it his "dream job."

However, as Kerby Neill later observed, "few people could read him like Terri and she was worried." Doc had stopped seeking treatment at the VA Medical facility, though remained in touch with his counselor, and continued taking two strong prescription medications for anxiety and insomnia. His first day of class was scheduled for Monday, August 25, and he left home that morning in what Terri later described as "great spirits." Unlike his usual thirty-minute drive to EKU, Doc was now just a few minutes from his new office. He never made it. Two days later in Georgetown, Kentucky, just north of Lexington, police found Doc's body in a motel room. He had died from a self-inflicted gunshot wound to the head from a 9mm pistol he purchased at a gun store the day before. He left no note.

His family was devastated. Terri, who Doc had recognized in the Preface of his book *Red Clay on My Boots* as having "fought the battle of Khe Sanh by my side for almost forty years," would now have another battle to fight, surmounting her own anguish and conflicting emotions in order to stay strong for her children and grandchildren.

Terri's dignity and a genuine compassion for the feelings of others during this darkest period in her life marked her as one of the most courageous women I have known, still the corpsman helper-healer she was when she first met Doc at the Great Lakes Naval Hospital over four decades before.

Despite knowing the extent of his PTSD-related psychological health issues, I could not, at first, believe he had acted on a self-destructive impulse. In shock, I postulated he had made enemies because of his outspoken views and was murdered. Any explanation was better than the truth. Soon, however, I accepted the facts, the hollowness of my personal loss and a deep despair at the utter waste of such a brilliant mind. His suicide was incomprehensible then, and will always remain so. I was not alone. Kerby Neill met Doc for lunch just ten days before his death. "I'm a clinical psychologist," Kerby said, "and I had no inkling that he was in the kind of distress he was in."[189]

Others tried to help me make sense of it. A message came to me from Dr. Kevin M. Gilmartin, former Marine and psychologist and expert on the topic of suicide from research for his book *Emotional Survival for Law Enforcement*. "It is almost impossible to detect suicidal intent in a noncrisis context," Gilmartin wrote. "Doc was a deep thinking, philosophical man capable of very intense and self-contained contemplation, who probably had reviewed and lived with his decision internally for years."[190]

Wandering Souls author Wayne Karlin observed that we Marines always saw our corpsmen as the strongest, the ones we could turn to. Doc, he said, remained that as a scholar, a healer in his passion to communicate the complex humanity of the Vietnamese. "There is some kind of sickening shift in the heart," Wayne wrote, "when you realize how each wound our corpsmen touched, physical or not, became their own. It's disheartening to realize that the war still has that power to reach over the stretch of forty years and snatch such a good person back."[191]

Doc's many friends in Vietnam had come to view him as "a living Buddha" for his compassion and generosity and took the news of his death with shock and deep sorrow. His dedication to those injured physically and emotionally by the war manifested itself daily across a broad spectrum, both in the United States and Vietnam. Thanks to the efforts of Kerby Neill, Doc's book, *Binding Their Wounds: America's Assault on Its Veterans,* was published in 2011.

From the day I first met him at Khe Sanh, until the end of his life, I saw Doc as a fearless and highly principled individual, and recognized it was the cruelest of ironies that the most inspired, introspective and caring among us were those most often selected as corpsmen. Most Navy corpsmen and Army medics who survived combat, have, like Doc, suffered painful, haunting memories for the remainder of their lives, blaming their "incompetence" for deaths they could not have prevented. It reminded me of a verse I'd once read about the sacrifices made by British soldiers in the nineteenth century: "The saviors come not home tonight. Themselves they could not save."[192]

Doc's funeral was held in Lexington on September 2, 2008, the mortuary overflowing with colleagues, students and friends. Terri had asked that I give the eulogy and Rick Noyes spoke before me, his heartrending words about the man who had saved his life at Khe Sanh leaving me shaken as I approached the podium. Despite a constricting throat, I was able to get through it and closed by saying:

> His extraordinary intellectual gifts and his confidence in
> the empirical process were always tempered by a calm spiri-
> tuality, which caused even a cynical, old pagan like myself to
> recognize there might be a place in this universe for both.
> I am eternally grateful for that, for the honor of his friend-
> ship, and for the simple pleasure of his company.

After the service, Doc's cremated remains were buried with military honors at the Lexington National Cemetery. As *Taps* played, a mournful chorus of sobs spontaneously rose from the crowd, mine among them.

Six weeks later, I traveled to the U.S. Military Academy at West Point, New York, where I had been invited to sign copies of *A Patch of Ground* at the Thayer Hall bookstore on campus. I later visited the cemetery, pausing first at the gravesite of Union Army Brigadier General Daniel Butterfield, who had written the musical composition *Taps*. As I wandered up to the northwest end of the cemetery, taking in all the illustrious names along the way, I soon found myself standing, by chance, at the tombstone of General William C. Westmoreland, who had died three years earlier at the age of ninety-one.

Just then, the sound of a bugler playing *Taps* unexpectedly wafted out of the fog from down the hill where a small, private, burial ceremony was ending. My emotions were still raw from Doc's funeral, and I began to cry at the sound of that first, long note. Suddenly I had a mental image of what it would have been like if Doc came upon me at that moment weeping at the grave of General Westmoreland. I would have never heard the end of *that*. For the next few minutes I was chuckling and crying at the same time. We two old buddies had gotten in one last, absurd joke.

Despite the seemingly callous nature of our dark, survival humor, Doc Topmiller was always serious and principled when it came to his profession as an historian. A few years earlier, while researching his book *The Lotus Unleashed*, he located the telephone number for retired General Westmoreland's residence in South Carolina and called to ask for an interview. He was surprised when the general personally answered the phone. After a few minutes of conversation, Doc recognized Westmoreland was suffering from dementia (he had by that time been diagnosed with Alzheimer's).

On a personal level, Doc had little respect for Westmoreland. And, while an unethical or spiteful person might have used some of the things the general was saying on the phone that day as an opportunity to embarrass him, Doc, first and foremost a serious scholar, courteously ended the conversation and hung up.

A few months after Doc's death, his University of Kentucky colleague, Peter Berres, traveled to Vietnam and spread some of his ashes at the site of the old Khe Sanh Combat Base. Though Doc and Tom Mahoney never met, Doc came to know everything about him and made extraordinary efforts, through his contacts in Vietnam, to bring Tom home. He had connected with Tom on a spiritual level that I was never able to achieve, or even understand, but one I accepted as being more profound than my own. As such, it is fitting that they are now together on that nearly forgotten field of battle.

Doc had been responsible for renewing my quest to find Tom after JPAC decided it was impossible to proceed. His death produced the opposite effect. I'd lost all desire to continue. It now seemed pointless.

22
WOUNDS THAT
NEVER HEAL

BY THE TIME OF DOC'S DEATH, I had spoken with several Marines who were on Hill 881 South the day Tom died, but none who had joined Frank Ahearn in trying to reach the body. I especially wondered how the three men who were wounded in that effort fared afterward. A quick check of names on the Vietnam Wall told me they had not succumbed to their wounds. Yet I remained disinterested in continuing this quest in the absence of Doc's guiding presence.

All that changed in June 2010 when I received an email from Carrie Williams, the daughter of Allen Williams, a name I immediately recognized as one of the three Marines listed in the Dorow report as having been wounded attempting to reach Tom. She'd located me from an online search and told me her father had been Tom's close friend in Vietnam and was living with guilt over his loss for the last forty-two years; refusing to discuss any details about that day other than saying, "I let Tommy down."

Allen, she said, was recently diagnosed as being in an early stage of Alzheimer's and doctors at the Los Angeles VA medical center told her there was a direct link between that disease and his PTSD-related depression. Allen agreed to start rigorously treating that depression, but did not know where to begin because he knew few Vietnam veterans, and none from his platoon. "I love my dad," Carrie wrote me, "but I don't really understand what he's going through. I hoped you might be interested in talking to him." I was immediately struck by her deep affection for her father and also Allen's courage, not only on that July afternoon in 1968 when he risked his life for

Tom; but now, in voluntarily reopening such an agonizing emotional wound.

Allen Victor Lee Williams III was born the son of a respected New York City psychiatrist and had educational and professional opportunities beyond the reach of most young Americans. Despite this, he joined the Marines as an enlisted man in 1967 to serve his country. The handsome, six feet two inch Allen was not a typical "grunt." One of his fellow Marines, Mark Milburn, who, despite receiving a number of serious wounds in Vietnam, would go on to have a distinguished career in law enforcement with Los Angeles County, later recalled how Tom Mahoney and others in First Platoon regularly asked Allen to read suspenseful paperback books to them, because of his dramatic and uncanny voice impersonations. "He always talked about becoming an actor when he got back to The World." Milburn said.[193] Frank Ahearn, too, recalled Allen as being "a fine Marine, a good person and very good for the morale of the unit."

I sent Allen a copy of *A Patch of Ground* and he responded a week later by email:

> Tom was my best friend in the Corps. A day never goes
> by that I don't think of him. I tried once to find his folks,
> but I stopped myself because I thought it would just make
> the pain worse. I suppose his people are gone by now. The
> whole experience at Khe Sanh and on the hills was awful.
> For a long time I thought of trying to talk to someone
> about it, but for the most part, I just buried it in some deep
> part of my heart.[194]

Allen knew how difficult our conversation was going to be, and so it was not until July 30, nearly two months later, that he was ready. I called and we spoke for over an hour as he worked forward through the anguish of always believing he had let his friend down.

After flying from Hill 881 South that night, the helicopter crew chief refused to let him get off at Hill 689 because of his wounded right arm. Allen pleaded that could do something to help, perhaps pull pins on grenades or carry water and ammo, but to no avail. As the chopper headed away from Khe Sanh to a hospital in a rear area, Allen felt more dejected than at any point in his life; angry with himself and frustrated that he hadn't refused Captain Black's order to leave the hill without Tom. "I just needed to do something right that day or I couldn't live with myself. I did not want to be the only one who survived. I just didn't want to be that one... [Here his voice broke off with emotion]."[195]

Allen was treated for his wound and returned to duty three weeks later, back with Bravo Company now stationed at Con Thien. A few days after his return, he was severely injured by an enemy mortar shell and immediately transported back to the United States where he spent months in treatment and rehabilitation.

On the day he was finally discharged from Saint Albans Naval Hospital in Queens, Allen took the subway home. He was in uniform and, despite the train car being crowded at the time, he vividly recalled how "the passengers literally (physically) pressed against one another to move away from me, as if I were a leper." It was, Allen added, "due to that ridiculous 'baby killer' stigma now borne by all Vietnam vets."[196]

After his discharge from the military, Allen stayed true to his dream of becoming an actor and went on to have a long, successful career in film and television, including scores of television shows, with regular cast roles in such acclaimed series' as *The Lou Grant Show*, *Knott's Landing* and *The Client*, and numerous major films, including *Being There* and *Against All Odds*. But he never mentioned his Vietnam service. "If I had," Allen said, "I would have been blacklisted."

I now better understood the tragic complexity of feelings that drove him to revisit this. While it might help mitigate the guilt, and thus the depression that accelerated his Alzheimer's, he also knew the disease would soon steal his memory, explaining to me: "I don't want to lose Tommy again." My mind went back to the grief I'd experienced in Vietnam on that July day in 1968 when I learned from the hospitalized Bruce Bird that Tom was dead, and how I struggled not to cry in front of my fellow Marines, provoking a beating rather letting that happen.

I suddenly recalled the words in the enemy report of Tom's death, describing how, just before he was shot, the soldiers said "his face was red and his eyes were blue like a mean animal." Tom's complexion was not abnormally ruddy nor his blue eyes cruel, except when narrowed in anger or anguish. That haunting description of his face, coupled with the despair he was feeling at the moment, and the fact that he sought to separate himself from other members of his platoon, made me wonder if Tom was crying in that last moment of life.

Allen and I had long since abandoned that macho reluctance to express such emotion in front of others and so sobbed silently on the phone for a minute longer before croaking simultaneous variations of "you take care" before hanging up.

On Veterans Day 2010, Carrie sent us both an eloquent message:

> I wish you had never had to endure the tragedy and turmoil
> of war, or had to grow up too fast, or lose your best friends
> in combat. I could never understand where you have been.
> I can only be grateful for the impact you both have made
> on my life. Thank you for your service to our country, for
> your love of each other, and the example you set for the
> next generation. The only real men I have ever known were
> Marines.

⚑ ⚐

While I was unable to find Richard Delucie, Wayne Sherwin and Richard Patten,[197] who also volunteered to go after Tom, I did locate Bruce Bird in 2013. I learned that he had excelled in track and baseball at New Jersey's North Plainfield High School, but did not make the football team because he was of less than average height. Bruce received his draft notice at age twenty-two, but decided to enlist in the Marine Corps because he "had been impressed with war movies about Marines in battle and liked the look of their dress blues uniform." After boot camp, he trained as an infantryman in special anti-tank weaponry and joined Bravo Company in November 1967, a week after Tom. At age twenty-three, Bruce was considered an old man in the platoon and "a kind of father-figure."

Like Tom, Bruce survived Con Thien, Hué and months of combat around Khe Sanh relatively unharmed before that July afternoon when he volunteered to go down the hill with Frank. Bruce was already wounded in the arm, the result of shrapnel from the NVA mortar shell that exploded among Second Platoon just minutes before.

After Richard Delucie was wounded, Bruce led the second attempt to reach Tom, slowly walking in a tight crouch to within ten feet of the body before a bullet struck the right side of his neck, spinning him 180 degrees and dropping him to the ground. Bruce watched as blood gushed from the wound onto the matted grass, recalling that it was "like they die in the movies, kind of slow motion with time to reflect on things like family and friends."[198]

Just as he was losing consciousness, Frank and Sherwin arrived and dragged him back up the hill where a corpsman quickly bandaged the wound. The bullet miraculously missed both his carotid artery and spinal cord by fractions of an inch, but the damage was extensive. Because so many Marines had been wounded by the earlier mortar fire, medevac choppers were already inbound. Bruce was put aboard the first one into the LZ, likely saving his life. He was given Catholic Last Rites before surgery in the hospital at Phu Bai and spent another three weeks bedridden.

Bruce was subsequently transferred to a hospital in the Philippines and then on to Okinawa for rehabilitation. Once fully healed, and because he still had forty-five days remaining before his DEROS, he was sent back to Bravo in Vietnam. Those still there from the fight on Hill 881 South were shocked to see him, believing he was dead before being choppered off the hill. He would participate in one more combat operation before returning to Camp Lejuene and discharge from active duty.

In civilian life, he worked simultaneously in an auto parts store and a chemical plant in central New Jersey until both businesses closed in 1998. Now unemployed and dealing with severe stress and

PTSD, Bruce suffered a stroke followed a few months later by a heart attack. His marriage soon ended and he moved to Florida to take care of his aging parents. When they died, he stayed.

"I knew Tom Mahoney and liked him." Bruce said. "He would do anything for anyone." When I asked Bruce why he'd volunteered to risk his life to retrieve Tom's body, he gave it a few moments of thought and then replied: "When a guy is dead, there nothing you can do for him. But you can't let the family get nothing. You can help make sure something goes home."

Khe Sanh historian Ray Stubbe observed that because the Marines could not easily adapt to the "atrocious battlefield environment" at Khe Sanh, their attempts to retrieve fallen friends often resulted in a vicious cycle of rescuers needing rescuers. "Time and time again," Stubbe said, "tradition and loyalty overcame reason or objectivity."[199]

From the time of the Hill Fights in April 1967, until the last days on Hill 689 in July 1968, the NVA used dead and dying Americans as deftly as any weapon in their arsenal. Nguyen Tien Thanh, a North Vietnamese soldier who participated in Tom's ambush and later fighting on Hill 689, recalled that their political officers told them (though incorrectly) that if an American recovered another dead American from the battlefield, the rescuer's tour in Vietnam was shortened by six months.[200]

Once in such traps, Marines became victims of their own stylized methods of fighting and reacted the way the enemy knew they would when struggling to retrieve a lost buddy, with emotion and bravado; effectively turning the Corps' most cherished virtue of *Semper Fidelis* into its deadliest liability.

From the time of the Civil War, up through the First World War, American war dead were collected by graves registration staff under brief humanitarian armistices allowed by both sides and buried on the battlefield. Attempts were made to have identification attached to individual bodies for later exhumation and reburial. On occasions where one side was forced to retreat and leave their dead, the victors often buried them in the same manner, as much through an unspoken code of honor as for hygienic reasons.

During this period, procedures for disposing of the dead were sometimes ignored, especially in remote locations. In November 1878, a reporter for the *Nevada State Journal* visiting the Little Big Horn battlefield in Montana two years after the fighting there, found the remains of several members of the Seventh Cavalry exposed to the elements: "The Indians, who are careful to guard their dead from the prowling wolf, either by placing the bodies on elevated platforms, or by burying them deep in the earth, must be astonished at such evidence of neglect on the part of people claiming to be their superiors."[201]

Ninety years later at Khe Sanh, another remote battleground which some in the media were comparing to Custer's Last Stand, the disposition of the dead was still a thorny subject. Captain William Dabney, commanding Hill 881 South during the siege, recalled that two of his gunnery sergeants were killed by an enemy shell and "there wasn't much left of them." Dabney, knew it might be weeks before the remains could be taken off the hill and it would be impossible to keep the rats away if they were stored in a bunker. He radioed the combat base for permission to bury them and was told that field regulations prohibited the practice and so permission was denied. Dabney ordered them buried anyway.[202]

During the Second World War, a highly mechanized and ruthlessly doctrinaire conflict, American fallen had been buried with as much decorum as was possible under the circumstances, and with a mind toward possible exhumation and reburial elsewhere at a later date. While American soldiers generally buried German and Italian enemy dead with a concern toward later identification, because of "racial and cultural differences" Japanese bodies were often burned or bulldozed into mass graves like trash.[203]

By the time of the Korean War, the American military had the transportation capability to bring bodies of combatants killed in action back to the United States almost immediately (called "concurrent return"), rather than burying them temporarily. This forced the military to explore new options for providing closure for troops left to continue the fight, leading to battlefield memorial services, instead of funerals. In December 1950, NATO forces, including elements of the First Marine Division, made a desperate departure from the Chosin Reservoir in North Korea where, enduring subzero temperatures, they were encircled by over 60,000 troops from the People's Republic of China.

First Marine Division commander Major General O.P. Smith ordered the frozen bodies of Marine dead transported out along with the wounded. The group slowly worked its way south for three days through a gauntlet of Chinese ground and artillery attacks. It may have been this test of will and loyalty, under the most grueling circumstances, that established a Marine Corps "tradition," and a *de facto* policy, of never leaving another behind—dead or alive.

Whatever the advent of that doctrine, it was understood by every Marine going to Vietnam that he would not be left there, a commitment that bound us together in a brotherhood of mutual trust. While encouraging this notion to foster *esprit de corps*, the Marine Corps actually had no official policy, largely because such guidelines were unnecessary before so many of these agonizing tactical situations arose at Khe Sanh.

Marine Brigadier General Jacob Glick, who was present at Khe Sanh Combat Base during the debacle at Hill 689 on April 16-17, 1968, when the bodies of over thirty Marines and corpsmen were left on the field for up to six days, later said the Division policy on recovery of MIA's and KIA's was not clearly defined. There was "a general understanding that the forces should not risk additional deaths and casualties unnecessarily to recover KIA's, but reasonable effort should be made to recover the MIA's; yet, we always recovered KIA's if we could."[204]

Colonel Frederick Knight, a Marine battalion commander in 1968, later wrote that the Third Marine Division commander, Major General Rathvon Tompkins, had a policy of recovering bodies as part of "the deep tradition of the Marine Corps taking care of each other, dead or alive."[205] General Tompkins' policy of bringing back all KIA's, Knight said, created problems for commanders who often "wanted to disengage to reduce casualties and seek a more advantageous tactical situation, but under that stricture, could not." Knight later advocated a policy of "weighing our traditions… against the utilitarian principle of the greatest good for the greatest number, and actions taken accordingly."

Tompkins' successor, Major General Raymond Davis, subscribed to the same "deep tradition," though more circumspectly. On July 10, 1968, four days after Tom Mahoney's body was left behind on nearby Hill 881 South, Davis visited Hill 689, where Marines there, having survived an enemy assault to recapture the hill, were still unable to retrieve the numerous American bodies outside their defensive positions. Lieutenant Colonel Archie Van Winkle, commanding the hill, spoke privately with Davis in the LZ near the General's helicopter. After Davis departed, Van Winkle returned to his command post and took his operations officer, Captain James McHenry, aside, saying, "Mac, he's not going to tell me that we have to get those bodies, but he is not going to let us leave until we do."[206] All but two of the bodies, both of which had been destroyed by bombing, were recovered the next evening.

Doc Topmiller, in his book *Red Clay on My Boots*, spoke of the lack of space inside the Regimental Aid Station at Khe Sanh during the siege, often requiring them to place corpses outside the doorway along the road on stretchers until a truck from the military morgue could get by to collect them—somewhat reminiscent of the streets of medieval Europe during the Black Plague. "Although the Marines are justly famous, and sometimes foolish, in their obsession to recover their dead from the battlefield," Doc wrote, "our trainers in the Field Medical School constantly cautioned us that we ministered to the living, saying 'dead people are a supply problem.'"[207]

In every classroom where tactical military theory is taught, few would consider it a good idea to stop in the midst of a skirmish to retrieve an obviously dead body. Because units depended on each other to accomplish their individual missions, this could result in loss of the battle and dramatically increase friendly casualties. Purists might even argue that going off to retrieve a dead body before a mission is completed constitutes dereliction of duty.

The reality of these situations is extraordinarily complex, often incomprehensible. While it was a fairly common occurrence at Khe Sanh for the enemy to move dead Marines and corpsmen as bait into lethal, prearranged zones of fire; only a small number of Americans throughout the length of the Vietnam War were put in a position to voluntarily endanger their lives to retrieve bodies from under such well-designed ambushes.

Only those who actually went forward into such a situation, like Lieutenant Frank Ahearn and the five Marines who volunteered to go after Tom, will ever really understand. It may have stemmed from a flickering hope he might still be alive; or some real-time, intuitive recognition that to do nothing would be impossible to live with the rest of one's life; or simply, because Tom would have done it for them. Whatever the reason, the rest of us can only marvel at the depth of courage and loyalty such a perilous, personal decision requires.

❧ ❧

Having spoken, by now, with a dozen surviving members of Bravo who had known Tom Mahoney in Vietnam, it was clear to me that he was the most trusted and well-liked member of his platoon. These men also felt he was the most emotionally stable among them, even after months of the worst combat of the war. This was articulated in Captain Black's words to Patricia Mahoney in the letter of condolence he composed five days after Tom's death, saying,

> Thomas was a sincere, hardworking young man who
> impressed everyone with his eager manner and courte-
> ous demeanor. He took great pride in doing every job well
> and constantly displayed those qualities of eagerness and
> self-reliance that gained him the respect of his seniors and
> contemporaries alike.[208]

So on that July afternoon when he was killed, they lost something much more than just another rifleman. It is an extraordinary tribute to his character that most of these battle-hardened veterans needed to fight through a veil of grief, some in tears, before they could speak of him over four decades later.

Such profound sorrow was not unique to a particular rank, culture or class, as I learned in June 2004 while gaining permission to reprint a photo for my book that was owned by famed photojournalist David Douglas Duncan. David responded to my letter by telephone from his home in the south of France, opening the conversion with a gruff: "So you didn't get your ass shot off at Khe Sanh, huh?"

He had photographed wars since the early 1940s, mostly for LIFE magazine, and I recalled seeing him in the COC bunker at Khe Sanh in February 1968. His subsequent books, *I Protest!* and *War Without Heroes,* included numerous photos he had taken during the siege, with one of Captain Harry Baig captioned, "Mad Mongol Renegade." Baig, the brilliant target intelligence officer who was largely responsible for the successful defense of Khe Sanh, had died in April 1971 under suspicious circumstances along with his wife and ten-year-old daughter, while visiting with them in Bangkok on a brief respite from a highly classified undercover mission for the CIA in neighboring Laos.[209]

David told me that after publication of these two books, he received a letter from Baig's father, Osman, a renowned, Sandhurst-educated general in the British Indian Army and later a distinguished Pakistani diplomat. Osman asked David to respect his recently deceased son's memory by removing the "Mad Mongol" reference, and threatened to use his influence to have future printings of the books stopped if he refused. David realized the elder Baig had no idea how instrumental his son had been in saving thousands of American lives during that battle, and so sent him other photos and tape recordings from his conversations with Harry at Khe Sanh. Osman soon re-contacted him and with great emotion said, "Thank you for giving me back my son."

Despite his patrician and military background, General Osman Baig's grief at the loss of his son was no less painful than that of Patricia Mahoney's. For as author Cynthia Enloe later wrote, "wars have their endings inside families."[210]

❡ ❡

The last time I saw Mrs. Mahoney was at my wedding in Grass Valley, California in September 1971. She, Claudia and Tom's grandmother had driven the two hundred miles from Oakland to attend and we had a chance to visit during the rehearsal dinner. Patricia looked wonderful and seemed happy for me, though I could not help but feel that, at some level, she must be wondering why it was not her own son's wedding she was attending—and I couldn't blame her.

Eighteen months later, when the final American POW was repatriated by North Vietnam, Patricia's last hope of ever again seeing her son flickered out, along with what emotional balance she still possessed. Over the ensuing years I would receive sad reports from mutual friends about her declining psychological condition. In late 2004, I had located Tom's sister Claudia, but could not bring myself to contact her because of my continuing survivor's guilt and an aversion to causing her further pain.

In February 2005, I finally made the call and learned that my anxiety had been unwarranted. Claudia was friendly and responsive to my questions, recounting the tragic story of the family's disintegration after Tom's loss and of Patricia's eventual death in 2001 at the age of seventy-nine. "Mom really never was the same again after that," Claudia said, "and as hard as I tried, I just couldn't ease her loss or pain. Unfortunately, she never would reach out for help and accept the fact that she was not the only one who had lost a son." In a real sense, Claudia not only lost a brother in 1968, but also a mother, when Patricia psychologically checked out of the relationship with her daughter, leaving the girl emotionally orphaned at the insecure age of fifteen. She had become one of a generation that author Michael Herr spoke of when he wrote, "Vietnam was what we had instead of happy childhoods."[211]

Claudia and my sister Sue had attended the same parochial high school for girls in Oakland and, during the time Tom and I were in Vietnam, were among just a handful of students whose brothers were at war. In the midst of an increasingly strident antiwar environment, which sometimes made them feel like "outsiders," they gravitated toward one another. Claudia later married Bill Harris, a former Marine who served in South Vietnam in 1966-1967 as an artilleryman at firebases along Highway 9. Sue was the maid of honor. Together, Bill and Claudia worked through problems the war had dealt them, and would have a son Nicholas.

When I told Claudia that my book was coming out soon and Tom was a big part of it, she candidly, but without rancor, explained that, even after forty years, she still resented her brother for being the catalyst for all this misery. I was once again staggered at the appalling residual effects of that war. When our phone conversation ended that evening, I believed it was the last time we would ever speak to one another. Nevertheless, I sent her a copy of *A Patch of Ground*.

Two weeks later I received a letter from Claudia saying how much the story meant to her and how, after becoming a parent herself, she better understood what it would be like to lose a child and the enormity of her mother's pain. "Precious life does go on," she wrote, "and it is so great to have you back in my life. Thanks to you for closing one door and opening another."[212]

Her eloquence and sincerity touched me deeply and I was pleased that the book was able, in some small way, to help heal such a deeply personal wound. No event since leaving the war has helped diminish my survivor's guilt more than Claudia's acceptance of me and the tacit forgiveness I felt.

23
AN EASY SHOT

DESPITE JPAC HAVING CONCLUDED in 2004 that further investigation into Tom Mahoney's loss should end because "there is no way to find the remains," they reopened the case in January 2007, sending a research team to Khe Sanh. They met at the interpretive center with "Mr. Cap and Mr. Ke," two long-time residents of Lang Ruon hamlet located down a steep slope on the north side of Hill 881 South, about five hundred meters from where Tom was last seen.

Mr. Cap told them that no villagers lived in the area during the fighting, and, after their return to Ruon in the early 1970s, he'd heard nothing about the discovery of remains or the personal effects of an American soldier. Mr. Ke added that they rarely went up the hill, now called "Ku Vo" by the locals,[213] except to collect metal to sell, and knew nothing of an American body left behind there. "Many buffaloes died," Ke explained, "and when people went to collect metal, they saw bones, but they were unsure what kind of bones they were."[214]

After visiting with these two elders, JPAC investigators again focused on locating the five men listed as Tom's ambushers in the *History of 246th Regiment*. This time they looked in places that these men lived before the war, rather than around Khe Sanh where they had conducted a pointless search in August 2004. They first met with Nguyen Duc Binh, a sixty-nine-year old retired lieutenant colonel, who, in July 1968, was deputy commander of the Tenth Company in the assault on Hill 689. He recalled that, in conjunction with that attack, the Ninth Company had been ordered to attack Hill 881 South "until liberated." Binh said he had not heard about a team killing an American on that hill and using the corpse to stage an ambush. However, he provided the researchers with several names of those who might know, among them were Le Duy Thuong and Nguyen Tien Thanh.

The investigators next visited Le Duy Thuong, a retired army major who had participated in the assault on Hill 689. A few days after that fighting, Le said, he met Nguyen Tien Thanh who told him he'd been part of a scout team that "killed one American soldier on Hill 845B [what the NVA called the western sector of Hill 881 South]" and later used the body as bait to ambush others. The investigators then went to Phuc Yen town near Hanoi to meet Nguyen Tien Thanh.

Thanh had been born there in 1946 and, after completing high school, began working in the construction trades. He joined the army in December 1967 and trained for eight weeks near Hanoi as a basic rifleman. On his trek south along the Ho Chi Minh Trail through Laos, Thanh was reassigned to the Ninth Company. He arrived in the Khe Sanh area in late March and recalled seeing the Lang Vei Special Forces camp, which had fallen just a month before, and Khe Sanh Combat Base, but from a distance, "because there were too many Americans around" to safely get a closer look.

Thanh's first taste of combat was on May 4, a month after the siege officially ended, probably at LZ Peanuts, adjacent to Hill 689, where they wiped out a U.S. Army artillery battery and the security force guarding it. He then fought a few miles to the southeast at "Highpoint 570" on June 7, corresponding to the horrific fighting at LZ Loon where forty-one Marines and corpsmen were killed along with at least one hundred fifty-four of Thanh's comrades. His company was then held in reserve until deployed on July 5 to encircle the Marines on Hill 881 South "to prevent them from supporting the U.S. forces engaged on Hill 689."[215] While the rest of the company lined up about two hundred meters behind, Thanh and four others approached the high point "to scout out the target status," concealing themselves in individual foxholes about thirty meters from the western entrance to the hill's fortification.

The next afternoon they saw a lone American outside the fortification. Their squad leader, Nguyen Van Luong, silently signaled the others to observe fire discipline, and a few moments later, Thanh said, "Mr. Luong shot him. The wounded soldier cried for help but that soon ceased." Knowing that his fellow Marines would soon try to retrieve him, Luong and Thanh ran out and grabbed Tom by the arms, pulling his body closer to their holes. The American, Thanh said, was already dead when they reached him, "a young, male Caucasian, tall and with a large build." They did not, he added, remove any items from the body.

The Americans began a recovery effort within ten to fifteen minutes, Thanh said, with his scout team fighting off "successive waves of U.S. troops" until approximately 8:00 p.m. when U.S. forces were helilifted off the hill. The rest of Thanh's platoon now moved up to occupy the deserted U.S. positions, leaving the next day to join in the fighting on Hill 689.

The JPAC investigators reported that Thanh did not see the American's body again, or learn anything later about the disposition of the remains, adding that Thanh expressed a willingness to assist in locating the remains, but was understandably concerned that he would not be able to find the precise location on the hill after such a long time. His concern was justified.

In addition to the usual reasons obscuring the clear retention of such details, including the passage of time, psychological and emotional stress and a natural proclivity among many war veterans to embellish, consciously or not, the difficulty and danger they faced; the Khe Sanh battleground presented unique problems. Fighting there was almost a daily occurrence and NVA units moved constantly and rapidly from one location to another on foot, often at night, in dense undergrowth through maddening geography where each parallel, rolling ridgeline looked much the same as the others, and then were left with little time to sleep. It was a rare individual, working under such conditions, who decades later could maintain a lucid recollection of where he or she was at any given time—or even what day it was.

Thanh was no exception. He was subsequently interviewed by JPAC on several occasions and his recollections changed often, a frustrating situation for me and those investigators, since he was the only known living eyewitness to Tom's death. For example, despite saying in February 2007 that Tom's body was intact when he left the hill, in a later interview Thanh said that U.S. aircraft "destroyed the battlefield" and that "the American soldier... was completely destroyed by the bombing and strafing."[216] During yet another interview with a JPAC researcher on July 21, 2008, Thanh changed back to his earlier account that he did not see the body again after moving up the hill and so did not know its eventual disposition.

I needed to clarify these issues and so, after locating Thanh in 2012, was able to remotely interview him with the help of my friend Gary Foster. Gary had not served in the military during the war, but traveled extensively throughout Vietnam over the years. His first trip there, at the age of twenty-three, was in 1972-1973, just two years before the South Vietnamese government fell to the communists. Later, a long-time employee of an international engineering service provider, whose professional assignments have taken him to scores of countries, Gary supervised the construction of modern Highway 9 through the Khe Sanh area beginning in 2000. There he became interested in the history of the place and joined the Khe Sanh Veterans Association as an associate member, where I met him at an Association function.[217]

Assisting Gary in these interviews was his old friend, Hoang Tran Dung, a native of Hanoi and former NVA soldier who had fought against the Americans late in the war, well after Khe Sanh was abandoned. Hoang was genuinely interested and very helpful; however, he is not a professional translator and so Gary sought the assistance of another acquaintance in Vietnam, Mike Najim, whose impeccable Vietnamese and professional interviewing skills made him perfect for the task. Mike had been raised in Florida and served in the U.S. Air Force from 1978 until his retirement in 2005. While in the service, he attended Vietnamese language school and began working for JTFFA, later JPAC, first going to Vietnam in 1992.

Armed with a list of questions I'd prepared, the three men visited Thanh's home where he welcomed them cheerfully, preparing glasses of hot chocolate and then pouring green tea into tiny cups after washing them ceremonially in the Vietnamese tradition. Thanh told Mike that on the afternoon of July 6, 1968, while they all aimed their rifles at Tom Mahoney, squad leader Luong took the shot hitting him twice in the heart.

Thanh explained that the AK-47 assault rifle was prone to jamming if the time of trigger depression is not long enough to allow the rounds to cycle through the chamber and the casings expelled. Luong, he said, was an expert at this "*Diem Xa*" technique, in which two bullets are fired in rapid succession with just the right amount of time on the trigger. "The American was only about ten meters away," Thanh said. "It was an easy shot for Luong."

Thanh then told Mike that he *alone* pulled the body downhill closer to his team's spider holes, first attempting to drag the corpse by the feet, but when that proved to be too difficult, pulled it along by the wrists. This version is not only different than the description in the *History of the 246th Regiment*, in which Luong and another team member, Tran Ngoc Long, moved the body, but also at odds with Thanh's earlier statements to JPAC that he and Luong moved it together. The scout team, Thanh said, then waited for the other Americans to come, opening up on them with rifle fire and hand grenades as they approached. The firefight lasted several hours, during which one of their members was killed and two others were wounded, though the U.S. bombers missed all their foxholes.

After the Americans withdrew, his team intended to stay there throughout the night, but was ordered away about an hour later "because the Americans had begun to bomb and shell the area." Thanh claimed he never saw Tom's body again and never returned to the positions they occupied during that firefight. I asked Mike to specifically inquire if the body was badly damaged by bombs, or was in "two parts" as a Marine helicopter pilot speculated in the Dorow report.

Thanh replied emphatically that the body was intact when he left the scene of the fight. Upon leaving the hill that evening, Thanh and his unit traveled about two hours before resting, and the next day joined in "the liberation of Hill 689." Following that battle, the NVA reclaimed recently abandoned Hill 861 which, along with Hill 881 South, had been captured from them by Marines during the bloody Hill Fights fourteen months earlier.

On August 2, both Thanh and Luong participated in an unsuccessful attempt to capture Hill 950. There, Thanh was badly wounded in the lower back by artillery shrapnel, requiring months of treatment in a subterranean hospital near Dong Ha. Once recovered, he remained with a unit in that general area. Thanh never saw Luong again after the fighting on Hill 950, but later heard he had been promoted to a regular army rank of "Senior Captain" and received special training as a sapper in a special forces unit. Thanh did not know when Luong left the army, or what he did afterward, but had heard at a recent reunion of the 246th Regiment that he died of lung cancer in 2009. I was disappointed to hear this because I'd hoped to record Luong's recollections as well.

Throughout 2006-2007 Doc Topmiller had used his network of contacts in Vietnam to try and locate Luong, who we believed was still alive at the time of our visit to Hanoi, and which I now learned he had been. This news raised the possibility that the mysterious, uniformed NVA soldier who had accompanied us up Hill 881 South in December 2007, and who smoked cigarettes continuously throughout the day, might have been Luong. However, when Gary and Mike showed Thanh photos of the soldier that I'd sent for the purpose of identification, Thanh said the man looked familiar, though he could not recall his name. He was perhaps another member of the team that ambushed the American, Thanh said, but "it was definitely not Luong."

Because Thanh was a practicing Catholic, his career in the military had not been easy. After the French defeat in 1954, the new Democratic Republic of Vietnam in the north regarded the Church as a reactionary force opposed to social progress and its members as enemies of the state. By contrast, in the south's Republic of Vietnam, Catholic influence expanded under the presidency of Ngo Dinh Diem, who promoted the religion to his western allies as a defense against the further spread of atheistic Marxism. Diem had lived for three years in a Catholic seminary in New Jersey just prior to assuming the presidency and his later discriminatory policies against non-Catholics, particularly Buddhists and Montagnard animists, would lead to national unrest and his eventual assassination in 1963.

In 1955, while tens of thousands of Viet Minh sympathizers were migrating from the south to the north under terms of the French surrender, approximately 600,000 northerners, mostly Catholics, were moving to the south. Thanh and his brother tried to leave that year, but made it only as far as Haiphong after which they returned home. During the ensuing years, Thanh, like many other young people in the north, did not have a strong desire to risk his life for those living in the south. But when the U.S. began bombing North Vietnam in March 1965, directly endangering Thanh's family, he joined the army along with tens of thousands of now highly motivated volunteers.

Once in the military, Thanh found himself discriminated against, deprived of promotion and harassed by political officers and fellow soldiers because of his religious beliefs and so took greater risks than others to prove his trustworthiness and competence. He eventually received five commendations, called *"Dung Si Diet My,"* translated by Mike Najim as, "Courageous One Who Killed Americans." Mike had interviewed hundreds of NVA veterans over the years and so was familiar with this type of commendation, which came in three levels of significance. Level 1, indicated the soldier killed three Americans, level 2 was earned by killing five, and level 3 at least seven. Thanh's commendations indicated he killed at least twenty-five Americans during the war. When Mike asked about this, Thanh agreed it was a reasonable figure.

What Thanh showed his visitors next astounded them. It was a framed photograph of him and six others in April 1969 being awarded their *Dung Si Diet My* medals by President Ho Chi Minh and Defense Minister General Vo Nguyen Giap—a young, beaming Thanh standing just behind Ho. Because of their accomplishments on the battlefield, the men were selected to attend special military training in the Soviet Union; however, as a Catholic, Thanh was not permitted to go. Despite this handicap to advancement early in his military career, Thanh's reputation for bravery allowed him to rise to the rank of major. He was discharged from active duty in 1976 and returned to the construction business where, over the years, he attained a relatively high standard of living for himself and his family.

Ironically, had Thanh's attempt to move to South Vietnam in 1955 been successful, he would likely have ended up fighting on the losing side. If he survived the war, he may have spent years in a reeducation camp and lived out the remainder of his life in abject poverty.

Gary, Mike and Hoang made their final visit to Thanh's home on January 21, 2014, forty-six years, to the day, from the beginning of the siege of Khe Sanh. After they had finished with the follow-up questions I'd prepared, Gary put his cell phone on speaker mode so I could talk directly to Thanh, via Mike's translation. I thanked him for trying to help us locate Tom's remains and said I hoped it was not a source of painful memories he would have rather forgotten. Thanh replied that it was quite the contrary, he felt it was important to discuss the war and pass those painful lessons on to our children. He then said: "Thank you for keeping your friend's memory alive." Though surprised by his comment, and touched by his sincerity, I was not feeling any particular kinship with this man who had directly participated in the killing of my friend. Nor was I feeling any hostility toward him. After a lifetime of beating myself up over Tom's death, I was feeling the best thing possible at that moment—nothing.

24
I'M THE GUY YOU'VE BEEN LOOKING FOR

ONE IMPORTANT QUESTION remained unanswered. If, as Lieutenant Dorow told Captain Black in the summer of 1968, a Marine recon team had gone to Hill 881 South and found Tom's body, where was it? In 2007, I emailed Michael Carlantonio, Tom's case officer at the U.S. Defense Department's Defense POW/MIA Personnel Office (DPMO) to ask if that issue was being explored. He replied that it had been, but with no success. "There are no military mortuary records to that effect or any information in USMC records," Michael said, adding that under normal conditions the remains of KIAs would have been brought back to the graves registration unit at Khe Sanh Combat Base and then moved to the military mortuary in Da Nang. But, because the combat base had just closed, "the chain of custody became muddled."[218]

Chaos at Khe Sanh during those last few weeks frequently caused such breakdowns in that process, as in the case of another Bravo Marine, Lance Corporal Charles Gatewood. During the 1968 Memorial Day fighting at Chop Non Hill, in which Bravo sustained over forty casualties, Gatewood, a friendly, eighteen-year-old, African-American from Chicago, was treated by a corpsman for a gunshot wound and, because he was ambulatory and did not appear to be in much pain, was directed to walk back down the hill where a landing zone had been established to medevac the wounded. Two Marines moving up the hill later stated they had seen Gatewood pass them[219] and the next day he was recorded in the unit diary as having been evacuated out to a medical facility.

Nearly three months later, on August 25, the commanding officer of the First Battalion received a message from Gatewood's family saying they had not heard from him since a letter dated May 24. First Lieutenant Stuart Dorow, who had investigated Tom Mahoney's loss just a month before, reviewed Gatewood's case and concluded that the delay in learning of his disappearance was the result of several problems. Both his platoon sergeant and squad leader had been killed in the fighting, thus eliminating his immediate supervisors. Continuity was further disrupted when Captain Black turned over command of Bravo Company a few weeks later and left Vietnam. Dorow added in his report that "a forward command" like Bravo, even in the best of circumstances, routinely lost contact with a medevaced Marine until the Division located him, or the medical facility where he was being treated sent information directly back to the evacuee's command. As such, it was normal for more than a month to elapse before a casualty would show up on a hospital admittance or transfer report, and "it was not considered an unusual time element" to wait until August 26 to request a follow up with Division headquarters on his whereabouts.[220] However, this remark seems a bit evasive, since Gatewood had been not been missing for "a month," but *three months*, still unnoticed.

Dorow did not go so far as to admit Gatewood was left behind, although he did change his official status to "Missing-in-Action." Steve Busby, who removed many of Second Platoon's dead from the hill that day, recalled that he and another Marine "carried out Mr. Gatewood and put his remains on a tank like the rest." A week later, when Steve learned that some of the dead bodies he had carried were still listed as MIA on the unit roster, he took it upon himself to write a memo to the battalion staff to help correct that status.[221] He never heard back from them.

If Gatewood died while walking back down the hill that day, was found by Busby and driven back to Khe Sanh base on a tank for transfer to a military mortuary, where was his body? It seemed reasonable to me that the body was either lost in transit, or misidentified by morgue staff and sent home as someone else. If so, could this have been what happened to Tom's body after allegedly being found by a recon team just a few weeks after Gatewood's disappearance?

Michael Carlantonio assured me that investigators at JPAC would continue to pursue the possibility that Tom's remains may have been recovered as claimed.[222] I then sent him all the information I'd received from Frank and Captain Black about the alleged recovery, including Frank's recollection that Dorow was "an exacting guy... almost to the point of compulsiveness."[223] Black added that Lieutenant Dorow ran things efficiently and had an especially tight handle on the paperwork. He inferred from Dorow's comments to him about Tom that he had been personally visited by a member of the recon unit that found the body. "Dorow didn't show me a memorandum or other written communication on it," Black later said, "but I had no reason to doubt what he told me. He would not have said something like that just to make me feel good, but only if it happened in fact."[224]

Captain Black immediately passed Dorow's information back to the men of Bravo Company who found some consolation in knowing that Tom's family would have something to bury. The Marine Corps, unaware that the body never made it home, was now officially satisfied that no further action was necessary. "That was the last I heard of the matter until thirty-six years later," Black said, "when Frank Ahearn informed me Mahoney still appeared on MIA lists."

Black agreed with Michael Carlantonio's remarks about the confusion at Khe Sanh, saying that information did not always get into the official unit records during such chaotic periods. In his own personal research of these records years later, Black found significant gaps for periods covering both the fighting at Hué in February and the abandonment of the hills around Khe Sanh in July.

He offered several possible scenarios, saying it was probably "ninety percent certain" that, despite the promise the operations officer Captain McHenry had obtained before Bravo ultimately left Hill 881 South that night, the First Marine Regiment would not have ordered a recovery mission to the hill, since they had returned to the Phu Bai area and were then under a different parent unit. He guessed the mission was ordered by either Colonel Barrow of the Ninth Marines, who had given Black the expletive-laced order to stop the rescue effort, or by the Third Marine Division upon receiving Dorow's report in late July.

Given these possibilities, Black deduced that the recovery effort would have taken place as early as July 12, the day the Marines finally abandoned nearby Hill 689, or as late as August 7, the last time Captain Black could have spoken with Dorow before leaving Vietnam. If the body was retrieved and properly handled, the military morgue where it was taken would have sent an official message to the First Battalion, First Marines regarding the disposition. If so, Black said, it then would have generated a "delayed and corrected" entry in the unit diary for Bravo Company. However, because Tom had already been dropped from Bravo's roll as a result of Dorow's July 27 finding of "KIA/BNR," as opposed to remaining on it as MIA, it may not have been entered in the diary.

When Captain Black left Hill 689, Lieutenant Edward "Bo" Stollenwerck replaced him as the company commander. The twenty-six-year-old Stollenwerck joined the Marine Corps after graduating from Mississippi State University and had been a platoon commander in Bravo since October 1967. I contacted Stollenwerck by telephone in April 2014, but he had no recollection of making or seeing a late unit diary entry about Tom Mahoney. Such a later recovery of his remains, he assured me, was something he would have remembered because he'd been on Hill 881 South the day Tom was killed would never forget the repeated efforts to reach the body.

He, however, was not surprised now to learn a recon team had gone there, because, he said, "the general understanding was that at some time, not specified, a recovery team would be sent to get his body." I asked his opinion of why, if the recon story was true, he did not know about it as commander of Bravo during that period. Stollenwerck suggested that Lieutenant Dorow may have told Captain Black verbally about the recovery while the two were at the battalion headquarters and the information never made it into the unit diary, or back to him in the field. Such records Stollenwerck said, were "notoriously incomplete," as he had learned when researching other matters related to his time at Khe Sanh, and he was convinced "many things occurred that were not reported at all or remained unclear."[225]

I was coming to the same conclusion on my own. Through the online Vietnam Project at Texas Tech University, I had checked microfilm records of command chronologies and after-action reports for the period in question, but found nothing about the recovery. On the chance that some of the records were still in paper form, I sought the help of the staff at the National Archives and Records Administration in College Park, Maryland, but they found no mention of it. The USMC Historical Branch researched all records they had relating to this, including "The Robert Barrow Papers," documents pertaining to the career of the Commandant, but found no mention of an order or a mission to recover American remains on Hill 881 South.

Captain Black suggested I contact Wendell "Hawk" Harkins in Cleveland, Georgia who he considered highly reliable. Harkins was the battalion administrative clerk at the time and so would have been familiar with all that went on within that unit. I contacted Wendell by phone and he had a clear recollection of a conversation with Lieutenant Dorow "in late July" who told him a "Black Knight chopper" recovered Tom's remains. Harkins was sure of the helicopter's call sign "because a Black Knight chopper had assisted us earlier in retrieving another Marine body."[226]

The only chopper unit calling themselves the Black Knights was the U.S. Army's Third Squadron, Fifth Cavalry, and I was excited to learn from their command chronology that elements of the unit were under the operational control of the Third Marine Division in Dong Ha during July 1968. Command reports on microfilm did not show a recovery being made on Hill 881 South during that time. I subsequently hired a professional military researcher to check the Third Squadron's daily unit diaries, which were still only in paper format, at the National Archives. That examination resulted in no mention of a mission to the area of Hill 881 South ordered by the Third Marine Division, or by way of a more impromptu request from the field. I then searched the July and August 1968 command chronologies of all battalion and force reconnaissance units in Vietnam at the time, but found no mention of a team being inserted on, or near, Hill 881 South, or the discovery of an American body.

If a recon team had not recovered the body, where did Lieutenant Dorow get that information? I was sure he could help resolve this issue and attempted to locate him, learning he had become a highly regarded physician in the state of Oklahoma, much admired for his civic and church work. Tragically, he had died of a brain tumor six years before, at the age of fifty-nine.

I now had nowhere else to turn in my search for answers.

❧ ❧

In April 2010, I received a message from Aloalo Maumausolo asking that I call him at his home in San Diego. I did not know him, but returned his call immediately and what he was about to say astounded me.

Aloalo had been born and raised in Hawaii and by his senior year of high school was an outstanding football player. After receiving a scholarship to Utah State University, a knee injury ended his athletic career and he returned to the islands where, still muscular and motivated, he enlisted in the Marines. He was subsequently selected for specialized training in parachuting, SCUBA and underwater demolition and upon arriving in South Vietnam, was assigned to Delta Company, Third Reconnaissance Battalion. Aloalo and I engaged in a bit more initial small talk before he paused for several seconds and then said, "I'm the guy you've been looking for." Chills ran up my spine and I was momentarily left speechless. After another few moments of silence he continued: "I found your friend."

In late-July or early-August 1968, Aloalo said, his six-man recon team was sent to establish a clandestine radio relay site on Hill 881 South. Just after dusk, as they approached the hill by helicopter, the pilot refused to land due to tricky winds and the potential for enemy ground fire, so the Marines rappelled down a rope line. Aloalo went first, and, as he was about to step on to ground, his foot landed awkwardly on something, knocking him off balance. He ended up on the ground in a sitting position with both feet now propped up on the object that had tripped him—a human body. "It was a good thing I had my rifle slung over my shoulder," Aloalo said, because, in the dim evening light he didn't know if the frightening shape he was now staring at was dead or alive and might have opened fire on it.

Corporal John J. Loughlin, the team leader, was soon at Aloalo's side and both men began examining the body, finding it to be intact "head-to-toe" and about six feet in length. The corpse, he said, appeared to have "a large burn" in the chest area (where Tom had been shot twice at close range). The rest of the skin was beginning to loosen and peel from decay, but, Aloalo added, "I'm sure it was a white guy." There was no clothing on the upper body, but some fragments of trousers beneath and no dog tags or other identifying information. After recovering from their initial shock, the men found the odor of death intolerable and, because they would be in the vicinity for several days, decided to bury the corpse. Aloalo recalled how he and Loughlin folded the body at the waist into a nearby spider hole and began chipping at the edges with their KA-bar knives to loosen enough dirt to cover the remains.

When the team left the hill and returned to their headquarters six days later, Aloalo assumed that team leader Loughlin reported the incident during debriefing. If he did, that information was either not recorded in the daily unit record or subsequently lost, and I have been unable to reach Mr. Loughlin to verify this. Aloalo's story was similar to what Dorow told Black and Harkins in the summer of 1968, that a recon team had gone to Hill 881 South, found Tom's body and "disposed of it." The vagueness of that term, I now realized, might be the reason there is no military mortuary record—the body never left the hill.

Aloalo had completely forgotten that ghastly discovery until decades later when, in the summer of 2006, he and his family were vacationing at the Grand Canyon and preparing to take a helicopter tour. Just as the chopper lifted off, he suddenly had a vision of that night on the hill and demanded the helicopter land at once. On the ground, he told his family: "I buried a guy in Vietnam. An American."

Suddenly all the macabre details came flooding back. His daughter, Trish Malimali, soon began browsing the recon company's website on her dad's behalf and found a message from Army Sergeant Ray Kern of JPAC asking if any former members knew about a Marine helicopter that was shot down near Hill 881 South in the summer of 1968. Eight bodies had been recovered at the time, but the copilot remained stuck in the burning wreckage and left behind. Aloalo phoned Kern and told him that, while he did not see any helicopter wreckage, he once found an American's body in that same vicinity and buried it. Kern continued to question him in great detail for over an hour.

The JPAC staff analyzed his answers, and soon Kern called to tell Aloalo that the only other body they were still looking for in that area was Tom Mahoney's, and the evidence strongly suggested it was the one he had buried. A representative subsequently mentioned my name to Aloalo as having been a friend of Tom's who had already gone to the hill in search of his remains. Trish began searching for me, which resulted in Aloalo contacting me in April 2010.

After speaking with Aloalo, I checked the records of Delta Company, Third Reconnaissance Battalion and saw that both he and Loughlin were listed as members of that unit in 1968. However, the unit records for July and August showed no mission to any hills west of Khe Sanh. I was not surprised by this because, in my long search for Tom, I had found that information from reliable human sources, often lacked support in military unit records. The JPAC also found Aloalo's statements credible and flew him to Vietnam to help locate the burial site. On May 30, 2010, their survey team arrived on top of Hill 881 South in four all-terrain vehicles.[227] Coincidently, or by design, the vehicles stopped at what was formerly the Marine's western sector,[228] within just a few meters of where Tom's body was last seen.[229] However, from there Aloalo led them on foot to a location on the former main position, roughly five hundred meters to the east.

The JPAC team was headed by forty-eight-year-old Army Staff Sergeant David White, a six-year veteran of JPAC field investigations. Among the documents White brought with him that day was the black-and-white high school graduation photo of Tom that I'd supplied them a few years before. Others in the group included an explosive ordnance disposal technician, an Army Special Forces medic and an Air Force photographer. Joining these Americans was a liaison team from the Vietnam Office for Seeking Missing Persons.

Aloalo soon identified a forty meter by fifteen-meter area, containing several still-visible spider holes, as the vicinity in which he had buried the body. *Agence France-Presse* news reporter Ian Timberlake watched as the team chopped through the grass before the explosives technician swept the holes with a metal detector. The detector whined like a baby, Timberlake later wrote, "signaling dirt-encrusted pieces of barbed wire and other war debris, but nothing that confirms precisely where the missing marine's remains lie."[230]

Traveling with them that day was Lee Huu Hanh, a sixty-four-year-old former NVA combat surgical nurse with the Ninth Company, 246th Regiment. Hanh then guided the investigators to an area about sixty meters downhill from the site Aloalo identified, where he claimed to have buried an American corpse in late July 1968.[231]

White had interviewed Hanh the night before and was told that on July 4, 1968, Hanh's company was preparing to attack the Marines on Hill 881 South when they shot and killed a lone American approaching their position. Hanh claimed that he "and two other soldiers" dragged the body far downhill to lure rescuers into an ambush. The following day, Hanh's company commander ordered him and two other soldiers, both of whom Hanh said were later killed in battle, to bury the body for sanitary reasons.

Hanh described the American as young, "approximately 18 years of age, handsome, and of large build," fully clad in a green uniform and combat boots. The dead man was not wearing a wristwatch, and Hanh did not check for items in his pockets. He did, however, remove "ID tags" from the body and gave them to his company commander who examined them briefly "then cast them down the hill."[232] They buried the body "approximately forty centimeters [about sixteen inches] deep" in an existing bomb crater on relatively flat ground about fifty meters from the easternmost high point of Hill 881 South.

Hanh's description of these events to Staff Sergeant White was considerably different than what he told JPAC investigators a year before, in January 2009, when they first spoke with him. During that interview, Hanh stated that sometime in the early summer of 1968 his unit shot and killed an American soldier halfway up the slope of Hill 881 South, then tied the body with rope and dragged it down to the foot of the hill as bait for an ambush. Hanh's unit withdrew the next day, but returned approximately fifteen days later to "re-station" the hill. At that time, Hanh said, he saw the body where they had left it. To his knowledge, no one ever buried it.

Nguyen Tien Thanh, who, as described earlier was interviewed for me by Mike Najim in 2013-2014, gave a statement to JPAC in 2008 saying Hanh had told him yet another variation of the story at a veterans gathering many years before. In that version, Hanh said that at some point after Tom's death in July 1968, his body, and that of a second American killed in the subsequent recovery effort, were dragged several hundred meters from the site of the fighting down to the bank of a stream and left there unburied.

This account is especially suspect because no American was killed in the effort to recover Tom's body and the nearest "stream" was over five hundred meters north, near the village of Lang Ruon, down an impossibly steep slope. While some of these discrepancies might be explained as having been corrupted by the passage of years or mistranslation, Hanh's stories seem to evolve over time to where he assumes the roles of Nguyen Van Luong and Nguyen Tien Thanh. Hanh's name does not appear in the unit history, or as being one of the five members of the scout team who shot Tom, and Nguyen Tien Thanh told JPAC that Hanh was not with his team the day Tom was killed.

Sergeant White did not seem to have been aware of Hanh's gross inconsistencies and so tried to reconcile the differences in the locations identified by Hanh and Aloalo. "If this is the same body Mr. Hanh buried," White wrote, "it is hard to explain how it was moved sixty meters up a slope and back to the surface"[233]

Hanh's credibility aside, a more glaring problem was not how the body Aloalo found had resurfaced and moved uphill after Hanh buried it, but how it moved over a quarter of a mile east, from where the Marines and NVA fought over it that afternoon! Despite these discrepancies, White told news reporter Timberlake that he believed there was enough evidence to recommend an excavation in the area indicated by Aloalo, with Hanh's site as a secondary, if needed.

To further complicate the issue, another missing Marine was last seen almost precisely where Aloalo indicated he had buried Tom. On April 30, 1967, during the Hill Fights to take 881 South from the NVA, and over a year before Tom's death, Private First Class Randy McPhee, a twenty-year old from Long Beach, California, was struck by shrapnel from several grenades. He was alive and curled up in the dense grass when last seen by a fellow Marine, who asked: "Randy, are you OK?" McPhee looked up at him and simply smiled.[234]

McPhee's body was probably destroyed during the massive American artillery and air pounding of that hilltop over the following two days and nights. Thirty-seven sets of pulverized human remains were found in the days following the bombardment, all believed to be American, but none could be identified as belonging to McPhee. Because he had died so many months before Aloalo and Loughlin's discovery in the summer of 1968, the JPAC report concluded it could not have been Randy McPhee because "the body would not still be intact as Mr. Maumausolo described."[235]

I was disappointed upon learning where Aloalo believed he had buried Tom, because I knew he had died over five hundred meters to the west of that spot and it did not seem logical that the NVA would employ at least two men to drag the body down one hill, across a saddle, and up another higher hill just to leave it on the open ground again for the recon team to discover a few weeks later. In addition, I had always wondered how Aloalo would be able to find the location of the grave, because his discovery of Tom's body and the burial had taken place in near-darkness, and he did not return to that area afterward.

Nevertheless, when I passed this information on to Captain Black, who was intimately familiar with the geographical layout of the place, he was unexpectedly elated, saying Aloalo's spot fit perfectly, except for its map coordinates, and that could be easily explained. Hill 881 South was actually an undulating east-west ridgeline containing several knolls of varying heights. The location Aloalo selected on the eastern knoll, Black said, was physically identical to where Tom was last seen on the western knoll, in that it was just below the crest and at the only other place along that ridgeline where the ground dropped off at the same sharp angle northwest into a valley.[236]

Aloalo's description of burying the body was also "highly plausible," Black said, because the recon team could not have brought the remains along with them while not yet having completed their mission. After returning to their company headquarters, they would have reported the finding during a routine debriefing. As the information was passed along through channels back to First Battalion, First Marines, it probably lacked detail. As such, Black concluded, "Stu [Dorow] probably told me, 'recon was up there. Found the body, buried it, and the Third Marine Division will go up there later to retrieve it.' And I came away from that brief conversation with 'recon found and retrieved it.'"

I agree with this analysis. Having spoken to Aloalo many times since our initial conversation, I'm convinced, as is Captain Black and JPAC, that he did bury the body of an American in the summer of 1968.

25
AN EVENING
LIKE NO OTHER

ON JANUARY 24, 2011, Allen Williams, Aloalo Maumausolo and I met with Tom's sister, Claudia at her home in Lake Forest, California. Much of Lake Forest is built over what had once been the El Toro Marine Corps Air Station, the place from which all our flights to Vietnam in 1967, including Tom's, had originated, giving our collective presence there the unmistakable feeling of a circle being completed—a journey's end.

Allen brought along his daughter Carrie Williams, and Aloalo his daughter Trish Malimali, which could not have been more fitting. Without the persistence of these two young women, searching for answers that might provide emotional healing for the fathers they so loved and admired, this gathering would not have happened. After Doc Topmiller's death in August 2008, I'd lost my motivation to pursue the search any further. Trish and Carrie, contacting me on behalf of their fathers just a few weeks apart in 2010, reignited my desire to see this quest through.

Claudia's genuine warmth and directness put us at ease within minutes of our arrival. Her devoted husband Bill, who had been a Marine in Vietnam, understandably worried that our presence might stir up too many emotionally painful memories for her, but was quickly supportive after seeing how moved she was by the remarkable nature of our meeting.

All phases of Tom's life and death were represented that night. Claudia and I had known him in his early years. Allen, a close friend in Vietnam, struggled mightily to recover him, and lived the rest of his life with undeserved guilt that he had let Tom down. Aloalo never knew Tom, but likely held the answer to what happened after his death. None of us knew what to expect, but soon experienced a sense of comfort and intimacy, despite being virtual strangers; a peculiar kinship of people who had encountered the unthinkable and endured. We had come that evening to learn more about Tom, the kind of person he was, and, perhaps, find relief from the sorrow and guilt, or in Aloalo's case, the unanticipated horror, that changed all our lives in that summer of 1968. It was as if we each held a piece of a puzzle and by working them around a bit, might bring this tragic story to an end.

I reflected on the notion that even if Tom's physical remains are never located, what I'd learned about human dignity and loyalty had already made this long personal journey worthwhile. To have found so many of those along the way, like Frank Ahearn and others in Bravo, as well as our former Vietnamese adversaries, whose humanity was strengthened rather than diminished by the horror and pain of war, seemed impossibly fanciful, and yet it was true. I now recognized that the world might be full of such extraordinarily compassionate people, heroically carrying heavy burdens of needless remorse. I thought of that June day in 1966 when I listened to Tom's high school graduating class sing *The Impossible Dream* with its starry-eyed stanza:

> *And I know if I'll only be true*
> *To this glorious quest*
> *That my heart will lie peaceful and calm*
> *When I'm laid to my rest.*

The following year, just nine days before Tom arrived in South Vietnam, Vice President Hubert H. Humphrey visited the U.S. Embassy in Saigon and, reinforcing such sappy sentimentalities, told the staff there that the war was "our great adventure and a wonderful one it is," and that American sacrifices in Vietnam would contribute "to the everlasting glory of this Nation."[237]

It reminded me of how bitter and angry I'd been in the years following Tom's death, blaming the institutions of our youth for filling our heads with such nonsense, then sending us off in a "quest" that was anything but "glorious." Before it was over, more than 210,000 young Americans had been wounded, died or gone missing and many others, like me, returned deep in the throes of what historian William Manchester once described as: "The supreme indifference of young men who have lost their youth and will never recover it."[238]

Yet, as I looked around the room that evening, a sense of Tom's presence, denied me years before at the two psychic gatherings in Vietnam, was now palpable and calming. I felt privileged to be in the company of such courageous and resilient individuals and to have known this lost young man who would, even decades later, remain so warmly remembered by his friends from the war for his fretful concern about their safety and a perpetual optimism which even the strain of combat was unable to steal from him until one July day when an ill-timed letter crushed his spirit. The room fell silent for a moment as we reflected on the ways Tom had so profoundly affected our lives and I allowed myself to slip into a callowness I'd not felt since before the war—before Khe Sanh. Now, home at last, I savored a tender bit of Irish verse:

For he gave all his heart and lost.[239]

EPILOGUE

In May 2010, a month after his return from Hill 881 South, Aloalo Maumausolo called to tell me JPAC had informed him that their investigation of the site had been "screwed up" and a new team was going back to do another survey. He was not given specifics about why they had to return, but was told his presence there again would not be necessary. I was relieved to hear this news because I had written JPAC a few months earlier expressing my hope they would not expend valuable time and resources searching a site that was over a quarter of a mile from where Tom fell. More than a year passed before I received a reply, a brief email message apologizing for their delay in responding and advising me that, despite my concern, they had approved Aloalo's site for future excavation.

I was not alone in my frustration. Donna Elliott, a former Army Reserve sergeant from Pleasant Grove, Arkansas, has been searching for the remains of her brother, Army Private First Class Jerry Elliott, who was last seen at the old French fort on January 21, 1968, as part of the ill-fated reinforcement effort to reach me and others during the desperate fighting in Khe Sanh village. Donna has done extensive research on Jerry's case and visited Vietnam numerous times.[240]

In 2003, locals at Khe Sanh led her to a grave not far from where her brother was last seen, claiming it held an American body that they'd inadvertently bulldozed up while quarrying roadway material, and quickly reburied. Because they believe the hills of Khe Sanh are haunted, the workers began burning incense sticks at the new grave each day to calm the American's restless spirit.

Donna reported this information to JPAC, but it would be another seven months before they excavated. After examining the remains at the Central Identification Laboratory, a JPAC representative told her it was, as she suspected, "a Caucasian," but would not confirm if it was Jerry or not. Donna had been present at the exhumation and saw a combat boot from the grave that was clearly not Jerry's foot size,[241] thus sparing her years of additional anxiety wondering if the remains were those of her brother. It was later determined through DNA comparison that it was not Jerry, and the identity remains a mystery.

Donna was also dismayed at what she considered JPAC's shoddy investigative methodology, which included a failure by them to interview the last American to see Jerry alive, and other incident survivors, until 2013. Their inability to locate his remains has, for Jerry's family, taken on grim urgency because the area where they stand the best chance of finding him is now completely covered with concrete as part of a memorial park and a seventy-foot-high war victory monument.

No country in history has committed more resources to finding its missing troops than the United States has done for those lost during the Vietnam War, and JPAC has many talented and dedicated researchers, military recovery specialists and field investigators who believe in the mission and perform their duty with skill and honor. However, dissatisfaction with the accounting command's management has been ongoing for decades and is well documented by federal oversight agencies.

As early as 1995, a Government Accounting Office review was highly critical of the JPAC leadership and methods. Two years later, the Chief of DPMO's Southeast Asia Archival Research Division produced a twelve-page internal memo chronicling the mishandling of cases and the inclination by some researchers to give greater credence to the often-unsubstantiated accounts of local Vietnamese, than to U.S. records and the first-hand recollections of American witnesses.[242] By 2010, Congress mandated that JPAC increase its successful recovery rate from an average of seventy a year to more than two hundred; but the number of recoveries did not change, and actually fell in subsequent years, despite JPAC's operating budget nearly doubling over the preceding decade.

Another internal memorandum, sent by a forensic anthropologist to the then-commander of JPAC in May 2011, outlined serious deficiencies occurring at the Central Identification Laboratory, including failure to update records on individual recovery efforts, the mishandling of remains, making determinations about sites when scientific data contradicted their conclusions, and management efforts to shield poor archaeological work from outside review.

Other complaints, included excavating incorrect sites and wasting funds on duplicative efforts due to shoddy methodology.[243] A Defense Department study of JPAC operations determined that, once a set of remains was recovered, it was taking the lab an average of eleven years to make an identification. In October 2013, an embarrassing scandal emerged when the Pentagon acknowledged that JPAC management, in an attempt to cover up their inadequacies, regularly staged elaborate, highly publicized, but phony "arrival ceremonies" with honor guards carrying empty, flag-draped coffins from military cargo planes to give the impression they were returning that day from old battlegrounds.[244]

Early in 2014, at the behest of Congress, the Secretary of Defense ordered the Pentagon to devise a plan to consolidate, under a single director, all entities involved in the search for MIA's and the remains of U.S. military dead. The mandate included finding ways to maximize the number of identifications, reduce duplicative functions and give more attention to cases that have been delayed or overlooked—providing new hope for Tom's family and friends.

In July of that year, a JPAC team returned to Hill 881 South and conducted a major excavation for Tom Mahoney's remains. Aloalo Maumausolo, and his daughter, Trish Malimali, were flown there courtesy of the U.S. government and watched for two days as archeologists dug at the sites he and Lee Huu Hanh had identified in the spring of 2010. Aloalo and Trish left the hill before the excavation was completed, but were told a few days later by a JPAC staff member that remains had been located at the site, and there was a strong possibility they were those of Tom Mahoney. [245]

I was astounded when Aloalo told me all this during a phone conversation on January 15, 2015. Though mystified at how Tom's body might have gotten so far from where he fell, I was delighted to be proven wrong in my calculations because it now seemed he was finally going to be repatriated after all these decades of searching. I waited each day thereafter for news that the Central Identification Laboratory in Honolulu had confirmed all this through DNA provided by Claudia.

Six weeks later I received an email message from Michael Carlantonio, Tom Mahoney's case officer. Michael was now part of the new Defense POW/MIA Accounting Agency (DPAA), which had officially replaced the DPMO just two months before. He advised me that JPAC had, as Aloalo Maumausolo told me in January, excavated the gravesites that he and Hanh identified. However, contrary to the optimistic news Aloalo had received earlier from someone at the Central Identification Laboratory, no remains had been found. "The graves," Michael said, "were empty." He then requested that I provide more information to help them further refine the location "and ensure we are digging on the correct hilltop."[246]

I was incredibly exasperated by this news because I'd been imploring JPAC for years to stop looking on the wrong hill and listen to those who had actually been there the afternoon Tom died. I reminded Michael of this and he advised me that he'd always felt the best evidence in the case indicated JPAC was at the wrong place, but that they had final decision-making authority with regards to field operations."[281] I immediately understood the implication of his words. After having read the Congressional investigation reports, I recognized that much of this inefficiency and dysfunction over the years had been due to a turf war between DPMO and JPAC, who shared many overlapping responsibilities.

A field team, Michael said, would be returning to the area twice in the summer of 2016. I quickly assembled and sent him all the information I had on the subject, including photos, maps, and diagrams, all of which I had previously supplied to JPAC in 2011. Their refusal to acknowledge this data had now cost four years and hundreds of thousands of dollars on a mission that was doomed to fail. I felt no sense of vindication, only a staggering disbelief that, as specialists in this profession, they could have missed something so obvious.

But I also couldn't avoid seeing an amusing facet to this. The Pentagon office of the Secretary of Defense, responsible for overseeing operations to locate missing American remains, is a thirty-minute drive from the National Museum of the Marine Corps, whose Vietnam War gallery features an exhibit of Hill 881 South. This unusual display allows visitors to pass down the back ramp of a CH-46 helicopter into a life-size diorama of the hill, accompanied by the realistic din of combat sounds and swirling, heated air to replicate the wash of rotor blades in that tropical climate. The first thing one sees see straight ahead as they disembark is a mural of a trail leading away from them, down a slight depression, and up to another hilltop in the distance. The summit there is a jumble of barbed wire, trenchlines and bunkers. On the far right side of that hill, just below the crest, and barely out of view, is the spot where Tom Mahoney was killed. From the museum's opening in 2006, until the time of JPAC's unsuccessful attempt to find Tom's remains in the summer of 2014 (digging at a location roughly equivalent to where the exhibit's helicopter is placed), nearly five million visitors have gazed out at the illustration of that distant hill. Among them must have been some Defense Department employees who had worked on Tom's case since the search began in 1994; yet no one had been able to figure out exactly where to look. Like some *Da Vinci Code* clue, it has been hiding in plain sight.

But here the story takes another improbable turn. In November 2015, the DPAA contacted the family of Army Staff Sergeant Billy D. Hill, in Poteet, Texas, to tell them they had recently identified Billy's remains through DNA comparison. Hill had been missing and was presumed dead along with Jerry Elliott at the old French fort after volunteering to risk their lives to come our relief in Khe Sanh village that day, and so this news was meaningful to me on a very personal level. Billy's ninety-one-year-old father, Billy Hugh Hill, was too ill to attend his son's funeral on December 18, 2015, but posed for a news photo, his arms around a meticulously folded American flag and a shadow box containing Billy's medals that he'd treasured for nearly five decades. Then, as if he had been waiting all those years until his son finally came home—the elder Hill died five days later. The DPAA representative told the family that, decades earlier, a bone collector from Quang Tri Province had been caught by authorities at an airport in Vietnam. His grisly contraband was turned over to U.S. officials in 1989 and soon became part of over one thousand sets of human remains backlogged and being warehoused by the JPAC in Honolulu.

For many decades, impoverished Vietnamese have believed, incorrectly, that U.S. MIA searchers pay for remains, and will even reward those finding a missing American by resettling them in the United States. Largely ignorant of human anatomy, they almost always bring in pig or cow bones; or those of unearthed Vietnamese, despite the latter remains being much smaller and with far less dental work than a typical American.

Unscrupulous bone traders perpetuate these rumors, motivating some to plunder cemeteries, and then present these remains, along with counterfeit supporting identification, such as dog tags and other U.S. military gear, in an attempt to deceive MIA specialists, and perhaps be rewarded. It is illegal in Vietnam to trade in human remains, and the government has made efforts to arrest those involved. A campaign of television and newspaper announcements, aimed at dispelling rumors that MIA searchers purchase remains, has had mixed results, especially among those living in economically distressed, rural areas of the country.

But the 1989 stash of confiscated bones is an astonishing exception to this pattern of fakery. Not only has it resulted in discovering Billy Hill, but also the identification earlier in 2015 of another American soldier, Army Sergeant First Class James Holt. Holt had been killed during fighting at the Lang Vei Special Forces camp just two weeks after, and three miles from where, Hill and Elliott were last seen. Sadly, there is no further information about how all these bones were collected, by whom, or where they were headed when confiscated at the airport; only that, in the late-1980s, several sets of American remains were known to have been provided to the U.S. government as part of Hanoi's overtures of reconciliation leading to the establishment of formal diplomatic relations in 1995.

Yet the DPAA did provide Donna Elliott with a tantalizing piece of information: More MIA's have been definitely associated with this cache of remains, though the names cannot yet be released. Could Tom Mahoney be among them? He fell less than four miles from Lang Vei, and five miles from the old French fort, and, as mentioned earlier, two village elders from Lang Ruon had told JPAC investigators in January 2007 that people had seen bones on Hill 881 South when they returned to the Khe Sanh area in the late 1970s, "but were unsure what kind of bones they were." Although it is a slim possibility, Tom's remains may already be at the Central Identification Laboratory in Honolulu.

❧ ☙

Over the last nine years, I have obtained information from interviews with Marines who knew Tom Mahoney, a North Vietnamese soldier who participated in the ambush that killed him, and JPAC's investigative reports. In addition, I have explored American and Vietnamese military records and other independent civilian historical research. In weighing these sources for consistency and credibility, the evidence strongly suggests to me that Tom's body was undamaged by bombs, left in the open by the NVA and buried within a few weeks by Aloalo Maumausolo and John Loughlin.

Having been to that sector of Hill 881 South in 2007, I believe that, if Tom's remains are not among those repatriated by Vietnamese authorities in 1989, there is a good chance they may still be at the location where he died, defined by map coordinates from American eyewitnesses and precise to within thirty feet. And, while there are several old bomb craters in that area of the hill, relatively few of them were created after the Marines abandoned Khe Sanh six days after Tom's death. If the NVA spider hole in which he was buried is no longer visible, a more likely offender would be the rudimentary dirt road shallowly scraped along that ridgeline, and so close to where Tom was last seen, it might actually cover the site. Until this new U.S. agency charged with locating and returning the remains of fallen Americans examines all pertinent facts in Tom Mahoney's case, it is my hope that this book may shake loose more information—perhaps even the final piece of the puzzle.

At times, the rational side of me is prepared to give up on this quest and hope that the precious resources of government instead be spent on cases with a better chance to locate another lost—but unforgotten—warrior, bringing relief to family and friends. But then I remember the words of Bruce Bird, who nearly died after volunteering to retrieve Mahoney, confirming how little the awfulness of war had changed my friend from our untroubled high school days in Oakland—and why I must continue:

"He was a nice, friendly kid who just wanted to be sure everyone was protected," Bruce said. "Tom would have done it for me."

THE END

ACKNOWLEDGEMENTS

I never cease to be astonished by the number of lives Tom Mahoney touched during his brief existence. Many of them have provided me with needed encouragement through periods when my willingness to continue faltered; at times despairing over the inability to locate an elusive clue, at other times frustrated by intractable bureaucracies or a Vietnamese mysticism I could not fathom. On occasion, I balked at drilling down too deeply into my own painful memories. In the end, however, this quest completely changed my perspective on the war and helped heal wounds in myself and others, wounds that were far deeper than I could have imagined them to be.

I am particularly indebted to three friends: Chaplain Ray W. Stubbe, Khe Sanh historian without whose lifetime of erudition and selflessness, the countless sacrifices made by young Americans during the struggle for Khe Sanh would never be known; author and journalist Gregg Jones, whose wise advice in helping make this narrative worthy of its unique subject matter cannot be overstated; and Gary Foster for all his assistance, particularly his tireless legwork in Vietnam without which this story would not be complete.

A special thanks to the staff at Hellgate Press, particularly publisher Harley Patrick, for the excellent and honest guidance he has provided me over the course of our long professional association. I also wish to thank the many helpful staff associates at the Marine Corps Historical Division, Marine Corps Historical Branch, National Archives and Records Administration at College Park, Maryland, Vietnam Center and Archive at Texas Tech University, Preston Library at the Virginia Military Institute and the Defense POW-MIA Accounting Agency, especially Michael Carlantonio and Hattie Johnson.

For all their help and inspiration over the years, I extend my heartfelt appreciation to my wife Becky, my children (Casey, Hilary and Colin), Frank Ahearn, Robert Black, Bruce Bird, Steve Busby, Caleb Cage, Kenneth Campbell, the Corporandy brothers (Tom, Bill and David), Dinh Van Toan, Tommy Eichler, Donna Elliott, Tom Esslinger, Ken and Amie Fernandes, Mike Fishbaugh, Kevin Gilmartin, Bob Ginther, Bob Guernsey, Joe Haggard, Wes and Donna Hammond, Wendell Harkins, Claudia and Bill Harris, Jim Hayden, George Herring, Hoang Tran Dung, Wayne Karlin, Jared Kelley, Kathleen (McCorry) Lopes, David Lownds, Mike Maier, Trish Malimali, Aloalo Maumausolo, Bruce Meyers, Mark Milburn, Minh Tan, Jack Mooseau, Mike Najim, Kerby Neill, Nguyen Buu Thuan, Nguyen Tien Thanh, Nguyen Thi Dieu Van, Tom Northrop, Rick Noyes, Raul Orozco, Steve Orr, John Pappageorge, Michael Reath, Gerry Rohlich, Robert Simpson, Seth Stamps, Kent Steen, Edward Stollenwerck, Walter Stone, Mark Swearengen, Sue Thomas, Terri Topmiller, Ernie Vaughn, Jim Velcheck, Carrie Williams, Allen V. Williams, Al Zehner and the wonderfully thoughtful faculty in the Department of History at Eastern Kentucky University.

BIBLIOGRAPHY

BOOKS

Michael Archer, *A Patch of Ground: Khe Sanh Remembered* (Hellgate Press, 2005)

Bao Ninh, *The Sorrow of War* (London: Secker & Warburg 1993)

Michael Beschloss, *Reaching for Glory: Lyndon Johnson's Secret White House Tapes, 1964-1965* (Simon & Schuster; Reprint edition 2002)

William Broyles Jr., *Brothers in Arms: A Journey from War to Peace* (New York: Alfred A. Knopf, 1986)

Lieutenant General Charles G. Cooper, U.S. Marine Corps (Retired) and Richard E. Goodspeed, *Cheers and Tears: A Marine's Story of Combat in Peace and War* (Trafford, 2002)

Robert Coram, *Brute: The Life of Victor Krulak, U.S. Marine* (Little, Brown and Company; First ed., 2010)

Peer DeSilva, *Sub Rosa: The CIA and the Uses of Intelligence* (New York: Times Books, 1978)

General Dong Si Nguyen, *The Trans-Truong Son Route* (The GIOI Publishers, 2005)

Edward Doyle, *The Vietnam Experience: Setting The Stage* (Boston Publishing Company, 1981)

Edward Doyle, Samuel Lipsman & Terrance Maitland, *The North* (Boston: Boston Publishing Company 1986)

Donna E. Elliott, *Keeping the Promise: The Story of MIA Jerry Elliott, a Family Shattered by His Disappearance, and a Sister's 40-year Search for the Truth* (Hellgate Press, 2010)

Cynthia Enloe, *The Morning After: Sexual Politics at the End of the Cold War* (University of California Press, 1993)

W.D. Ehrhart, *Passing Time: Memoir of a Vietnam Veteran Against the War* (February 2012)

Bernard Fall, *Street Without Joy* (Mechanicsburg, PA: Stack pole Books 1994)

C.R. Figley, *Introduction: Stress Disorders Among Vietnam Veterans: Theory, Research, and Treatment*, New York: Brunner/Mazel, 1978

Harold P. Ford, *Revisiting Vietnam Thoughts Engendered by Robert McNamara's In Retrospect*, https://www.cia.gov/library/center-for-the-study-of-intelligence/csi-publications/csi-studies/studies/96unclass/ford.htmsigma

David Halberstam, *Ho* (New York, Random House, 1971)

Chris Harman, *The Fire Last Time: 1968 and After* (London and Chicago: Bookmarks: 1998)

Michael Herr, *Dispatches* (NYC: Avon Books 1978)

George C. Herring, *America's Longest War: The United States and Vietnam 1950-1975* (McGraw-Hill 2002)

Brigadier General Hoang Dan and Captain Hung Dat, *Highway 9—Khe Sanh Offensive Campaign: Spring and Summer 1968*, Vietnam Institute of Military History, Hanoi, 1987).

Hoang Ngoc Lung, *The General Offensives of 1968–69*. McLean VA: General Research Corporation (1978).

Gregg Jones, *Last Stand at Khe Sanh: The U.S. Marines' Finest Hour in Vietnam* (Da Capo Press, 2003)

Howard Jones, *Death of a Generation: How the Assassinations of Diem and JFK Prolonged the Vietnam War* (New York: Oxford University Press 2003).

Wayne Karlin, *Wandering Souls: Journeys with the Dead and the Living in Viet Nam* (Nation Books 2013).

Stanley Karnow, *Vietnam: A History* (Penguin Books, 1997).

Michael P. Kelley, *Where We Were in Vietnam: A Comprehensive Guide to the Firebases, Military Installations and Naval Vessels of the Vietnam war 1945-75* (Hellgate Press, 2002).

Victor H. Krulak, *First to Fight: An Inside View of the U.S. Marine Corps* (Naval Institute Press, Annapolis, MD 1999).

Gary Kulik, *War Stories, False Atrocity Tales, Swift Boaters, and Winter Soldiers—What Really Happened in Vietnam* (Washington D.C. Potomac Books, Inc., 2009).

Mark Lane, *Conversations with Americans: Vietnam Veterans' Shocking Testimony of Atrocities and Massacres During the War* (Simon & Schuster, 1970).

Lanning, Michael & Cragg Dan, *Inside the VC and NVA: The Story of North Vietnams' Armed Forces* (Texas A&M University Press, 2008)

Lien-Hang T. Nguyen, Hanoi's War: An International History of the War for Peace in Vietnam (University of North Carolina Press, 2012).

Robert Mann, *A Grand Delusion: America's Descent Into Vietnam* (Basic Books, 2002

William Manchester, *Goodbye, Darkness: A Memoir of the Pacific War* (New York, NY: Dell Publishing, 1980).

Alfred McCoy, *A Question of Torture: CIA Interrogation, from the Cold War to the War on Terror* (Owl Books, 2006).

H. R. McMaster, *Dereliction of Duty: Johnson, McNamara, the Joint Chiefs of Staff, and the Lies That Led to Vietnam* (Harper, 1998).

Robert S. McNamara and Brian Van DeMark, *In Retrospect: The Tragedy and Lessons of Vietnam* (Vintage Books, 1996.)

Edward F. Murphy, *The Hill Fights: The First Battle of Khe Sanh* (New York: Ballantine Books, 2003).

Bernard C. Nalty, *Air Power and the Fight for Khe Sanh* (Office of Air Force History, United States Air Force, Washington, D.C., 1986).

Michael Norman, *These Good Men: Friendships Forged from War* (Random House Value Publishing, 1991).

Tim O'Brien, *The Things They Carried* (New York, NY: Broadway Books, 1998).

Rick Perlstein, *Nixonland: The Rise of a President and the Fracturing of America* (New York: Scribner, 2008).

Robert Pisor, *The End of the Line: The Siege of Khe Sanh* (Ballantine Books, 1983).

John Prados and Ray W. Stubbe, *Valley of Decision: The Siege of Khe Sanh* (Annapolis MD: Naval Institute Press, 1991).

Thomas Ricks, *The Generals: American Military Command from World War II to Today* (Penguin, 2013).

Rudolph Rummel and Nghia M. Vo, *The Vietnamese Boat People, 1954 and 1975-1992* (McFarland, 2006).

Jonathan Shay, *Achilles in Vietnam, Combat Trauma and the Undoing of Character* (New York, Scribner 1994).

Neil Sheehan, *A Bright Shining Lie: John Paul Vann and America in Vietnam* (New York: Random House, 1988).

Moyers S. Shores III, *The Battle for Khe Sanh* (History and Museums Division, Headquarters, U.S. Marine Corps, Washington, D.C., 1969).

Jack Shulimson, *U.S. Marines in Vietnam: The Defining Year 1968* (History & Museums Division, Headquarters U.S. Marine Corps Washington, D.C. 1997).

Lewis Sorley, *A Better War: The Unexamined Victories and Final Tragedy of America's Last Year in Vietnam* (Harcourt, Inc., 1999), p.30.

Lewis Sorley, *Westmoreland: The General Who Lost Vietnam* (Boston: Houghton Mifflin Harcourt 2011)

Ronald Spector, *After Tet: The Bloodiest Year in Vietnam* (New York: Free Press 1992)

Ray W. Stubbe, *Battalion of Kings: A Tribute to Our Fallen Brothers Who Died Because of the Battlefield of Khe Sanh, Vietnam, First* ed. (Wauwatosa, WI: Khe Sanh Veterans, 2005)

Ray W. Stubbe, *Pebbles in My Boots Vol. 2* (Wauwatosa, WI, 2011)

Ray W. Stubbe, *Pebbles in My Boots Vol. 3* (Wauwatosa, WI, 2014)

Ray W. Stubbe, ed., *B5-T8 in 48 QXD: The Secret Official History of the North Vietnamese Army of the Siege at Khe Sanh, Vietnam, Spring, 1968* (Wauwatosa, WI: Khe Sanh Veterans, 2006)

Robert J. Topmiller, *Red Clay on My Boots: Encounters with Khe Sanh 1968 to 2005* (Minneapolis, MN: Kirk House Publishers, 2007)

Robert J. Topmiller, *The Lotus Unleashed: The Buddhist Peace Movement in South Vietnam, 1964-1966* (University of Kentucky Press, 2002).

Robert J. Topmiller and T. Kerby Neill, *Binding Their Wounds: America's Assault on Its Veterans*, Paradigm Publishers 2011)

Nick Turse, *Kill Anything That Moves: The Real American War in Vietnam* (Picador, 2013).

United States Marine Corps, *Small Wars Manual* 1940 (Watchmaker Publishing, 2011)

Jack Valenti, *A Very Human President (*New York City, W.W. Norton 1995)

Tim Weiner, *Legacy of Ashes: The History of the CIA (Random House LLC, 2008)*

William C. Westmoreland, *A Soldier Reports* (Doubleday, 1976)

Terry Whitmore and Richard Weber, *Memphis-Nam-Sweden: The Story of a Black Deserter*, University Press of Mississippi, 1997)

ARTICLES & STUDIES, FILMS

Francis B. Ahearn, *A Two Dollar Officer*, unpublished memoir, September 4, 2003

Robert Black, *Closing the "End of the Line,"* Shipmate magazine, November 2000

Malcolm W. Browne, *Battlefields of Khe Sanh," New York Times*, May 14, 1994

Peter Brush, *"The Withdrawal from Khe Sanh."* http://www.vwam.com/client/contentclient.php?intIdContent=22

Peter Brush, *The Unexploited Vulnerability of the Marines at Khe Sanh* (Vietnam Magazine, August, 1997) pp.58-60.

Lieutenant Colonel Mathew Caffrey, Jr. USAFR, "Toward a History-Based Doctrine for Wargaming," *Aerospace Power Journal*, Fall 2000.

Philip Caputo, "The Unreturning Army," *Playboy magazine*, January 1982.

Lieutenant General John A. Chaisson, USMC, Historical Center, Oral history, 1975.

Major Norman L. Cooling, *Hue City, 1968: Winning A Battle While Losing A War*, 2001 https://www.mca-marines.org/gazette/hue-city-1968-winning-battle-while-losing-war

Col. William H. Dabney, USMC (Ret.), Interviewed by Jim Dittrich, *Cold War Oral History Project, Center for Military History and Strategic Analysis* (Virginia Military Institute Archives, Military Oral History Collection) September 8, 2005.

C.R. Figley, *Introduction: Stress Disorders Among Vietnam Veterans: Theory, Research, and Treatment,* New York: Brunner/Mazel, 1978.

William Conrad Gibbons, *The U.S. Government and the Vietnam War: Executive and Legislative Roles and Relationships, Part IV: July 1965–January 1968* (Princeton University Press 1995 http://books.google.com/books?id=J5RJtcGuNzkC&dq.

Colonel James W. Hammond, Jr. USMC (Ret.), *War by the Box Score,* unpublished essay, 2010.

Hearts and Minds, 16mm, 112 minutes, BBS Productions, United States, 1974.

George Magazine, "A Special interview with General William Westmoreland," November 1998

Lieutenant General Dang Kinh, " The Tri-Thien-Hue Battlefield (Installment 1)" *People's Army* newspaper, 27 Jan 2008, translated by Merle Pribbenow. *http://www.qdnd.vn/qdnd/baongay.psks.phongsu.28802.qdnd*

Marc Levy, "An Interview with Bao Ninh: Part One," *The Veteran: Magazine of the Vietnam Veterans of America* (Fall/ Winter 1999)

PTSD Continues to Afflict Vietnam Veterans 40 Years After the War, http://www.latimes.com/nation/nationnow/la-na-nn-ptsd-vietnam-20140808-story

Colonel D.E. Lownds, taped historical interview (debriefing), 29 July 1968, Headquarters Fleet Marine Force, Pacific.

Ian MacKinnon, "Forty years on, Laos Reaps Bitter Harvest of the Secret War," *The Guardian* (London), December 3, 2008

Paul D. Mather, LTC, USAF (Ret.), *M. I. A.: Accounting for the Missing in Southeast Asia*

Colonel Bruce F. Meyers USMC (RET) *Reflections of a Grunt Marine* (unpublished memoir, 2013)

Combat Stress Among Veterans Is Found to Persist Since Vietnam, http://www.nytimes.com/2014/08/08/us/combat-stress-found-to-persist-since-vietnam.html?_r=1

John Olsson Interview, March 2007 http://digitaljournalist.org/issue0107/olsontext.htm

John Prados, *Khe Sanh: The Other Side Of The Hill,* The VVA Veteran, Jul-Aug 2007

President's Commission on Mental Health, *Mental Health Problems of Vietnam-Era Veterans,* Washington: February 15, 1978).

Rudolph Rummel, *Statistics of Democide.* http://www.hawaii.edu/powerkills/NOTE5.HTM

Rudolph Rummel, *Statistics of Democide* http://www.hawaii.edu/powerkills/SOD.TAB6.1A.GIF

Admiral U.S. Grant Sharp, *We Could Have Won In Vietnam Long Ago,* Readers' Digest Magazine, May 1969

Neil Sheehan, New York Times Book Review, *Conversations with Americans,* December 27, 1970 *New York Times,* January 24, 1968, pp. 1

Clark Smith, *"The Soldier-Cynics: Veterans Still Caught in the War,"* Southeast Asia *Chronicle,* Issue No. 85, August 1982.

S.C. Spring, K. Harris and J.R. Lind, *Case Study Of A Two-Company NVA Attack On A Marine Company In A Defensive Position On Foxtrot Ridge* (United States Air Force, Project Rand, November 1971)

South Vietnam. Pre-1975: Report of Death, case of Lance Corporal Thomas P. Mahoney III 2375990, USMC; South Vietnam. Pre-1975: Change of MIA Status to KIA; and *South Vietnam. Pre-1975: Circumstances Indicate Subject was KIA (BNR* [Body Not Recovered]*).*

Stubbe, Ray W., *Khe Sanh and The Mongol Prince* (unpublished manuscript, 2002)

W.J. Tiffany and W.S. Allerton, *Army Psychiatry in the Mid-1960's,* American Journal of Psychiatry 1967, p. 810-821.

Ian Timberlake "Not Forgotten: Remains of US Soldier Sought in Vietnam" *Agence France-Presse* (AFP), June 5, 2010.

TIME, "The Red Napoleon," June 17, 1966.

James Turner Interview, Texas Tech University, The Vietnam Archive, Oral History Project, conducted by Steve Maxner, December 5, 2001:

Peter Zinoman, *The Colonial Bastille: A History of Imprisonment in Vietnam 1862-1940* (University of California Press, 2001).

CHAPTER NOTES

1.

1 David and Tom Corporandy email to author, December 2, 2011.

2 Kathleen (McCorry) Lopes email to author, October 17, 2008.

3 Bill Corporandy and Tom Corporandy email to author, December 2, 2011.

2.

4 Bernard Fall, *Street Without Joy* (Mechanicsburg, PA: Stack pole Books 1994), p. 28.

5 The use of "South" is to distinguish it from Hill 881 North, located about a mile away. On U.S. Army Map Service topographic maps used during the war, hills were named for their altitude in meters above sea level. For example, Hill 881 South was eight-hundred eighty-one meters, or 2,890 feet, high.

6 During the two-week struggle for the high ground west of Khe Sanh, one hundred fifty-five Americans would be killed and another four hundred twenty-five missing or evacuated with wounds. Estimates of NVA casualties, difficult to calculate due to their practice of disciplined withdrawals and battlefield burials, ranged from five hundred to a thousand.

7 Soren Kierkegaard, *Journals and Papers, vol. 5, entry no. 5556, 1840-1842, eds. Howard V. Hong and Edna H. Hong (1978).*

3.

8 Tim O'Brien, *The Things They Carried* (New York, NY: Broadway Books 1998), p. 21.

9 First Battalion, First Marine Regiment Command Chronology, November 1967.

10 Ibid., p.5.

4.

11 Lawrence Ferlinghetti, "#64" from *A Far Rockaway of the Heart,* New Directions, 1997.

12 H. R. McMaster, *Dereliction of Duty: Johnson, McNamara, the Joint Chiefs of Staff, and the Lies That Led to Vietnam* (Harper, 1998) p. 63; William C. Westmoreland, *A Soldier Reports* (Doubleday, 1976) p. 53; Thomas Ricks, *The Generals: American Military Command from World War II to Today* (Penguin, 2013) p. 217 states that "Maxwell Taylor arguably was the most destructive general in American history."

13 Niall Ferguson, *Kissinger, 1923-1968: The Idealist* (Penguin 2015).

14 Neil Sheehan, *A Bright Shining Lie: John Paul Vann and America in Vietnam* (New York: Random House, 1988) p. 629.

15 Victor Krulak, *First to Fight: An Inside View of the U.S. Marine Corps* (Naval Institute Press 1999), p. 199. NOTE: Krulak proved to be correct. By 1972, the allies had managed to reduce the enemy manpower by perhaps 25 percent at a cost of over 220,000 U.S. and South Vietnamese dead.

16 Krulak, *First to Fight*, p. 210.

17 William Head, *Bloodshed and Bitterness: The Battle for Khe Sanh, Diversion or a Second Dien Bien Phu? www.virginiareviewofasianstudies.com*

18 Westmoreland, *A Soldier Reports* p. 339.

19 Jack Shulimson, U.S. *Marines in Vietnam: The Defining Year 1968* (History & Museums Division, Headquarters U.S. Marine Corps Washington, D.C. 1997), p. 69.

20 John Prados and Ray W. Stubbe, *Valley of Decision, The Siege of Khe Sanh* (Naval Institute Press 1991) p. 191.

21 Lewis Sorley, *Westmoreland: The General Who Lost Vietnam* (Boston: Houghton Mifflin Harcourt 2011), p. 175.

22 Ray W. Stubbe, *B5-T8 in 48 QXD, The Secret Official History of the North Vietnamese Army of the Siege at Khe Sanh, Vietnam, Spring, 1968* (Khe Sanh Veterans, Inc. Wauwatosa, WI 2006), translations by Sedgwick D. Tourison, Jr. and Robert J. DeStatte, p. 10.

23 Ibid., p. 15.

24 Ibid., p. 16.

25 John Prados, *Khe Sanh: The Other Side of the Hill*, The VVA Veteran, Jul-Aug 2007, p. 4.

5.

26 Former Lieutenant Robert Simpson, Delta Company, First Battalion, Twenty-sixth Marine Regiment, email to author, November 22, 2007.

27 Stubbe, *B5-T8*, p.12.

28 *New York Times*, January 24, 1968, pp. 1, 3.

29 Colonel William H. Dabney, USMC (Ret.), Interviewed by Jim Dietrich, *Cold War Oral History Project, Center for Military History and Strategic Analysis* (Virginia Military Institute Archives, Military Oral History Collection) September 8, 2005.

6.

30 Francis B. Ahearn, *A Two Dollar Officer*, unpublished memoir, September 4, 2003.

31 Lien-Hang T. Nguyen, *Hanoi's War: An International History of the War for Peace in Vietnam* (University of North Carolina Press, 2012), p. 309.

32 Shulimson, U.S. *Marines*, p. 166.

33 Mark Milburn email to author June 19, 2010.

34 Frank Ahearn email to author May 14, 2014.

35 Robert Black email to author August 12, 2012.

36 Frank Ahearn telephone call with author October 29, 2014.

37 Robert Black email to author August 6, 2005.

38 Ken Fernandes email to author, August 17, 2015.

39 *An Interview with John Olsson*, March 2007, http://digitaljournalist.org/issue0107/olsontext.htm.

40 Ahearn, *A Two Dollar Officer*.

7.

41 Sorley, *Westmoreland*, p. 171.

42 Prados and Stubbe, Valley *of Decision*, p. 299.

43 Declassified memorandum December 23, 1968 from Major Harry Baig, Headquarters, United States Military Assistance Command, Thailand, Joint United States Military Advisory Group, Thailand to Headquarters USMC, Historical Records Branch, G-3 Division.

44 Nguyen Duc Huy, *Major General Nguyen Duc Huy: A Life in the Military*, Second Edition, with Additions and Corrections (People's Army Publishing House, Hanoi, 2011), translated by Merle L. Pribbenow, p. 69.

45 Stubbe, B5-*T8*, p.79.

46 Dabney, Oral Interview.

47 Ibid., p. 79.

48 Pisor, *The End of the Line*, p. 218.

49 Stubbe, *B5-T8*, p. 82. NOTE: On April 5, 1968, MACV prepared an "Analysis of the Khe Sanh Battle" for General Westmoreland. The report, classified SECRET (declassified by the NARA on November 20, 1997), noted that intelligence from many sources indicated conclusively that the North Vietnamese had planned a massive ground attack against the base. The attack was to have been supported by armor and artillery. Having to push up the attack date to January 20 from early February, and losses inflicted on the enemy in the opening days of the attack, were of sufficient magnitude to cause the enemy to abandon this plan.

The Spring-Summer 1968 Khe Sanh – Route 9 Offensive Campaign history notes that the NVA retained the option that, "at some point," if American reinforcements and supplies could not be drawn up Route 9 into the traps prepared for them, and "if conditions were favorable," they would attempt to "liberate Khe Sanh." They kept a specific order of battle for their plan to take the base, should that command be given: "The 9th Regiment would be reinforced by sappers who would attack along the primary direction from the south and southeast and the 66th Regiment would attack at the west and southwest and the 24th Regiment would be a reserve force."

50 Stubbe, Ray W., *Khe Sanh and The Mongol Prince* (unpublished manuscript, 2002), p. 28.

51 Colonel James W. Hammond, Jr. USMC (Ret.), *War by the Box Score,* unpublished essay, 2010.

52 *The Wall Street Journal*, February 24, 1968.

53 George C. Herring, *America's Longest War: The United States and Vietnam 1950-1975* (McGraw-Hill 2002) p. 223.

8.

54 Author's interview with Colonel Bruce F. Meyers, September 2, 2013.

55 Shulimson, *U.S. Marines*, p. 312.

56 Ibid., p. 313.

57 Stubbe, Battalion *of Kings*, pp. 305-307.

58 Stubbe, *Battalion of Kings*, p.1.

59 Ahearn, *A Two Dollar Officer.*

9.

60 Shulimson, *U.S. Marines*, p. 318-319.

61 Ibid., p. 320.

62 Stubbe, *B5-T8*, p. 52.

63 Steve Busby email to author July 23, 2006.

64 Tom Northrop email to author July 18, 2014.

65 Milburn email to author August 25, 2105.

66 U.S. Library of Congress, DOD/DPMO Research and Investigation Team Research Report June 20, 2005 into the case of Lance Corporal Charles Gatewood.

67 Shulimson, *U.S. Marines*, p. 321.

68 Ibid., p. 322.

10.

69 Jim Hayden email November 30, 2012.

70 Brush, Peter, "*The Withdrawal from Khe Sanh*." http://www.vwam.com/client/contentclient.php?intIdContent=22

71 Hayden email November 30, 2012.

72 Ibid.

73 Stubbe, *B5-T8*, p. 87.

74 Ken Campbell email to author August 26, 2005.

75 Ahearn, *A Two Dollar Officer.*

11.

76 Robert Black email to author, August 13, 2004.

77 Ahearn, *A Two Dollar Officer.*

78 Letter Ken Fernandes to Patricia Mahoney dated July 24, 1968.

79 Ken Fernandes email to author, July 16, 2014.

80 Northrop email July 18, 2014.

81 Allen Williams interview with author July 30, 2010.

82 Robert Black email to author, November 2, 2008.

83 Allen Williams interview, July 30, 2010.

84 Author interview with Nguyen Tien Thanh July 8, 2012, with translator Mike Najim.

85 U.S. Library of Congress, DOD/DPMO Research and Investigation Team Research Report 03-016; Vietnam Historical Reference to Battles at Hill 845 in Quang Tri Province, Case 1224-0-01 (hereafter referred to as "JPAC Research and Investigation Team Research Report").

86 James P. McHenry, *The Last Battalion Out of Khe Sanh*, unpublished memoir, 2013, p.2.

12.

87 Ken Campbell email to author, October 13, 2006.

88 Allen Williams interview, July 30, 2010.

89 Ahearn email to author May 14, 2014.

90 Tom Northrop email to author July 18, 2014. Tom Northrop was wounded on Hill 689 the day after Mahoney's death. After being hospitalized, he returned to duty with Bravo Company and left Vietnam in September 1968.

91 First Marine Regiment Command Chronology, July 1968.

92 McHenry, *The Last Battalion*, p.4.

93 Ernie Vaughn email to Frank Ahearn, October 11, 2005.

94 Robert Black, "Closing the 'End of the Line,'" *Shipmate Magazine*, November 2000, pp. 13-14.

95 Black, *Closing*, p. 4.

96 *Vietnam Weekly*, July 16, 1968.

97 "Analysis of the Khe Sanh Battle," April 5, 1968, prepared by MACV for General Westmoreland. Just through the siege months between late-January and early-April 1968, the CIA had concluded NVA losses ranged from 50 to 65 percent of the personnel committed to the Khe Sanh operation, including in replacements which averaged from 190 to 380 troops a day. Thus, the total number of NVA troops engaged in the battle during just that seventy-seven day period may have been as high as 44,000.

98 Shulimson, U.S. *Marines*, p. 324.

99 Sorley, *Westmoreland*, p. 173.

100 Krulak, *First to Fight*, p.220.

101 Ibid., p. 204. Krulak retired in 1968. Two others involved in trying to change the Johnson Administration's policy of attrition, Admiral U.S.G. Sharp and Commandant Wallace Greene, Jr., also retired that year.

102 Sorley, *Westmoreland*, p. 197.

103 *Hearts and Minds*, 16mm, 112 minutes, BBS Productions, United States, 1974.

104 "A Special interview with General William Westmoreland," George *Magazine*, November 1998.

105 Cecil B. Currey, interview with General Vo Nguyen Giap in Hanoi December 12, 1988, published in VIETNAM magazine April 1991, p. 22.

13.

106 Our suspicions about the danger of complacency, and the increasing drug use in Headquarters Company 26th Marines, proved tragically correct. In February 1969, two months after Steve and I left Vietnam, our unit sustained heavy casualties when their camp was overrun by the enemy. Two Marines responsible for watching the road on which the enemy soldiers approached that night, had smoked dope in the guardhouse. They were later found dead, their throats slashed by the VC.

107 Telegrams to Mrs. Patricia Mahoney July-August 1967 from Twelfth Marine Corps District, Alameda, California.

108 Investigation findings from First Lieutenant Stuart A. Dorow to the commanding officer First Battalion First Marines, July 27, 1968, Subject: "Report of death; case of Lance Corporal Thomas P. Mahoney III."

109 Claudia Harris telephone call with author August 21, 2015.

14.

110 Karnow, *Vietnam: A History* (Penguin Books 1997) p. 361.

111 Smedley D. Butler, *War is a Racket* (Feral House, 2003), p. 23.

112 CBS Radio broadcast December 29, 1943

113 Chris Harman, *The Fire Last Time: 1968 and After* (London and Chicago: Bookmarks: 1998), p. 176.

114 Herring, *America's Longest War*, p. 342.

115 Rudolph Rummel, *Statistics of Democide*. http://www.hawaii.edu/powerkills/NOTE5.HTM.

116 Robert J. Topmiller interview KOLO TV, Reno, Nevada, August 12, 2008.

117 Rudolph Rummel and Nghia M. Vo, *The Vietnamese Boat People, 1954 and 1975–1992* (McFarland, 2006).

118 Ibid., p. 338.

119 Washington Post, March 31, 2014.

15.

120 Clark Smith, "The Soldier-Cynics: Veterans Still Caught in the War," *Southeast Asia Chronicle,* Issue No. 85, August 1982.

121 Rudyard Kipling address to 1907 graduating class of McGill University, Montreal, Quebec, Canada.

122 Alan Zarembo, *PTSD Continues to Afflict Vietnam Veterans 40 Years after the War,* http://www.latimes.com/nation/nationnow/la-na-nn-ptsd-vietnam-20140808-story.html.

123 Op. cit.

124 Jonathan Shay, *Achilles in Vietnam, Combat Trauma and the Undoing of Character* (New York, Scribner 1994), p. 179.

125 Email from Jim Hogan to Frank Ahearn, September 16, 2008.

126 Joint POW-MIA Accounting Command (JPAC) Research and Investigation Team Research Report, Case 1224, February 1993.

127 Shay, *Achilles*, p. 20.

128 Ahearn, *A Two Dollar Officer.*

129 Robert Black email to author June 19, 2014.

130 JPAC Research and Investigation Team Research Report, February 2005.

17.

131 Robert J. Topmiller, *The Lotus Unleashed: The Buddhist Peace Movement in South Vietnam, 1964-1966* (University of Kentucky Press, 2002).

132 Robert J. Topmiller and T. Kerby Neill, *Binding Their Wounds: America's Assault on Its Veterans*, Paradigm Publishers, 2011) p. 6-12.

133 Ibid. p. 22.

134 Topmiller, *Red Clay*, p. 15.

135 Ibid., p. 120.

136 Ibid., p. 119.

137 Ibid., p. 197.

138 Robert S, McNamara, *In Retrospect: The Tragedy and Lessons of Vietnam* (Vintage Books 1996).

139 Admiral U.S. Grant Sharp, *We Could Have Won In Vietnam Long Ago*, Readers' Digest Magazine, May 1969.

140 Harold P. Ford, *Revisiting Vietnam: Thoughts Engendered by Robert McNamara's In Retrospect,* https://www.cia.gov/library/center-for-the-study-of-intelligence/csi-publications/csi-studies/studies/96unclass/ford.htmsigma.

141 Peer DeSilva, *Sub Rosa: The CIA and the Uses of Intelligence* (New York: Times Books, 1978).

142 Also coincidentally, for the first twenty years of his life McNamara had resided at 1036 Annerley Road in Oakland, less than a mile from the Fairmount Avenue home where Patricia Mahoney was then living, and where Tom was later be raised.

143 Topmiller and Neill, *Binding,* Foreword, p. *x.*

144 Topmiller, *Red Clay,* p. 18.

145 Chamberlain speech dedicating a monument to the 20th Maine on October 3, 1889, Gettysburg, Pennsylvania.

18.

146 Robert Black email to author May 17, 2007.

147 Hoang Tran Dung email via Gary Foster January 21, 2014.

148 Marc Levy, "An Interview with Bao Ninh: Part One," *The Veteran: Magazine of the Vietnam Veterans of America* (Fall/ Winter 1999).

149 *New York Times,* April 29, 2010.

150 Michael Lanning & Dan Cragg, *Inside the VC and NVA: The Story of North Vietnams' Armed Forces* (Texas A&M University Press, 2008), p. 92.

151 While members of other branches of the U.S. military were only required to remain in Vietnam for twelve months, Marines had thirteen month tours. This was because early in the war the Defense Department assumed as a part of the Navy, Marines would arrive by transport ship and that the transit should not count toward the twelve-month deployment. The rule was never changed even when all Marines began arriving by air like the other branches.

152 Nguyen Tien Thanh interview with Mike Najim, January 21, 2014.

153 Wayne Karlin, *Wandering Souls: Journeys with the Dead and the Living in Viet Nam (*Nation Books 2013) p. 329.

154 Bao Ninh, *The Sorrow of War*, Secker & Warburg, London 1993) p. 4.

155 Shulimson, *U.S. Marines*, p. 177.

19.

156 Dabney, Oral History.

157 Ibid.

158 Stubbe, B5-*T8*, p.11.

159 Ibid., p.12.

160 Ibid., p. 95.

161 Taped Historical Interview Documentation Sheet of interview conducted at Marine Corps Base, Twenty-Nine Palms, California, March 15, 1968. Subject: Communications Problems at Khe Sanh. Interviewee Sergeant Harry E. Stroud. Interviewer Staff Sergeant William J. Enochs. Transcribed by Ray W. Stubbe.

162 Dianne Williamson email to author March 13, 2008.

20.

163 Army Map Service (AMS), Series L7014, 1:50,000 Sheet 6342 III, Huong Hoa, Edition 5-AMS, 1968, XD 773441 and XD 7720 4405.

164 Wayne Karlin email to author, October 26, 2008.

165 Kenneth J. Campbell, *A Tale of Two Quagmires: Iraq, Vietnam, and the Hard Lessons of War* (Paradigm Publishers, 2007) p. 36.

166 Mark Lane, *Conversations with Americans: Vietnam Veterans' Shocking Testimony of Atrocities and Massacres During the War* (Simon & Schuster, 1970).

167 Neil Sheehan, "Conversations with Americans," *New York Times Book Review*, December 27, 1970.

168 Lane, *Conversations*, p. 74.

169 Gary Kulik, *War Stories, False Atrocity Tales, Swift Boaters, and Winter Soldiers—What Really Happened in Vietnam* (Washington D.C. Potomac Books, Inc., 2009) p. 218.

170 Ibid., p. 230.

171 Nick Turse, *Kill Anything That Moves: The Real American War in Vietnam* (Picador, 2013)

172 Kulik, *War Stories*, p. 199.

173 Steve Busby email to author December 23, 2005.

174 Terry Whitmore and Richard Weber, *Memphis-Nam-Sweden: The Story of a Black Deserter*, University Press of Mississippi, 1997).

175 Kulik, *War Stories*, p. 154.

176 Rudolph Rummel, *Statistics of Democide*. http://www.hawaii.edu/powerkills/ NOTE5.HTM

177 Alfred McCoy, *A Question of Torture: CIA Interrogation, from the Cold War to the War on Terror (Owl Books, 2006)* p. 69.

178 Shay, *Achilles*, p. 35.

179 Sheehan review of *Conversations with Americans*.

180 William Broyles Jr., *Brothers in Arms A Journey from War to Peace* (New York: Alfred A. Knopf 1986) p. 250.

181 Allen Williams interview July 30, 2010.

182 Ken Campbell email to author March 23, 2013.

183 *The New York Times*, February 12, 1968.

21.

184 Stubbe, *The Mongol Prince*, p.12. Before being commissioned as an officer in May 1960, Baig married the socialite daughter of Count Nicholas de Rochefort, a CIA staffer, and was subsequently assigned to the Intelligence Research Officer Course at Ft. Holabird, Maryland. Baig later joined the Third Marine Division's counterintelligence team, personally exploring much of the area south of the DMZ in 1964 and taking copious notes which would become invaluable to commanders in that theater when Marine combat units arrived a year later.

185 Jared Kelley email to author November 30, 2009.

186 Topmiller & Neill, *Binding Their Wounds*, p.3-5.

187 Ibid. p. vvi.

188 Kerby Neill email to author September 23, 2013.

189 *Lexington Herald-Leader*, May 29, 2011.

190 Kevin Gilmartin email to author September 9, 2008.

191 Karlin email to author October 26, 2008.

192 A.E. Houseman, *"1887"* from *A Shropshire Lad* (Heritage Press, 1951)

22.

193 Mark Milburn email to author, June 19, 2010.

194 Allen Williams email to author, June 25, 2010.

195 Allen Williams telephone interview July 30, 2010.

196 Ibid.

197 The Dorow report mistakenly showed the spelling as "Patton," rather than Patten. I would later learn he died in 2004.

198 Bruce Bird interview January 21, 2014.

199 Ray Stubbe letter to author, August 6, 2012.

200 Nguyen Tien Thanh interview with Mike Najim, January 21, 2014.

201 *Nevada State Journal*, November 18, 1878.

202 Dabney oral history.

203 Michael Sledge, "*Soldier Dead: How We Recover, Identify, Bury and Honor our Military Fallen* (Columbia University Press, 2005) pp. 253-254.

204 Shulimson, *U.S. Marines*, p. 314.

205 Ibid., p. 316.

206 McHenry, *The Last Battalion, p. 5.*

207 Topmiller, *Red Clay*, p. 54.

208 Robert Black letter of condolence to Mrs. Patricia Mahoney July 12, 1968.

209 Stubbe, *The Mongol Prince*, p. 28.

210 Cynthia Enloe, *The Morning After: Sexual Politics at the End of the Cold War* (University of California Press 1993).

211 Michael Herr, *Dispatches* (NYC: Avon Books 1978), p.244.

212 Claudia Harris letter to author August 7, 2005.

23.

213 "Ku Vo" can be translated into English as "Old Vo" and, though I have not been able to pinpoint the derivation of the name, one intriguing possibility is that the hill is now named for General (Vo Nguyen) Giap, perhaps another strange vestige of the war. Giap died in October 2013 at the age one hundred two.

214 JPAC Research and Investigation Team Research Report April 19, 2007.

215 JPAC Research and Investigation Team Research Report Case # 1224, July 22, 2008.

216 JPAC Research and Investigation Team Research Report, Case # 1224, April 19, 2007.

217　In addition to numerous professional articles for engineering publications, Foster has written pieces about modern Khe Sanh published in the organization's official publication *Red Clay*, a book about aviation during the Vietnam war titled, *Phantom in the River: Flight of Linfield Two Zero One*, and is currently working on a novel centering around the siege of Khe Sanh.

24.

218　Michael Carlantonio email to author August 21, 2007.

219　Stubbe, *Battalion of Kings*, p. 339.

220　Report of Missing: Case of Lance Corporal Charles H. Gatewood 2381218/0311, USMC, by First Lieutenant Stuart A. Dorow, 14 September 1968 (Library of Congress).

221　Steve Busby email to author September 5, 2009.

222　Michael Carlantonio email to author August 21, 2007.

223　Frank Ahearn email to author December 29, 2012.

224　Black email to author January 15, 2013.

225　Edward Stollenwerck email to author April 10, 2014.

226　Wendell Harkins interview with author February 6, 2013.

227　JPAC Research and Investigation Team Research Report, Case #1224, August 19, 2010.

228　At AMS, Series L7014, 1:50,000 Sheet 6342 III, Huong Hoa, Edition 5-AMS, 1968 coordinates XD 77162 44025.

229　At AMS, Series L7014, 1:50,000 Sheet 6342 III, Huong Hoa, Edition 5-AMS, 1968 coordinates XD 7720 4405.

230　Ian Timberlake "Not Forgotten: Remains of US Soldier Sought in Vietnam" *Agence France-Presse* (AFP), June 5, 2010.

231　At AMS, Series L7014, 1:50,000 Sheet 6342 III, Huong Hoa, Edition 5-AMS, 1968 XD 77768 43768.

232　JPAC Research and Investigation Team Research Report, Case #1224, August 10, 2010.

233　Ibid.

234　Edward F. Murphy, *The Hill Fights: The First Battle of Khe Sanh* (Ballantine Books 2003) p.154.

235　JPAC Research and Investigation Team Research Report, Case #1224, August 10, 2010.

236　Black email to author April 11, 2010.

25.

237 Carl Solberg, *Hubert Humphrey: A Biography* (W.W. Norton, Co. 1984), p. 312.

238 William Manchester, *Goodbye, Darkness: A Memoir of the Pacific War* (New York, NY: Dell Publishing 1980) p. 300.

239 *The Collected Poems of W.B. Yeats* (Scribner; 2nd Revised edition, 1996) "Never Give All the Heart."

EPILOGUE

240 Donna E. Elliott, *Keeping the Promise: The Story of MIA Jerry Elliott, a Family Shattered by His Disappearance, and a Sister's 40-year Search for the Truth* (Hellgate Press, 2010).

241 *Stars & Stripes* 9/23/13 http://www.stripes.com/news/families-express-frustration-with-jpac-s-efforts-to-recover-war-missing-1.242757.

242 Dr. Timothy Castle, the Chief of DPMO's Southeast Asia Archival Research, memo to Lt. Col Mann, DPMO Plans and Policy, Case 2052, April 28, 1997.

243 http://www.stripes.com/news/pacific/internal-memo-alleges-jpac-ethics-violations-mishandling-of-military-remains-1.264355.

244 http://www.stripes.com/jpac-admits-to-phony-ceremonies-honoring-returning-remains-1.246322.

245 Maumausolo phone call to author January 15, 2015.

246 Michael Carlantonio email to author March 20, 2015.

INDEX

Page locators in italics indicate maps and photographs.

ABOUT THE AUTHOR

MICHAEL ARCHER grew up in northern California and served as a U.S. Marine in Vietnam during 1967-1968. His books include *A Patch of Ground: Khe Sanh Remembered*, an acclaimed first-person account of the infamous seventy-seven-day siege of that American combat base; *A Man of His Word: The Life and Times of Nevada's Senator William J. Raggio*, about one of Nevada's most courageous, honorable and admired citizens; and *The Long Goodbye: Khe Sanh Revisited*, chronicling the author's search for answers to a friend's mysterious death at Khe Sanh. Michael lives in Reno and, in addition to his writing, is a staff member with the Senate Committee on Finance at the Nevada State Legislature.